FRANCE

'Loved it. An essential guide
— the French will complain.'
Andrew Neil

First edition published for the first time by Gibson Square

Available as an e-book

info@gibsonsquare.com
www.gibsonsquare.com
Tel: +44 (0)20 7096 1100 (UK)
Tel: +1 646 216 9813 (USA)
Tel: +353 (0)1 657 1057 (Eire)

ISBN 9781783340842

FRANCE

A Nation on the Verge of a Nervous Breakdown

JONATHAN MILLER

GIBSON SQUARE

FRANCE:
A NATION ON THE
VERGE OF A
NERVOUS
BREAKDOWN

I recently made an appointment to visit my lawyer. I was told to ignore the sign on the front door announcing that the office was on strike. It was a national day of action protesting proposed reforms to the legal profession. Instead I should knock discreetly at the side entrance and someone would let me in. The office was pretending to be on strike, while conducting business as usual. In France, not everything is always as it seems. In a country where people claim to be revolutionaries but are terrified of change, boast of their social model while condemning young people to mass unemployment, and claim to be the best cooks in the world, while a million people a day eat at McDonald's, there is much that is paradoxical, even psychotic.

When I bought my modest *maison* in France 15 years ago, equipped with rusty O-level French, I was seduced by the beauty of the country, discouraged by the difficulty of communicating effectively with French people, and entranced by the otherness of everything. Like many English people newly arrived in France, I imagined I had stumbled into a kind of paradise. Learning the language was both a challenge and a pleasure. The first 10 years are the hardest, but fluency (or an approximation of fluency, which is all I claim) is the very best tool for understanding the French, whose beautiful, romantic language is an insight into their soul. I have discovered the French to be warm, funny and generous. But I also learned how France really is and understood how their language has prevented them from seeing the world realistically, often isolating themselves within a francophone discourse that can be pretty remote from the harsh global reality and indeed is often delusional.

In 2014 I was elected to my local council - an experience that has given me introductions to many politicians and a new window into the endless contradictions of French life and the refusal to confront reality. It is fundamental to the French sickness that they believe that they are unique in seeing the world as it is, and everyone else is mistaken. As any psychiatrist can tell you, it is the patient who denies he is ill who is likely to be sicker than the one who accepts having some problems.

I have often heard people who do not really know the French say that 'the French hate the English.' This is complete nonsense. On the whole I think they rather like us. I have certainly never encountered any visceral anti-British sentiment in my years in France although they do like to tease us, if not as much as we sometimes tease them. The relationship is much more complicated than that. And our own relationship to the French is also nuanced. What's clear is that we often struggle to understand one another.

The French are often adorable, but also frequently infuriating, often naïve, even infantile, hopelessly romantic, deeply neurotic and capable of holding numerous incompatible thoughts in their head at the same time. They admire principles, even when they may not work when applied in practice. The French talk often of their exceptionalism. And they are exceptional, but not always in a good way. The impossibilities of the French idea of themselves are startling. It is a country of great beauty, but where villages are dilapidated, millions of dwellings abandoned and suburban homeowners fortify themselves behind exterior walls that are made of untreated *parpaing* (breeze blocks), especially in the south. It is a state that claims to be *laïc* (prohibiting the state from recognising religion or even ethnicity) yet where millions in public funds are spent restoring cathedrals, even as Muslim girls are sent home from school for wearing headscarves and skirts that are deemed provocatively too long. In Britain girls are sent home for skirts that are too short.

To explore the endless paradoxes of France is to discover a nation that is dysfunctional and frequently self-destructive and where, it is said, the customer is always wrong. Arriving in France is like putting your watch back 50 years, to Britain in the 1970s. Whose carrots, as they say in one colourful idiom suggesting a situation that has become hopeless, are cooked (*les carottes sont cuites*). France is a country blessed with natural and human resources, with a cultural heritage admired everywhere. It is a society nominally committed to equality, liberty and fraternity, but it is failing to reliably deliver any of these things to many of its 65 million people.

This work will doubtless be decried by some as French-bashing and it is true that it is often critical. But I make no claim that the French are unique in the world in being prisoners of their own mythology. I do not say that France is better or worse than the Britain or the United States, which I also know well. The French do not in any case need me to bash them since there are plenty of French writers and intellectuals who have made a career out of it. And there is always scope for the French to bash the endless foibles, hypocrisies and contradictions of America and Britain. Indeed, they seem to relish doing so. I merely take France on its own terms, and try to measure the gaps between the country's unlimited potential and its often pitiful performance.

The selection of entries can justly be criticised as personal, haphazard, capricious and even irrational, in part a *contradictionary*, mostly *un dictionnaire égoïste* - an egocentric dictionary, influenced by my own experiences, the places I have visited, the people I have met, my immersion in and seduction by the French language and not least by my own location in the Languedoc, on the less fashionable side of the Rhone Valley, in one of the poorer parts of France. It is definitely not written from the perspective of Paris. I have tried to go from the particular to the general and the reverse, seeking to relate these stories to the bigger contemporary narrative of France. If I am negative and sometimes snarky, it is because from the beginning of this project I have been fuelled by rage at a political class that has ignored the real problems of the country, while feathering its own nests. I am afraid the snark is a bad habit acquired as a newspaper reporter.

The rose-tinted view of France offered by sentimental writers like Peter Mayle (*A Year in Provence*, 1989) and many others has not been helpful to understanding this country. France is an easy country to romanticise, but it is doing it no favours to overlook the present position. Yes it is often beautiful and full of charm, but not always. Can France be saved? Possibly. I conclude my tour with an Afterword, a modest manifesto. I reckon this to be good advice, but doubt it will gain much traction.

A woman in the village café, overhearing one of my morning rants about the conceits, paradoxes and misapprehensions of France, asked me bluntly: 'If you don't like it, why do you live here?' The answer is that I love France, the French, their language, their music and art and literature, their extraordinary countryside, their ancient villages, their cheese and their wine - indeed, I have been in love with this country and its people since I first came here on a family holiday, aged 10. But the more I have come to know about France, and the greater my admiration for ordinary French people, the greater my contempt for its elites, who have betrayed the country and its future. Like the Bourbons, they have learned nothing and forgotten nothing. The late Tony Judt, a superb historian of France, wrote that reading the history of interwar France, 'one is struck again and again by the incompetence, the *insouciance* and the culpable negligence of the men who governed the country and represented its citizens.' My argument is that France occupies once more what Judt identifies as the terrain of 'collective and individual irresponsibility'. *The Economist* in 2012 said that France was a time-bomb at the heart of Europe. It has become even more dangerous since, to itself and others. The French need a slap, at least, if not a decent kicking, to break their hallucinatory cycle. This is a nation with the potential to be great, that is failing. It is heartbreaking to witness this.

Author's Note

The book is organised alphabetically, in French. Within the text French words are in italics, *followed by the author's translation into English. The headings are followed by an explanation in English, sometimes literally translated but often not. Words in* A different type *cross-refer to related entries.*

A

AFFAIRES
BUSINESS AND FUNNY BUSINESS

An *affaire* is a business, an *homme d'affaires* is a businessman - but often, an *affaire* is a scandal. Scandals in France are often tangled, and are typically named after their central personalities or feature, hence the historic *Affaire* Dreyfus, the current *Affaire* Bettencourt, the recent Sarkozy-Kadhafi *Affaire*, and the long-running Bygmalion *Affaire*. Each of these has its own Wikipedia page attempting to make sense of the typically tortuous plot and cast, but neither these accounts nor the vaguely-sourced and often tendentious information relayed by the media are always convincing.

Current *affaires* run the gamut from swindling rich widows, secret political financing, everyday bribery, money laundering, tax evasion, banking, football match-fixing and inevitably sex (see Dominique Strauss-Kahn). Sometimes there may be less to these affairs than meets the eye and the actual scandal is imaginary, the invention of prosecutors and journalists pursuing political vendettas. Pedants distinguish between great political and financial *affaires* and purely criminal *affaires* of banditisme (gangsterism). It is sometimes hard to see a great difference. *Affaire* can also be used to evoke a romantic affair, or liaison, not uncommon in France. If your employer is generous you will fly *classe affaires* (business class) on Air France but if really generous he will not make you fly on Air France at all.

L'AFRIQUE
THE HEART OF FRENCH DARKNESS

La Françafrique is French shorthand for France in Africa. Much of north and west Africa was under French rule in the 19th century and first half of the 20th, and although the colonial ties were dissolved (and in the case of Algeria, brutally so), the political, linguistic and emotional connections are perhaps as strong as ever. Also, the conflicts. On a trip to Mali, I visited the *grand marché* in the centre of Bamako where as I walked through the market, there were murmurs of *toubabou, toubabou* (white man, white man). On one side of the market, on the rue Mohammed, is the *Grande Mosquée* (Great Mosque) tallest building in the country; facing it, on the avenue de la République, is the French-built national assembly, with odd Moorish flourishes on a building that looks to have been modelled on a suburban French high school. The market itself is rooted in an Africa with roots more ancient than either Islam or democracy. Traders deal in everything from animist fetishes, the skins of leopards, the heads of monkeys and potent spells. And there are magnificent, explosively colourful woven and dyed textiles.

Mali was already too dangerous for me to visit Timbuktu, a lifetime ambition. At the last minute, my wary pilot discovered 'technical problems' with his King Air turboprop that would make the trip impossible. The road was insecure and westerners daring to travel it regarded as kidnap fodder. I left Mali optimistic, nevertheless, writing in the *Washington Post* that it still had a chance to become a west African success story. I thought the country might be capable of finding a social compact, under a government that while far from perfect, was at least vaguely democratic. In retrospect, I should have seen the coming catastrophe. Mali was crawling with spies. Mysterious Cubans and Americans were installed at corner tables in the best restaurants. The music was incredible, but the atmosphere on the streets was menacing. In 2013, Mali's government fell, faced with an Islamist insurgency that seized Timbuktu and much of the north.

President François Hollande has deployed French forces to Mali to combat the Islamist extremists in the Sahel, and has established military bases throughout former French Africa, and beyond. His predecessor, NicolAs SArkozy, with British and American help, deposed Muammar Gaddafi in Libya in 2011 although with disastrous consequences. There are now Islamic State enclaves on the Mediterranean coast and a tidal wave of migrants is crossing the sea seeking asylum in Europe, and straining France's relations with Italy, where most of them land. The French are entangled as far east as Djibouti in the Horn of Africa where they maintain a *demi-brigade* of their Foreign Legion and operate a secretive drone and special forces base in partnership with the United States Africa command. France looks warily at Africa, no longer for the possibilities of commercial exploitation that inspired the French African empire in the first place, but because it is a menacing continent across just a short stretch of sea from France itself.

Parisians sometimes express their disdain for the *rustiques* (rustics) of France by muttering *l'Afrique commence au sud de la Loire* (Africa begins south of the river Loire).

AGRICULTURE
SEMI-GOVERNMENTAL

The French are some of the most urbanised people on earth yet still cling to a romantic notion of themselves as PAYSANS (peasants, people of the soil). Rural employment is only 3 per cent of the workforce (versus 1 per cent in the U.K., 2 per cent in the U.S.A.) yet there is a quasi-religious respect for *terroir* (the soil, the countryside) shared by even those who rarely go near it.

The rustic pretensions of France conceal an agricultural sector that is becoming highly industrialised. If you drive through the centre of France you will see enormous fields of wheat and sunflowers, onto which the French pump vast quantities of water, often wastefully in the heat of the day, whence it largely evaporates. This is a highly effective food machine that makes the French largely self-sufficient in terms of their basic food supply (though they say that in time of war, it is wise to go long on cooking oil and sugar). The French process vast quantities of foodstuffs, including dairy products, cereals and wine and the sector accounts for roughly 15 per cent of French exports.

The fetishisation of agriculture has major political consequences. Farmers are often angry, blockading roads and demanding subsidies to protect them from the marketplace. Blockades of motorways in the north of France and around Lyons by angry farmers in 2015 produced promises of new subsidies. PRESIDENT FRANÇOIS HOLLANDE promised to put pressure on supermarkets to raise prices and said schools, prisons and hospitals should buy only French meat. Utterly illegal under EU rules but a good headline. The farmers rejected the offer by closing the frontiers with Germany and Spain, ransacking trucks in search of agricultural goods coming into the country, which they regard as unfair competition. Farmers also frequently dump tons of manure in public spaces to protest their miserable lot. There are, naturally, no arrests. The police are too busy keeping Uber closed to keep the frontiers open.

All French presidents have attended the annual agriculture salon in PARIS and are photographed admiring French-built combine harvesters and posing with fat cows, goats, and sheep. The French are the largest beneficiaries of the EU's common agricultural policy but a lot of the subsidies go straight to the cereal barons with very little, in reality, trickling down to the milk producers and producers of beef or the remaining *paysans,* who continue to till their tiny plots, milking their cows, dutifully sowing their crops of winter wheat and sunflowers, and closing highways.

AÏGO BOULIDO
FOUL PANACEA

When I was sick, a kindly villager made this for me and I was cured. This potion of Provençal origin is made of garlic (lots), herbs of the garrigue, olive oil, egg white and the mint-like salvia plant (*sorge*). It is traditionally consumed on Christmas day after the excesses of la grande bouffe (the great feast) eaten on Christmas Eve. Also prepared as required throughout the year as a remedy for almost anything. French people make extravagant claims for traditional remedies but this one really works, if you can bear to let it pass your lips. If it isn't dégueulasse (disgusting), it isn't working.

Recipe: more garlic than you'd think humanly possible, thyme, sage, a cup and a half of salt water, pepper, a splash of olive oil, egg yolk (one or two), croutons from a baguette deep-fried in olive oil. If the garlic will not drive away demons than at least it will repel relatives who don't care enough about you.

AIRBUS
(OVER-) REACHING FOR THE SKY

The French-based aircraft manufacturer faces turbulence. Its new military air-lifter, the A400M, is 10 years late, and 6.2 billion euros over budget. It is still not convincingly airworthy, one recently crashing, killing its crew, when faulty software shut down the fuel supply. The pride of the fleet, the giant A380 super-jumbo, has sold poorly and may never be profitable. Smaller Airbus jets have done much better, becoming the staple of regional and low-cost carriers and there are strong hopes for the new A350 inter-continental twin-jet. Being French, Airbus planes have dispensed with the traditional control yoke and replaced it with a side-mounted joystick like those used by video games. A tray table has been put where the column used to go, which makes it easier for the pilots to eat their meals.

Airbus has become a vast and complicated business, and would be proof that it is possible to run a world-class enterprise mostly out of France, except that there is energetic outsourcing of actual production to China and the United States. Airbus head-quarters at Blagnac airport in prosperous Toulouse is the centre of an economic microclimate. Toulouse has an actual rush hour because so many people have real jobs, and you can buy A&W

Root Beer in the expat shop that caters for all the Americans who work there, some of them alumni of Boeing.

AIR FRANCE
EMPLOYEE-BENEFIT SCHEME MASQUERADING AS AN AIRLINE

Snooty personnel and a dubious safety record. 'Avoid at all costs,' says one of my French neighbours, whose monthly trips to China he schedules via Germany, after too many disrupted journeys on the national carrier. Aviation Week recently wondered whether Air France was destined to follow Pan Am into bankruptcy. Air France is being slaughtered by EasyJet on its domestic routes yet its pilots recently staged disruptive strikes to stop the airline from expanding its own low-cost subsidiary, Transavia. Management capitulated and France now has no chance of launching a major low-cost competitor. The disruptive strike was a further blow to what remains of customer loyalty.

Air France mimics in so many ways the activity of an airline, but it is really a PARAÉTATIQUE (semi-governmental) enterprise operating a lavish employee benefit programme, which also flies 245 aircraft. The crash in 2009 of an Airbus A330 into the Atlantic due to pilot error, killing all 228 aboard, was a disaster for the airline's reputation. Another catastrophe was narrowly averted in spring 2015 when an Air France crew set a course to fly into an African volcano, and were about to do so, before being alerted by their instruments to pull up. It is not clear that the loss of an Air France Concorde in 2000, killing everyone on board and more people on the ground, was entirely the fault of Air France, as there was debris on the runway that damaged the aircraft. But before the crash, American safety regulators had warned Air France on four occasions of potentially catastrophic safety problems with its Concorde fleet.

Postings on the Professional Pilots Rumour Network, an online forum for airline pilots, reflect widespread contempt for the management of Air France and the professional competence of its pilots. According to Atlantico, Air France's operating costs per seat per kilometre are three times higher than Ryanair and twice as high as EasyJet, while senior Air France pilots work far fewer hours than their counterparts at British Airways and are paid more (200,000 euros per year for senior officers). Air France also owns the Dutch carrier KLM, whose management is not in love with its French bosses.

ALGIERS
ONE-TIME JEWEL IN THE COLONIAL CROWN

Annexing Algeria was seen as a civilising mission, although this was a view to which few actual Algerians ever subscribed. After bloodily settling the country in 1830, it was declared nothing other than a *département* of France itself and the vast resources and expanse of the country were annexed and then ruthlessly exploited. With insouciant respect for the environment, the French even tested atomic weapons in the Algerian desert. Inevitably, there was a violent war for Algerian independence and eventually the French were kicked out and the country has been independent since 1962.

The film The Battle of Algiers (Gillo Pontecorvo, 1966) is everybody's first reference for this brutal war, whose echoes continue to resonate. Algeria remains a multi-faceted headache for the French. There are millions of people living in France who claim Algerian roots, many of them Muslim, others the descendants of the French immigrants who colonised the country and were forced to leave and others of Spanish, Italian and Jewish origin. The European Algerians forced from the country after independence are called *pieds-noirs* ('black boots') and have themselves suffered from discrimination in France. France, still dependent on Algeria for oil and gas, is a major security and has sensitive, almost indefensible borders with Libya, Tunisia, Niger, Mali, Mauritania and the Western Sahara, all of them infested with Islamic militants for whom France remains an eternal enemy.

ALLEMANDS
LES BOCHES - FEARED, UNLOVED

The French do not love the Germans, although they fear them, grudgingly respect them and have shackled their national interests to them for 60 years. Appeasing the Germans has been and remains at the very centre of post World War Two French policy. The institutions that form the kernel of today's European Union were at the heart of this policy of rapprochement, starting with the Coal and Steel Community, which evolved into the European Economic Community and then the European Union and the common currency zone. This worked well for the French until Germany was reunified, after which the relationship between the two nations has become increasingly lopsided, not evidently to the advantage of the French.

The contemporary entanglement with Germany is rooted in the early medieval foundations of Charlemagne's Carolingian empire and the outcome of the *Guerre de Cent Ans* (100 Years' War, 1337 to 1453) of the Plantagenets against the Valois, after which France turned its back on its links with England, to look east. Today this strategy is never questioned, which is a pity as the relationship is obsolescent. The French have deluded themselves into believing that they can stand up to the Anglo-Saxon monolith, by aligning with the Germans. Even if this strategy had ever been plausible, the fall of the Berlin Wall and the subsequent relaunch of Germany as an economy vastly more powerful than France has put the French into a subservient relationship that is leading it nowhere other than into servitude.

ALTERMONDIALISTES
OTHER-WORLDLY ECOLOGISTS

The French version of a tree-hugger. Perhaps they cultivate a little organic cannabis behind the *yourte* (yurt). A movement opposed to *ultra-libéralisme* (Anglo-Saxon economic liberalism), capitalism generally, money, fracking, genetically modified foods, *altermondialisme* is closely related to *Zadisme*. The spiritual home of the *altermondialistes* is the plateau of Larzac in the south, where José Bové, the militant ecologist, once drove a tractor into the Millau branch of McDonald's to protest junk food.

ALTRAD, MOHED
BEDOUIN MILLIONAIRE

France's most successful Arab immigrant. His story is inspiring. Doesn't know his own birthday - either 1948 or 1951. Born in Syria, orphaned, attended school clandestinely, immigrated to France where he studied engineering at the University of Montpellier before working in information technology for Alcatel and Thomson. Bought a failing scaffolding company in southern France and built it into a global construction-support business with 17,000 employees. Author of three acclaimed novels and a management book. Owner of Montpellier Hérault Rugby club. Given the Légion d'Honneur by Jacques Chirac in 2005. He was named World Entrepreneur of the Year by Ernst & Young in 2015.

What! How could this be? A Frenchman, named world ENTRE-PRENEUR of the year? It seems impossible. The French don't even have a word for entrepreneur, according to former American president George W. Bush. The French political class was delighted, taking it as evidence that France was 'open for business'. Altrad was quoted praising France for putting him on the road to success and said he hoped his story could inspire the country to believe in itself. None of this made sense to me so I phoned Altrad and found his views were much more nuanced. He is indeed grateful for having found asylum in France after his disturbed childhood, but is not exactly brimming with enthusiasm for the business climate in France. I asked him to explain the paradox of France, a country with such unlimited potential that always seems to underperform. 'I'm not a politician, I consider myself first of all a writer and then a businessman, but there is a paradox and it can be very dark,' he tells me. 'The problem is cultural. The French have always had a problem with money. When you are rich and successful you are suspicious. In other countries to be successful is seen as a good thing.'

Yes, his Altrad Group employs 17,000 people, but only 3,000 in France. Wage overheads - social charges and taxes - are twice as high in France as they are in the UK and Germany. 'Another problem is the French political class,' he says. He is careful not to be partisan but believes that all French politicians have difficulty understanding where the wealth of a nation might originate. Politicians have no understanding that businesses cannot be taxed indefinitely, he said. 'Unemployment and poverty has increased for 30 years in France. The country has a debt of 2,000 billion euros. I want to be constructively critical. It is difficult to avoid hurting feelings. But the politicians don't understand the huge consequences of constantly increasing taxes. The only place where you can make value is companies.'

As if to prove his point about the suspicion of wealth and wealthy people in France, in a profile in the newspaper *Libération* in 2013, an unnamed socialist deputy launched an astonishing attack on Altrad, claiming he 'believed nothing' of Altrad's biography. The newspaper cited other unnamed critics accusing Altrad of using a ghostwriter to achieve his literary success, of being a member of the Assad clan that has ruled Syria for decades, and of money-laundering on his route to success. I repeat these accusations with great reluctance, because I can find no evidence to support any of them. What is illuminating is the naked hatred directed at those who achieve success in business in France. And it is worse for Altrad, who is an Arab. The newspaper may claim that it was merely repeating the claims of others but this won't do. *Libération,* which receives 10 million euros of subsidies a year from the state, offered no proof whatsoever for its defamations but compounded this terrible journalism by awarding anonymity to the person who made them. And this is a newspaper whose snooty political reporters think that voters have no right to know about the adulteries of their presidents.

Altrad is a very good businessman and writer who has employed thousands of people and has been gracious to his adopted country. His story is exceptional and inspiring and France needs more like him. But he has some money, so the French left hates him and is utterly unscrupulous in its attacks.

AMERICAINS, LES
BARBARIANS AND MYTHIC SUPERHEROES

Not one or the other, but both at the same time. French people adore all manifestations of American popular culture including line dancing, McDonald's and trick-or-treating. Alarmed, their governments have implemented measures to restrict imports of American cultural products: American rock music is so popular that radio stations have been ordered to play less of it. America is seen as France's original ally and the special relationship between France and America is believed to be firmly anchored in the Statue of Liberty in New York harbour, a gift of the people of France to the United States. Yet the French also resent and fear America.

The French are grateful to have been saved from the Germans twice in the 20th century by American armies, yet these memories also provoke a certain ambivalence. There is shame that such a rescue should have been necessary in the first place. After the second war, France did not exactly make life easy for the Americans, ordering their military out, withdrawing from the NATO military command structure, and cozying up to the Russians. The British became the best friends of the Americans. Today, America is seen as the cradle of ultra-liberalism, menacing the French way of life, but also as the only ally ultimately strong enough to be indispensable, when push comes to shove.

There is genuine affection, too. There is a 94-year-old man in my village who still talks about the day in 1944 that the Americans arrived and gave him chewing gum. American exiles in Paris - James Baldwin, Gertrude Stein, Ernest Hemingway, Henry Miller, and many others - helped define the city's cultural identity. American movies, music, video games and social networks suffuse France. French gangsters used to drive American cars and middle-aged Frenchmen still buy Harley-Davidson motorcycles. Yet Americans are also seen as dangerous economic predators and for decades the French have been terrified by the *Défi Americain* (American Challenge), which was defined in an influential 1967 book by the journalist and politician Jean-Jacques Servan-Schreiber.

ANGÉLISME
IGNORING REALITY
A specific French psychosis involving the wilful refusal to confront reality, to substitute sentiment for moral, human or practical consequences, credulity and utopianism for what is otherwise self-evident, *angélisme* represents the triumph of naïvety over objectivity. When a gang of drug dealers in a nearby town was involved in torturing one of their mules who had failed to deliver a consignment of cocaine from Brazil, much of local opinion reverted to an *angéliste* analysis in which the brutal behaviour of the perpetrators was explained to be a consequence of their unhappy childhoods.

L'ANGLAIS
THE ENGLISH LANGUAGE
After my French friends grew weary of trying to teach me French, and found that my own approximate version of it had become minimally acceptable for rudimentary communication, they demanded that I start teaching them English. So I organised

a series of classes in my *chai* (winery) and quickly learned that teaching is hard. There was no lack of enthusiasm from my pupils, only bafflement at my indifferent pedagogy. Eventually I decided that the best way to teach them English was to persuade them that they already knew it.

Georges Clémenceau, prime minister of France during the Great War, once described English as *jamais que le français, mal prononcé* (nothing other than badly-pronounced French). And this is not as ridiculous as it sounds. By various counts, there are 40,000 words in common between English and French. So my technique was to use English words that are cognate in French, to overcome the *difficultés* (you see how it works?) and show that it is *possible* (*idem*) to communicate in English, using mostly words they already knew in French. After I had *persuadé* (there I go again) my students, the problem became, as Clemenceau noted, the pronunciation. The English language presents *problèmes* (!) to French people. They find it hard to *prononcer* (!!) the 'th' letter combination. I taught them not to worry, that this (*zat zis*) makes them sound *adorable* (!!!) when they speak English. Think of Peter Sellers's Inspector Clouseau in the *Pink Panther*: 'I am from the Nice *telefern* company. I have come to fix your *fern*.'

Part of the problem for French people who want to learn English is that it is often very poorly taught in French schools. (The reverse is also true.) Typically students learn English in groups of 30 for an average of 50 minutes, three times a week. After the recent round of BAC exams, 12,000 students signed a petition to the minister of education protesting that the English exam was too hard. They'd been asked to interpret a passage from *Atonement* by Ian McEwan in which the word 'cope' appeared. There is no exact equivalent in French although *se débrouiller* and *s'en sortir* will do. Students complained the question was *incompréhensible* (!!!!). Indeed, many teachers seem determined to make it as difficult and boring as possible (see My TAILOR is RICH bUT MY ENGLISH is POOR).

French people who move to England usually master our

language quite quickly, being immersed in it. I have lost count of the number of French families who have asked me to organise home stays in England, so their children can advance. Still, English remains a challenge. It doesn't help that the French elite has often been hostile to English. In 2006, former President Jacques Chirac walked out of an EU meeting when the French head of a European business group spoke English. 'I was profoundly shocked,' said Chirac. It was considered headline news when prime minister Manuel Valls spoke a few words of English in London in 2015 (he also recited a few words of Chinese, in Shanghai). One of the most elite colleges in France, L'École Nationale d'Administration (ENA) is to make competence in English compulsory only from 2018. It is amazing that they have waited this long.

ANGLAIS EXPATRIÉS EN FRANCE, LES
THE ENGLISH IN FRANCE

We English are admired, mistrusted and misunderstood, simultaneously. Loved or not, the English have again invaded France and are unavoidable. You can tell an English person in France by sight alone. We announce ourselves by the way we walk, the way we dress, and by our unquenchable thirst for the local plonk. *Les Anglais ont toujours soif* (the English are always thirsty) say the French. There are cricket clubs in the Drôme and the Dordogne, English newspapers produced in France for English people, and, inevitably, 'we speak English' signs in the windows of all estate agents. The latest French census picks up only a hundred thousand or so British people fully resident in France but the data is fishy (I have seen how these censuses are compiled). I am doubtful the official statistics are correctly capturing the scale of English and British immigration to France and especially the significant number of people with properties and interests in both countries. I'd guess there are between 250,000-400,000 Brits in France, full or part time.

British people have transformed much of rural France and a house that is freshly painted is likely to be occupied by British people (or possibly Germans, Dutch or Scandinavians, who are also in love with France). The French prefer to guard their affluence behind shabby exteriors, lest it attract the interest of the *fisc* (tax authorities). Some British people have made an effort to integrate, learn French, and make French friends, others have stayed in anglophone bubbles. There are many like my English neighbour who will not or cannot learn French. He has not been invited inside a French person's home in 20 years (and neither has he invited anyone from the village into his).

ANGLETERRE
ENGLAND

Perfidious appendage to Europe, adrift in the north Atlantic, England is the number one destination for French people fleeing economic stagnation at home. Yet we still have a reputation for being dangerously mercantile, for bad food and for imposing military humiliation on the obviously superior French. *Les rosbifs* (the roast-beef eaters) are *tous riches* (all rich), according to Flaubert. That's a misunderstanding. French women say *les Anglais ont débarqué* (the English have landed) when their period has started, an unsubtle reference to the sanguinary arrival of English soldiers on French soil. That's mistrust. Many French people think that all of the United Kingdom is England although rugby fans recognise that Scotland and Wales are separate nations. A surprising number of French people have never been to England, even those who live in the north of France. But this is changing. The low-cost flights that used to be entirely filled with English passengers are now equally patronised by French people returning 'home' to London after a weekend with their family in France, or French people experimenting with long weekends in London. Barbour jackets and British motorcars are the height of chic among upper-middle class French people who like to drop

English words into the conversation in much the same way that English people play with French. Clémenceau described England as a *colonie française qui a mal tourné* (a French colony turned bad) but the French never really colonised England, it was the Normans, who were not French, but Vikings. See *Londres*.

ANGOISSE
ANXIETY - A CHRONIC FRENCH CONDITION

The French are world-champion neurotics and seem rather proud of it. They have a lot about which to be miserable and anxious. Contemporary writers like Michel Houellebecq and Eric Zemmour reflect the existential angst that permeates the French mentality. The French find work itself to be oppressive. The media often occupies itself with exposés of employers (France Telecom is frequently cited) whose working practices supposedly contribute to depression and suicide. There are conflicting data sets floating around. Some seem to suggest that the French are no more depressed than the Americans or the Brits. Others that the French are truly sad. My own psycho-pathological diagnosis tends more to seeing French *névrosité* (neurosis) as psychotic and delusional rather than merely depressive. Obviously, the French have good reasons to be anxious and depressed, as a consequence of the grim position in which their country finds itself. The paradox is that many French people do not think that France is actually in such a position, so perhaps their delusions protect them from anxieties. (My qualification for offering this analysis is that my father was a psychiatrist.)

APARTHEID
FRANCE'S NOT QUITE FRANCE

My friend Nicola, a Brixton-born Englishwoman of Jamaican ethnic origin, and a naturalised French citizen who speaks perfect French, tells me she has never encountered overt racism in

France, but I suspect it is because French people regard her as English, not black. It's clear that black sub-Saharan Africans occupy a marginal place in society but those who are not Muslim less than those who are.

Prime Minister MANUEL VALLS in January 2015 described neighbourhoods like Mosson in Montpellier and Clichy-sous-Bois outside Paris as places of 'social, geographic and ethnic apartheid' ('*Un apartheid territorial, social, ethnique*'). He was attacked by former president NICOLAS SARKOZY who said it was an error to have used this word. 'I'm disturbed by the use of this expression and that the prime minister of the republic could use such a word,' he said. But it is hard to dispute that Valls accurately characterised a problem that other politicians prefer to ignore. Apartheid means 'the state of being apart' in Afrikaans and it is 100 per cent accurate to use this term to characterise the situation in France. Though there is no law enforcing racial segregation - quite the contrary, it is strictly prohibited - denial of *de facto* discrimination is hardly credible. See *BEURS, GHETTOS*.

ARMES
A NATION OF GUN-LOVERS

The French love weapons and celebrate the right to armed revolution in the refrain of the national anthem, *LE MARSEILLAISE (aux armes, citoyens)*. I know very few people who do not have a *carabine* (rifle) or a *fusil* (shotgun) tucked away. Officially, there are 33 guns per 100 people in France, compared to 6 in Britain and 88 in the United States. Unofficially, I expect there are considerably more. Technically, you do need a licence. Naturally, when I came to France, I wanted to join in. When I went to the doctor to ask him to sign the form allowing me to buy a gun, he asked me if I had ever had the desire to shoot anyone. '*Souvent, j'ai une longue liste,*' (frequently, I have a long list) I replied, hoping he recognised that I was joking. 'No problem, that's normal,' he said, grinning, signing the form and pounding it with his official rubber stamp. I hope he was joking, too. At my interview with the licensing officer at the gendarmerie, I was asked if I had ever been in prison. 'Not yet,' I said. That seemed to be an adequate answer. I confess to have become quite attached to my modest armoury. Should law and order break down entirely, I will not be unprepared. Shooting turns out to be highly therapeutic and quite demanding. But one is not allowed to shoot at targets with a human form. When I asked the president of my gun club if I could use imported American zombie targets he said, 'absolutely not.' 'But they're already dead,' I said. He was unmoved.

Selling weapons to dictators has long been a pillar of the French economy. (The same charge can be levelled against the Americans and British.) Following recent huge pressure from the United States, they recently only reluctantly agreed not to sell Mistral helicopter-carrier warships to Vladimir Putin's Russia, following his invasion of Crimea and eastern Ukraine. They are now negotiating to sell the ships to the Chinese. Jokes about French tanks having more reverse gears than forward ones are not fair. The modern French arms supermarket includes missiles, ships, aircraft, armoured vehicles and battlefield command and control equipment.

The Paris Air Show every two years, which I used to attend when I was writing about aerospace, is perhaps the world's most elaborate arms marketplace. The food in the hospitality chalets is also very good, even if some of the catering companies responsible are British. President François Hollande (François of Arabia) has emerged as France's arms salesman in chief, cozying up in particular to Saudi Arabia, Egypt, Qatar and the United Arab Emirates. French arms deals have traditionally been accompanied by massive bribes of which few details ever emerge since they are classified *secret défense* (defence secrets). French Exocet missiles sold to the Argentinian dictatorship caused havoc for the Royal Navy during the Falklands war.

ARROGANCE
THE FRENCH ARE NOT POLITE

The Pew Research Centre in Washington D.C. in 2013 surveyed 7,600 people in eight European countries and discovered that the British and Germans judge the French to be the most arrogant people in Europe. The French themselves were divided between those admitting that they are the most arrogant and those maintaining they are the least. I find my neighbours and southerners generally not to be at all arrogant, although my winemaker neighbour Jean-Claude Mas launched a range of wine called The Arrogant Frog, which has become wildly successful, especially in the United States. Parisians may be the problem - they are often disliked even by the French. In 2015, the French government, disturbed by reports that tourists have been put off by the arrogance of many French people, launched a campaign to train-workers to be more polite. We shall see how this goes.

ARTE
EXCELLENT BUT LARGELY-UNWATCHED FRANCO-GERMAN TV CHANNEL

Pronounced 'are-tay.' A Franco-German TV station conjured up by president FRANÇOIS MITTERRAND and German chancellor Helmut Kohl, at the height of the Franco-German romance. It was to be an element within a larger project to protect French and German language and culture, and thwart the domination of English. In addition to the TV station, German students were supposed to be taught French and vice-versa. Most students on both sides of the border were smart enough to realise it was more useful to take English. But Arte lives on. The German and French media experiment has sometimes almost immeasurably small ratings, which are unlikely to grow when all of television is moving away from the broadcasting model to the on-demand model. Arte is, nonetheless, excellent. It has many eclectic shows and even some American films. It was well in advance of the BBC in showing the

Danish police procedural *Forbrydelsen* (*The Killing*). It broadcasts a gorgeous, full-strength HDTV signal, which makes its wonderful, Attenborough-free natural history documentaries highly viewable. Although its coverage of economics is predictably Marxist, Arte is much more convincingly a public service than the BBC, eschewing the derivative, populist drivel that is a mainstay of the Beeb, and is infinitely better than the pablum broadcast on the regular French channels. It is not clear why it is not available in the UK, or indeed outside France and Germany. The station could transform itself into a serious pan-European public broadcaster but seems to remain tied to promoting Franco-German amity to a tiny audience of die-hard fans.

ARTISAN
SOMEONE DRIVING A VAN AND MCDONALD'S

Artisanal describes products or services that are really rather ordinary or worse: approximative building skills, disengaged cooking, all are too often described as artisanal. This word, of noble origin, hijacked by low commerce, is also infiltrating English, in equivalent misuse. In the United States, McDonald's has recently introduced an artisanal hamburger. Everyone in France with a van, from plumbers to stonemasons, describes themselves as an *artisan*. Artisans frequently work on their own since they say it is too expensive and risky to hire anyone to help them.

ASTÉRIX
EMBLEMATIC FRENCHMAN CREATED BY FRENCH PEOPLE FROM ELSEWHERE

Created by René Goscinny, a Franco-Polish Jew who spent his youth in Argentina, and Albert Uderzo, a Franco-Italian. Their comic book character of Astérix the Gaul is arguably the totemic image of the Frenchman in popular culture. The indomitable, mustachioed Astérix was projected into public consciousness first in the famous comic albums (bandes dessinées), then on film, later at the eponymous theme park outside Paris and in video games. Myths have power even if they are just myths and Asterix has profoundly influenced the French self-image while becoming a French cultural export and brand in its own right. Do not dismiss these brilliantly written and beautifully drawn books as merely for children. They are social satires and rewarding reading at any age. The English versions of Asterix by Anthea Bell and Derek Hockridge are the most brilliant popular translations of French into English ever achieved, defying Vladimir Nabokov's insistence that translations be literal. They transmit the humour and style of the original without paying too much attention to the particular. Idéfix, Asterix's dog, in English becomes Dogmatix - both are puns, the French from *idée fixe* (fixed idea) and the English a play on the word dogmatic. The best of all the books is *Astérix chez les Bretons* (*Asterix in Britain*), a great and funny romp in which the English drink *eau chaude avec un nuage de lait* (hot water with a cloud of milk, tea not yet having been discovered by the English). *Un nuage du lait* is a phrase instantly recognisable to all French people.

ATLANTICO
THE BEST FRENCH POLITICAL WEBSITE, MOSTLY IGNORED BY THE FRENCH POLITICAL CLASS
Indispensable, must-read antidote to much of the French media. Except with little apparent influence against the overwhelmingly leftist French media. The reform-minded digital daily argues for liberalised markets, flexible labour codes, other structural reforms, and reveals abuses in France. Lacks much humour.

AUBRY, MARTINE
SOCIALIST POLITICIAN, ARCHITECT OF ECONOMIC DECLINE
A destroyer of French prosperity, Martine Aubry, the mayor of

Lille, is a hard-left socialist party apparatchik, whose rigid socialism epitomises the delusions of the French governing class. Notorious author of the 2000 law imposing a 35-hour week, which she promised would create 700,000 new jobs, which it didn't. Unemployment has subsequently risen and Aubry remains a pillar of the socialist party left wing. The daughter of Jacques Delors, former president of the European Commission, she was minister of employment and solidarity from 1997-2000. Unsuccessful contender for French presidency. Political foe of FRANÇOIS HOLLANDE, MANUEL VALLS and EMMANUEL MACRON, whom she believes to lack ideological purity. See TRENTE-CINQ HEURES.

AUTOCARS
FRANCE DISCOVERS THE INTER-CITY BUS

France is terrified of inter-city buses. They have been considered dangerous, unfair competition to the state railway, SNCF. There have been buses to Spain, Britain, Belgium and Italy, under EU open-market rules. But they were prohibited from allowing passengers to board in, e.g. Paris, and dropping them off in Toulouse, on the way to Spain. This is despite the fact that French companies like Transdev are world leaders in public transportation, albeit abroad. In a rare example of real reform, the market for inter-city buses will be liberalised and should be in full operation by 2016, allowing journeys between France's major cities at half the price of the train, and perhaps creating 10,000 jobs. But for the moment, the details remain unclear and only journeys of more than 200km will be permitted, so even if a bus is travelling from Montpellier to e.g., Marseille, it may not be possible to drop off or pick up passengers in Nîmes. For shorter trips, a new regulatory authority is to be established to arbitrate disputes between the railway and the bus companies. As if France does not have enough regulators.

AUTO ÉCOLES
DAYLIGHT ROBBERY

Interminable and exorbitant is how victims describe the process of obtaining a driving licence in France, where the heavily regulated driving schools gouge their customers and subject them to endless hours of instruction at 45 euros per hour. French drivers are much better than they used to be since thousands of speed and red-light cameras have been deployed in recent years, yet roughly one-third more French people die on the roads proportionately than in Germany or the United Kingdom, so it is not clear that interminable instruction is producing better drivers. Candidates can wait five months for a driving test in Paris, three months elsewhere. Reforms have been promised but remain undelivered. A competitor to the driving school cartel has proposed offering courses of equal quality at 35 euros per hour but this has been fiercely opposed. It typically takes 18 months and fees of more than 1,000 euros to prepare for the exam.

AUTO-ENTREPRENEUR
LEGAL STATUS PREVENTING SUCCESS

This new category of self-employment was supposed to encourage small businesses by exempting them from the worst of France's Procrustean employment laws. But like so many so-called reforms, it has been eviscerated by the socialists. The reform was introduced by former president Nicolas Sarkozy to encourage sole-entrepreneurs to emerge from the clandestine economy (le noir) and engage with the tax and benefit system through a streamlined, economical process. This was just getting into operation when President Hollande took over and comprehensively gutted it, with the help of France-Inter, the state radio network, which launched a vicious campaign accusing auto-entrepreneurs of presenting unfair competition to established firms. The then-prime minister Jean-Marc Ayrault cracked down, putting ceilings on the amount that could be earned (no more than the minimum wage), sharply raising *COTISATIONS* (social charges) and imposing new layers of regulation. So a lot of people who were thinking of going the auto-entrepreneur route have changed their minds and still work on the *noir*.

AUTOROUTES
MOTORWAYS: RACE TRACKS, GIANT CAR PARKS

French motorways are fabulous. They are surfaced like billiard tables. Most of the network is privatised and the tolls are heavy. Paris to Clermont-Ferrand, 424 km, costs 36.50 euros. The *autoroutes* shame the congested British motorways and crumbling American ones. But there are black spots. The Paris ring road (*le boulevard PÉRIPHÉRIQUE*) is in dire condition. And when the French all go on holiday at the same time, the *autoroutes* can become the world's finest car parks. On some summer days there are 1000km of jams. As the motorways have become infested with speed cameras, the French have largely stopped using them as race tracks but the British continue to drive like lunatics the second they get off the shuttles from England, and the Germans are even worse.

AVIATION
INVENTED BY THE FRENCH

To the chagrin of the French, it was the American Wright brothers working from their bicycle shop in Dayton, Ohio, who achieved the world's first sustained powered flights in 1903. But the French had been first into the air in 1782 in a balloon created by the Montgolfier brothers. Two years later, a Frenchman flew the first dirigible over the English Channel. By 1890, Clément Ader had demonstrated heavier-than-air flight but his aircraft wasn't stable and flew for an insignificant distance. In 1909, Louis Blériot won a prize of £1,000 for flying the first heavier-than-air aircraft over the English Channel. Today the French make some of the world's best fast combat jets, airliners, helicopters, business jets, light aircraft and rockets. The Ariane 5 heavy satellite launcher had by 2015 accumulated a record of 54 consecutive successful missions. The successor, the Ariane 6, is intended to be entirely reusable, challenging the American entrepreneur Elon Musk, whose own SpaceX rocket has so far led the way in this field. A rare French success story. See AIRBUS.

AVOCATS
IRRATIONAL PROFESSION

Lawyers are obsessed with their own privileges within a system that is secretive, politicised and often manifestly unjust. The big cases drag on for decades. The system is still reverberating from the miscarriage of justice in 2004 in Outreau near Boulogne where a zealous young magistrate prosecuted 18 people for child abuse. They subsequently spent years in jail - one died in custody - before the case collapsed. Eleven years later, the affair continues to drag on with inconclusive efforts to prosecute the magistrate responsible for the miscarriage of justice and repeated accusations that his superiors have evaded responsibility for the affair.

The legal profession is riddled with restrictive practices and opacity. Lawyers refuse (claiming it would be unethical) to work as in-house counsel for companies, which hire English, Dutch, German and American lawyers instead. Many French lawyers are simply not that smart, evidently. The most numerous type of lawyer in France is the *avocat*. There are roughly 50,000 of them (although England has twice as many solicitors) who may offer legal advice, draft contracts and have a right of audience before all criminal, civil and administrative courts. To become an *avocat* is not considered especially difficult and below the level of the elite *cabinets* (firms) there are large numbers of them with little to do except launch various vexatious proceedings and organise their fellow professionals to obstruct reforms. For the consumers of legal services, the structure of the profession is confusing and imposes costs. The execution of legal judgements is reserved to a specialised type of lawyer called a *HUISSIER* and property conveyancing is reserved to yet a third type of lawyer called a *NOTAIRE*. Efforts to introduce competition among these three branches, even to allow mixed *cabinets* (offices) in which all three might work together, in order to lower costs to consumers, have made only modest progress.

AYRAULT, JEAN-MARC
FAILED PRIME MINISTER

Failed, almost ridiculous prime minister, in office from May 2012 to March 2014 before being unceremoniously dumped by President FRANÇOIS HOLLANDE. A high-school German teacher and union activist, Ayrault rose through the ranks of the Socialist party to become mayor of Nantes and while holding onto that job, also a member of the National Assembly. With less charisma than the president himself, it can only be imagined that Hollande put Ayrault in place to make himself look more glamorous. It is not even clear that Ayrault can speak German. In Berlin on an official visit, he spoke only French and used an interpreter to talk to Chancellor ANGELA MERKEL. After all economic conditions deteriorated under his government, Ayrault was replaced by the interior minister, MANUEL VALLS, who is a much tougher character but whose own sacrifice would seem inevitable as Hollande seeks to blame everyone else for the problems of the country.

B

BACCALAURÉAT
SECONDARY-SCHOOL DIPLOMA THAT COUNTS FOR NOT MUCH

A feared school matriculation examination that prepares French students to take exams but not always much more. Françoise Sagan failed hers and went on to write the miserabilist bestseller *Bonjour Tristesse* (Hello Sadness). Émile Zola also failed yet went on to become one of the greatest of all French writers. The *bac* is roundly criticised as a deeply compromised examination of doubtful utility in preparing French high school students for the opportunities and cruelties of modern economic life. The criticism is not new. More than 100 years ago, Flaubert advised, 'thunder against it.' Oddly, the *bac* is now admired outside France more than within it. Some British schools have begun experimenting with an internationalised version, as an alternative to A-levels. Harsh grading of mathematics and philosophy papers is blamed for provoking pointless neurosis among the most gifted students taking the most academic versions of the exam. But at the same time, the OECD says French students perform better at maths than students in South Korea, Britain, Germany or Finland.

Although the image abroad of the *bac* is of a highly inflexible and unchanging system, characterised by rigour, the French have quietly abandoned the one-size-fits-all approach and almost everyone passes one version or another. There are now both traditional academic *bacs* and also applied *bacs*, one even allowing for a speciality in hotel management. For those aspiring to the GRANDES ÉCOLES there is a further gruelling course called PRÉPA. Finally, after repeatedly skimming the cream in exam after exam, the French end up with an elite that is academically brilliant but otherwise often mediocre. French people who flee say that employers in France are obsessed with exam results whereas those in Anglo-Saxon countries are more interested in practical ability, personality, potential and commitment.

French local newspapers publish special supplements every July with the names of all those who have passed the *bac* and the grades they have achieved. The son of one of my neighbours who received an exceptionally high score in maths got a telephone call from the Minister of Education, congratulating him.

BANDES DESSINÉES
COMIC BOOKS, WORKS OF ART

Comic books, sometimes political, sometimes romantic, often pornographic and sometimes brilliantly political as in the work of Julien Berjeaut (Jul), the author and illustrator of *Il faut tuer José Bové* (JOSÉ BOVÉ Must Die), a satirical *tour de force* mocking the conceits of the environmentalist *ultras*. ASTÉRIX is among the best-known and best-selling series of *bandes dessinées*, alongside Tintin, which is of course Belgian.

BANDITISME
ORGANISED CRIME

The romantic image of French criminals - gangsters who knew to wear a good suit and hat - is the invention of the film industry and journalism. Bandits in France are actually pretty sordid. The celebrated Traction Avant gang (named after their preferred model of Citröen) after the Second World War was made up of former *milice* (right-wing militia), collaborators with the Nazis whom even the Nazis found uncontrollable. They changed sides at the end of the war to become *résistants* in time for the liberation, then evading any accountability for their wartime crimes, adapted to the changed environment and resumed their vicious criminality. Near my village there is a memorial to a gendarme gunned down by the gang in 1947 as he signalled them to stop for speeding. Jean-Luc Godard immortalised the notorious gangster Pierrot le Fou (real name Pierre Lautrel, 'Peter the madman'), and also the actor who played him, Jean-Paul Belmondo, in an eponymous film (1965), although completely changing the story. Lautrel was found guilty of three murders and dozens of hold-ups and became one of the last Frenchmen to be guillotined, in 1956. The gangster genre has been a stylish mainstay of French film and television. Highlights include *Diva* (Jean-Jacques Beineix, 1981), *Mesrine* (Jean-François Richet, 2008) and today's long running series *ENGRENAGES*.

BANQUES
INCENDIARY FINANCIAL INSTITUTIONS

French banks long ago gave up much financing of small business and much prefer playing in the global financial casinos. They sell consumer products such as car loans, insurance and mortgages, but only to those who are exceptionally well-qualified, meaning they must have permanent employment contracts and preferably be civil servants. French bank managers seem to have no discretion to finance business customers outside of narrow guidelines. An acquaintance with assets of millions of euros tells me his own application to borrow a few hundred thousand euros for a business project was met with a flat refusal as the limit would be no more than 50,000 euros. The manager had no discretion to consider the circumstances. Banks of course close at lunch time and often on Mondays.

The French love to blame Wall Street and City of London banks for inflicting *ULTRA-LIBÉRALISME* (extreme capitalism) on the world, but for naked criminality it is hard to beat the performance of France's own financial institutions. The most notorious episode in recent history was in May 1996 when the magnificent Paris headquarters of Crédit Lyonnais was destroyed by a fire that burned for 12 hours, usefully destroying virtually all of the bank's archives and computer records. Crédit Lyonnais corruption was absolute: involved in money-laundering; served as a piggy bank for political allies of former President François Mitterrand; perpetrated a massive fraud involving the sale of Adidas to the colourful businessman Bernard Tapie. Tapie crops up elsewhere in this book for his involvement in football match fixing (see Foot, Christine Lagarde). Crédit Lyonnais also sponsored the Tour de France, appropriately since the cycle race was itself completely corrupt. Crédit Lyonnais has been reinvented as LCL and continues to operate as a retail bank in France.

More recently, BNP Paribas was fined $9 billion by the US District Court in New York for laundering money on behalf of Sudan, Iran and Cuba. France's third-largest bank, Société Générale, is notorious for having employed the trader Jérôme Kerviel who lost 5 billion euros in misjudged equity trades that apparently were unnoticed by any of his superiors. It is fair to say that nobody in the world outside Société Générale believes a word of the bank's explanation for how this was allowed to happen but happily for my own modest deposit there, at least nobody has yet burned the bank to ground.

BASTILLE, LA
BIRTH OF FRENCH REPUBLICANISM, SORT OF

According to French mythology, the storming of the Bastille on July 14, 1789, was the foundation event of the First Republic. This is not quite the complete picture. The Bastille was the citadel of monarchic power in Paris but its seizure did not mark the end of the monarchy. In any case, the only occupants liberated were a handful of old men, some of whom did not wish to leave. Informed of the event, Louis XVI asked the Duke of La Rochefoucauld: *'C'est une révolte?' 'Non, sire, c'est une révolution.'* ('Is it a revolt?' 'No sir, it's a revolution.') But the monarchy clung on for another three years until 1792 when citizens stormed the Tuileries, slaughtering 600 of the King's Swiss guard, and the First Republic was proclaimed.

BAYARD, PIERRE
SUBVERSIVE LITERARY CRITIC

A genial, brilliant Parisian literary critic and psychoanalyst, and an indispensable guide to surviving in French intellectual circles. Oscar Wilde warned against reading books before reviewing them, but Bayard pushes further, saying you need not read them ever. His exegesis *Comment parler des livres que l'on n'a pas lus?* (*How to Talk About Books You Haven't Read*), classifies all books as HB (heard-of book), SB (skimmed book), UB (unknown book) and FB (forgotten book). He goes on to note his opinions on some specific books. *Ulysses* he notes as an HB++ meaning a book he has heard of for which he holds an extremely positive opinion. Proust is doubly classified as an SB and an HB++. His point is that it is not necessary to have read a book to put it into a literary context but he raises some broader questions on the way, such as what does it mean to read? Bayard is also author of *Who Killed Roger Ackroyd?*, a parodic structuralist investigation of Agatha Christie's classic, in which he suggests that Hercule Poirot identified the wrong criminal, driving him to suicide. To bring Bayard up to date, it could be argued that the beauty of his method is that it also works with films, music, television programmes, the Internet. Once one has mastered the art of placing things in context, the details can be consulted on Google.

BB
BRIGITTE BARDOT, SEX SYMBOL, BATTY OLD WOMAN

People with enormous numbers of animals and difficult relations with human beings are frequently deranged. An example is Brigitte Bardot, 80 in 2015, a sex symbol who established St Tropez as the most glamorous seaside resort in the world. (It is no longer glamorous at all but infested with Russian oligarchs). BB, pronounced bay-bay, is a devoted supporter of JEAN-MARIE LE

PEN, the National Front founding leader. She's nuts, but kind to donkeys, and we'll always have *Et Dieu créa la femme* (*And God Created Woman*, Roger Vadim, 1956).

BCBG
POSH

Bon chic, bon genre (very stylish, well-born). French equivalent of a Sloane Ranger (British) or yuppie (American). Pronounced bay-cee-bay-shay.

BELGIQUE, LA
BELGIUM, OBJECT OF MOCKERY

Good food, confusing country, butt of French jokes. ('Why do Belgian dogs have flat heads?' 'Because they run after parked cars.') Belgium is not really understood by the French and the Belgians themselves are even more confusing. Some speak French but are not really French. Others speak Dutch but are not really Dutch. The French don't really like the idea of Brussels as the capital of Europe, insisting the European Parliament divide its time, at high expense and inconvenience, between the Belgian capital and the second European Parliament site in Strasbourg, in Alsace. The French nevertheless respect Belgian *gaufres* (waffles), *moules* (mussels) and *frites* (French fries). Ill winds often blow from Belgium. Waterloo was where Napoléon was definitively defeated, and the Germans who helped defeat him returned to Belgium in 1914 and 1940 with disastrous consequences for France. Belgium uses the Napoleonic code and is supposedly *laïc*, (the state recognising no religion) but *laïcité* in Belgium is not quite the same flavour as in France, since Belgium remains a communitarian kingdom with no Republican nonsense about everyone being equal. Lots of people sometimes thought to be French are actually Belgian, like Hercule Poirot, Tintin, Jacques Brel, Georges Simenon, René Magritte, Claude Lévi-Strauss, Eddie Merckx,

Marguerite Yourcenar, Plastic Bertrand and Stromae.

BELLE ÉPOQUE, LA
HISTORICAL BOOKEND

Much to admire, especially as this was when my house was built with its 4.3 metre high ceilings and glorious salons (all for the price of a two-bedroom flat in East London). Retrospectively romanticised, The *Belle Époque* (beautiful era) between 1871 and the start of the Great War was the high-water mark of French culture, prosperity, industrial revolution and imperialism. Although unique in detail, it was concurrent with other similar golden eras in Britain and the United States, and was a product of an unusual period of peace between the end of the Franco-Prussian war and the Great War. Without doubt, PARIS attracted many of the greatest musicians, painters, writers and capitalists, eager to invest in progress in all dimensions. The Paris *Exposition Universelle* (World's Fair) in 1899, framed by the Eiffel Tower, seemed to put Paris at the centre of the world but this was to be the bookend to an era of disproportionate French cultural and artistic influence, which was followed by a century indisputably American. In any case, the heritage of the *Belle Époque* tells only part of the story. The art, music, architecture, cuisine and technology of the *Belle Époque*, seen through the prism of Paris, is in sharp contrast to the precariousness and exploitation of the poor described by ÉMILE ZOLA, and the sheer primitiveness of the south, described by Robert Louis Stevenson in *Travels with a Donkey in the Cévennes* (1879): the epoch was not so *belle* for everyone. The THIRD REPUBLIC would not survive the wars that were to follow and while the heritage of the period is incomparable, nobody today thinks of Paris as the centre of the world, or even of Europe. Rather, Paris has become something of a museum of its vanished greatness.

BENJAMIN, WALTER
WITNESS OF PARISIAN GREATNESS

In 2014, I drove two hours from my village to the Spanish border then took the winding coastal road to Portbou, where Walter Benjamin died in obscure circumstances on 26 September 1940. Benjamin, a German and a Jew, was fleeing from the Nazi invaders of France, but his papers were not in order and the Spanish border guards ordered him to return to France the next day. He was dead hours later, aged 48, perhaps a suicide. Benjamin left behind the unfinished manuscript of *The Arcades Project* (*Passagenwerk*), a never-finished but monumental history of the emergence of Paris as the capital of the 19th century. It was inspired by Charles Baudelaire's *Les Fleurs du Mal,* which, wrote J.M. Coetzee, 'in Benjamin's eyes first revealed the modern city as a subject for poetry.' Coetzee notes somewhat acidly that Benjamin did not appear to have read Wordsworth, who'd had a similar insight 50 years earlier. Benjamin's manuscript was hidden in the *Bibliothèque Nationale* (French national library) by his friend Georges Bataille, and was discovered after the war. Published only in 1982, and in English translation 20 years later, and more than 1,000 pages long, the *Arcades Project* is a monumental collage, melding literary and architectural criticism, history, Marxist critical theory and encyclopaedic quotation that often overwhelms Benjamin's own spare reflections. In their introduction to the English edition, the translators Howard Eiland and Kevin McLaughlin describe the project as 'the blueprint for an unimaginably massive and labyrinthine architecture - a dream city.'

My pilgrimage was to visit the Israeli artist Dani Karavan's breathtaking memorial to Benjamin, named *Passages*, a reference to both Benjamin's unfinished masterwork and of his flight to exile. It is an installation seemingly as inscrutable as Benjamin himself. At the end of the first of Karavan's three passages, on a sheet of glass offering a view of a whirlpool far below, Karavan has etched the words of Benjamin himself: 'It is a more arduous task to honour the memory of anonymous beings than that of famous persons. The construction of history is consecrated to those who have no name.'

Benjamin was buried in an unmarked grave in the section of the municipal cemetery reserved for non-Catholics. Visitors are urged to honour the Jewish tradition by leaving a stone on the marker. I placed a piece of basalt from my village on his memorial stone and mourned.

BERN, STÉPHANE
PRESENTS THE EUROVISION SONG CONTEST

The most brilliant French radio and television presenter, a monarchist, presenter of the Eurovision Song Contest, host of sadly terminated midday show on France Inter called *Le Fou du roi* (the court jester). Bern is funny, gay, and was decorated with the MBE by Her Majesty Queen Elizabeth II in June 2014 during her visit to Paris. He explained to her that he had made a programme about Queen Victoria for French television. 'She seemed truly interested. She had this astonishing ability to make you feel like you were the most important person she had met all day.' Presented a jolly programme on France 2 about Louis XVI in 2015 suggesting he was not such a bad guy after all.

BEURS
'ARABS' WHO ARE NOT REALLY ARABS

Unloved descendants of north African immigrants, *les beurs* are a generation born in France, but in spite of France's claim to equality for all, often self-defined and defined by their fellow French citizens as not quite French. Officially, they do not exist. There is no official or administrative count of citizens of north African origin, but independent data suggests there are more than four million. Simple observation shows they are poorer, less educated, more often unemployed and increasingly radicalised and estranged from the republic of equality.

The political class pretends that this community does not really exist. Republican doctrine does not recognise multiculturalism and the census does not count people by their racial identification or origin. The evident reality is that *les beurs* occupy a wholly different space to the so-called FRANÇAIS DE SOUCHE (French people by roots). They are poorer, more poorly housed and educated and earn less, if they are employed at all. Other immigrant groups in France - the Portuguese, Italians, Spanish - have largely assimilated. Not so *les beurs*. There is a separateness that is palpable. Of course there are exceptions, and this is hardly a uniquely French problem, but the chasm between this community and the rest of France is enormous and seems to be widening.

The word *beur* is a contortion of the word Arab, taken from the mostly obsolescent VERLAN *argot* (slang). Specifically it has described the descendants of north African immigrants, although in practice it is used to describe anyone whom the French might describe as Arab. The notion that north Africans from Algeria, Tunisia and Morocco, who constitute the majority of France's immigrants, are Arabs, is contestable, although they do speak distinctive versions of Arabic.

French national football teams, in which players of immigrant origin are heavily represented, are sometimes referred to as the '*black, blanc, beur*' in an ironic reference to the '*bleu, blanc, rouge*' of the national tricolour. There is a radio station called Beur-FM, determinedly secular, with a playlist heavy on Arab pop music and an agenda focused on defining a '*nouvelle génération*.' The station supports women's rights, offers horse racing tips on its web home page, and the only visible headscarves are in the ads for Islamic dating sites.

BHL
BERNARD-HENRI LÉVY

The global brand of a French public intellectual. Too grand to describe himself as a journalist, and very rich since he inherited about 100 million euros, Lévy, always known as BHL, is a celebrity-philosopher, essayist and controversialist who has parlayed his bilingualism to straddle the gap between Paris and New York. He has a website on which he confidently pronounces in English and French on topics from Heidegger to Greece. Editors like him because he tickles the readers with views that are sometimes as ridiculous as they are elegantly stated. In Paris he is a columnist and talk-show stalwart and has advised ARTE, the TV channel paid for by French and German taxpayers. In New York he is seen at parties with Arianna Huffington (and, for a while at any rate, with Daphne Guinness, the granddaughter of Diana Mosley), for whose eponymous online journals he pronounces frequently. It is hard to identify BHL with any consistent school of thought other than strong self-belief in his rightness on everything, underpinned by a dark view of the past, very much coloured by memories of the Holocaust. His identity as an egotistical neoliberal humanitarian interventionist puts him on the same piste as Tony Blair. A Jew, he is not apparently sufficiently self-aware to see anything paradoxical in his consistent advocacy of western military intervention in the murky affairs of the Islamic world. BHL is a style icon, being ruggedly handsome, and always wears his trademark, immaculate, tailored white shirt open halfway down his chest. MICHEL HOUELLEBECQ, his frenemy, has written of BHL: 'You dishonour even the white shirts you wear. An intimate of the powerful who, since childhood has wallowed in obscene wealth, you are… a philosopher without an original idea.' BHL is also an enemy of the controversial anti-Zionist comedian DIEUDONNÉ.

BISES, BISOUS
POIGNÉE DE MAIN
KISSING - 182 BILLION KISSES
HANDSHAKES - A SOCIAL OBLIGATION

Who to kiss, how many times, when? When I was elected to my

local council, with 10 male members and nine women, it was apparent that all the men were required to kiss all of the women at the start of every meeting. Some of the men, who had known each other a long time, also kissed one another. In our part of France, three kisses are the norm. Hence, before any business could be transacted, at least 270 kisses were exchanged. The maths are fuzzy but one can estimate that the population of France (65 million), each kissing, say, 10 times per day (this is just a guess), could collectively be kissing up to 3.5 billion times a week, exchanging some 182 billion kisses a year. But the figure is conjectural because in parts of Corsica, it is customary to kiss five times, in much of northern France four times, twice in the southwest and three times in the Midi. The Bretons make do with one. It is hard to see how any of this contributes to national productivity, although it is very sweet.

Avoid use of the synonym *baiser*, which also means to fuck.

If kissing is reserved for people who you already know, *poignée de main* (shaking hands) is ubiquitous and you will shake hands with anyone with whom you have even a passing acquaintance. Walking through my village to the bakery in the morning, I will shake hands with up to a dozen people. Failure to observe this ritual can be taken as an insult. Arriving at work, it is customary to shake everyone's hand. I find this custom extremely agreeable as it establishes a direct and human contact that is a formal recognition of mutual respect. It is typically accompanied by the phrase *comment allez vous?* (how are you?) or more informally, *comment ça va?* (how's it going?). I prefer to *vouvoyer* (using the formal *vous*) as it indicates respect. The handshake must always be accompanied by eye contact. Those who you do not know must also be acknowledged. At the very least, you must offer a *bonjour* (good day). If you ask a conductor at a railway station for directions without prefacing your question with a *bonjour*, he or she is likely to be insulted. These rituals are indispensable social signals. When I am in England I reflexively shake hands with many people who do not expect it, evidence, I suppose, that I am going native. It goes the other way, too. Marie-Jo, a French friend who has lived for 20 years in England, tells me she once asked an official at the Gare du Nord for advice, forgetting the obligatory *bonjour*, and could tell at once that the official was distressed. 'I felt ashamed,' she later admitted. 'It was as if I had ignored his humanity.'

BOBO
CHAMPAGNE SOCIALIST

The *bourgeois-bohème* is a privileged, comfortably off champion of the workers, although unlikely to know any as such. Family money is often in the background. Educationally privileged, the *bobo* works in government or the media. Self-situates politically well to the left and culturally to the bohemian. A typical *bobo* might be a film director living in a smart, Brooklyn-style loft in the posh, artsy Paris suburb of Montreuil. There's a comfortable contract with the irrelevant but state-subsidised ARTE television channel, a heavy bookshelf and, on his feet, 500-euro hand-made English shoes. Our *bobo* voted at the last presidential election for Jean-Luc Mélenchon, candidate of the Left Front, *la gauche de la gauche* (the left of the left - hard leftist).

BOLLORÉ, VINCENT
POLITICALLY-CONNECTED BUSINESSMAN

A capitalist who infuriates the French because he has survived all attempts by the taxman to take him down. Industrialist, friend of former President NICOLAS SARKOZY, despised by the left for having made a fortune despite all the obstacles that make this so hard in France. He has a law degree from Nanterre (not the smartest university), started with a family fortune and made it vastly bigger. The notorious/celebrated (depending on your point of view) corporate raider has profited handsomely by outwitting less agile opponents. The *patron* (boss) of media companies VIVENDI AND

Canal⁺, Bolloré is the 329th richest person in the world, according to Forbes. He is currently manufacturing electric cars in Italy (although some will soon be made in France by Renault, under contract) for deployment in the expanding Paris *autolib'* car sharing scheme. His Bluecar uses an innovative lithium metal polymer battery, coming soon to London. With typical swagger Bolloré admits the Bluecar is a gamble but says even if he loses the bet, he will still be rich. His other friends include, inter alia, the supermodel Vanessa Modely.

BOONE, LAURENCE
ECONOMIC ADVISOR TO FRANÇOIS HOLLANDE

In June 2014, Boone was appointed member of François Hollande's kitchen cabinet, and subsequently named *sherpa* to the president (personal representative of a head of state) responsible for preparing his participation in the annual G8 international summit. Aged 46 in 2015, she is a graduate of the University of Paris at Nanterre, holder of further degrees from London Business School and the University of Reading and a former chief European economist for Merrill Lynch. Attended the 2015 elite Bilderberg summit in Austria in 2015 alongside various prime ministers, chief executives and, inevitably, Henry Kissinger. Since it does not appear that the president has any coherent economic policy at all, either her advice is ignored or she is merely expanding her impressive CV. Cynics note that she is very pretty.

BOURBONS, LES
FAILED FRENCH ROYAL DYNASTY THAT LOST ITS HEAD

The decadent royal family whose greed and selfishness condemned France to Republicanism. Or at least this is the history taught in French schools. The Bourbons have been systematically traduced by Republican historians, but the truth is more nuanced. The Bourbon Henri IV, 'Good King Henry,' seemed to launch the French monarchy on a new path when the family replaced the somewhat deranged Valois dynasty on the throne of France in 1589. Louis XIV, the Sun King, was on the throne for 72 years during which France was the leading European power. Louis XV, his great-grandson, inherited a kingdom that was financially stagnant as a result of military adventurism and was forced to return the Austrian Netherlands (Belgium and a bit) to Austria and New France in North America to Spain and Great Britain.

Louis XVI was guillotined on what is now the Place de la Concorde on 21 January 1793. '*Le roi est mort, vive la nation,*' screamed the mob as he was decapitated. His wife, Marie Antoinette, followed him to the scaffold a few months later. She is notorious for having proposed, when informed that the people had no bread, *Qu'ils mangent de la brioche* (let them eat cake). Yet there can be little doubt that this quotation was entirely invented by Jean-Jacques Rousseau as there is no trace of it in contemporary reports.

Despite his subsequent Republican demonisation, Louis XVI was a deeply cultivated and intelligent man (though he required instruction in the mechanics of conceiving a child with Marie Antoinette), fluent in many languages. His efforts to reform the country were undermined by the nobility and never went far enough to appease the growing popular disgust with the regime. Yet he was a patron of science and technology, vaccinating himself against smallpox to demonstrate to his sceptical subjects the value of scientific medicine. He sponsored the Montgolfier brothers' first flights, was patron of the legendary sea voyages of Jean-François de la Pérouse and left an architectural legacy that is still admired by millions of tourists a year. He was also sponsor of the guillotine as a humanitarian method of execution, and experienced first-hand whether it succeeded.

BOVÉ, JOSÉ
GREEN POLITICIAN AND MILITANT

A reactionary ecologist with a moustache straight out of ASTÉRIX, and a founding father of French militant anarchist-ecologism. Aged 61 in 2015, he has participated in destruction of genetically modified crops, destroyed a McDONALD's in Millau, France, with a tractor, has served prison terms for these and other actions. Has travelled to Ramallah in the occupied territories to demonstrate solidarity with Palestinians. Has claimed that attacks on synagogues in France were orchestrated by Israel. Founding member of ATTAC, a group campaigning for taxation of financial transactions. Although appearing French and nativist, he spent years as a child in Berkeley, California, where his parents worked at the university. He speaks English fluently and, beneath the pretence of being a *PAYSAN*, is thoroughly bourgeois. He is currently banned from entering the United States, as well as a Member of the European Parliament as a member of the ultra-left green party, Europe Écologie.

BOVARYSME
THE ENDLESS FRENCH CAPACITY FOR SELF-DELUSION

A flight to the imaginary and romantic. Derived from GUSTAVE FLAUBERT's novel *Madame Bovary*: the heroine's retreat into a world of fantasy, provoked by dissatisfaction with reality, ends in SUICIDE. Bovarysme remains a fundamental French condition. See *ANGÉLISME, ANGOISSE, MISÉRABILISME, SUICIDE.*

BRETON, ANDRÉ
FOUNDER OF SURREALISM

Died aged 70 in 1966, author of the *Manifeste du surréalisme* (Surrealist Manifesto), a striking philosophical document inspired by the Marquis de Sade, Charles Baudelaire, Arthur Rimbaud and Dante, *inter alia*. Poet, art collector, contemporary or colleague of

Louis Aragon, Claude Lévi-Strauss, Leon Trotsky and Salvador Dali. Surrealism has powerfully influenced art, literature, theatre, music, film and politics and continues to do so. Expelled from the communist party, Breton eventually drew the only possible surrealist conclusion and became an anarchist. It is quite possibly true that modern France is itself a surrealist state, an attempt to resolve the contradictory conditions of dreams and reality. See Haïti.

C

CALAIS
IGNORED TERMINUS

Mary Tudor said Calais would be engraved on her heart after it was seized by the French in 1557. In 2015, the city is under siege once more and it is not clear that the French remain in full control. Migrants from the Middle East and Africa have invaded the outskirts seeking clandestine passage to England and disputatious dock workers routinely block the ferry port and tunnel. Human rights organisations condemn the squalid migrant camps on the outskirts. By the summer there were violent daily confrontations between migrants and lorry drivers and the migrants repeatedly breached the tunnel's security perimeter. French police are often conspicuously absent from these confrontations, apparently quite happy for the migrants to get to Britain and become somebody else's problem. Meanwhile, migrants are dying trying to get to England, eight in eight summer weeks. Very little of this is reported in the French national press. The situation in Calais makes French claims to be a *terre d'asile* (land of refuge) seem rather hollow. See: *Tunnel sous la Manche*.

CAMUS, ALBERT
FRENCH HUMANIST WRITER

Died a very French death in 1960 in the passenger seat of his publisher Michel Gallimard's Facel Vega motorcar. A contemporary of JEAN-PAUL SARTRE and a lion of post-war literary Paris, Camus has stood the test of time better than Sartre mainly because he never made a fool of himself apologising for totalitarianism. Famously preferred football to theatre. Born in Algeria, he played goalkeeper for *Racing Universitaire Algerois*, won the

Nobel prize for literature and accepted it with grace (Sartre later turned it down - to snub Camus?). After his death there were various theories that he had been assassinated by the Russians, but the application of Occam's Razor to these theories suggests it was merely Gallimard showing off his iconic French Grand Tourer, driving 180 km per hour and hitting a tree. SARTRE lived on for another 20 increaingly vapid years. The late, great Tony Judt, eminent historian of France, kept a picture of Camus on his desk.

CANARD ENCHAÎNÉ
SATIRICAL, COMPROMISED WEEKLY NEWSPAPER

Sometimes funny weekly newspaper and often less seditious than it appears. *Private Eye* is the closest British equivalent. Established in 1915, it carries no ads and breaks many scoops of which some seem to be spoon-fed rather than uncovered. There is a *face cachée* (hidden side) to the *Canard Enchaîné* (literally, duck in chains) according to the journalists Karl Laske and Laurent Valdiguié in their book, *Le Vrai canard* (*The Real Canard*, 2008) who accuse it of an opaque financial structure and too-cozy relations with politicians. There's little doubt that the journal has allowed itself to be used to settle scores and, notoriously, to convey government disinformation (e.g. the invented story that British intelligence was responsible for sinking the RAINBOW WARRIOR). *Le Canard*'s punning headlines are masterpieces but the wit, while rapier-like and cruel, really serves no purpose other than to boast how clever the magazine is. The paper's annual parties, which are lavish affairs befitting a journal that reputedly makes gigantic profits, attract many members of the very establishment elite who are mocked. All these accusations are sniffily denied by the journal, which calls them 'just gossip.' *Le Canard*, of all journals, is of course hardly in a position to denounce gossip, its own stock-in-trade.

CAPITAL SOCIAL
LIVING FRANCE

A sociological concept coined by the French. Alexis de Tocqueville in the 19th century (*Democracy in America*, 1835) admired the strong social networks in America and their social importance was subsequently elaborated by the sociologist Pierre Bourdieu in 1972. If these informal networks of citizens have subsequently weakened in America, in France my empirical observation is that they remain resolutely strong. At its most fundamental, social capital is manifested simply by the willingness of people to talk to one another in informal encounters. This is very much part of the fabric of life in a French village where people wish each other good day and look one another in the eye as if they mean it. It is also visible in the strength of the voluntary sector. Although the French have a reputation for leaving everything to the all-powerful state to organise, I have become convinced this is not true. My own village of 2,500 people is extraordinary in its level of community engagement with associations covering sports, culture, heritage, music, senior citizens and a twin-city programme. Nearly 300 people turned up for a community concert and dinner in my garden - more than 10 per cent of the population. Friends who live in other villages tell me that the sense of community cohesion is equally strong there. Of course such collective activities exist in other countries, but I have the impression that they remain especially resilient in France - an example of real community *solidARITÉ*, as opposed to the ersatz variety espoused by politicians. A weakness is that the French seem far less active in charitable activities that the British and Americans, a consequence of their belief that social distress is a matter best addressed by the all-powerful state.

CAPOTE ANGLAISE
CONTRACEPTIVE

The French slang term for a *préservatif* (condom). A *capote* is literally a cape or hood. In English, oddly, a condom is sometimes referred to as a French letter.

CATASTROPHE
A STORM IN A TEACUP

When a French person declares *une catastrophe*, do not worry. It is not a nuclear power station melting down, or a war being declared. In French, *catastrophe* is likely to mean that someone has curdled the hollandaise sauce. Or more likely, in the land of ubiquitous McDonald's, spilled the ketchup. An example of a *faux ami* (false friend) - a word that does not mean exactly the same thing in English and French.

CDD, CDI
THE TWO TYPES OF EMPLOYMENT IN FRANCE

The local computer repairman, like almost every French tradesman I know, works alone. Hiring someone is just too risky. 'I would have to take a pay cut to hire someone and then if they were no good I couldn't fire them,' he explains. The French talk constantly about the evil of the so-called zero-hour contracts used in the UK but their own system encourages an equally precarious situation for employees. A *contrat de travail à durée déterminée* (CDD) is a fixed-term contract uniquely for temporary employment. A CDD employee can be used as a temporary replacement for a permanent employee on parental or sickness leave, to fill a gap in case of temporary increase in activity, for seasonal employment or in the case of specialists, to fulfil a precise and specific activity for a duration not to exceed 36 months. It is forbidden to replace a striking worker with an employee on a CDD. All other employees must be covered by a *contrat à durée indéterminée* (CDI), which guarantees a job for life except under specific circumstances when the employee may be terminated or made redundant. These circumstances, and the compensation payable for termination, are rigorously regulated. Employers prefer to employ workers whenever possible under a CDD and young people are disproportionately employed under these arrangements, if they are employed at all. Many are forced to accept jobs as sub-minimum-wage *stagiaires* (interns), for a duration not to exceed six months. CDD contracts and employment as an intern are typically not recognised by banks as a basis for a mortgage loan hence those employed under these arrangements are significantly excluded from home ownership. Although the objective of the French law is to promote employment stability, it perversely produces both high unemployment and precarious temporary employment.

CDG
FRANCE'S FILTHY GATEWAY

Arriving from Bamako, Mali, at 6 a.m. at Charles de Gaulle airport is one of the most dispiriting experiences I can remember. CDG features crumbling buildings, scowling officials, chaotic security lines and filthy food. This is unfortunately the first view of France available to its 65 million passengers a year. The old Terminal One, a rat's maze of concrete and perspex tubes, is almost unnavigable, but at least still standing. A chunk of the newer Terminal Two simply collapsed shortly after it opened, killing several passengers. All the contradictions of modern France are on display. Eighty baggage handlers have been arrested for stealing from passenger luggage in six years, Air France or the air traffic controllers or the taxi drivers are frequently on strike, the toilets are dirty, the catering disgraceful. Aéroports de Paris (ADP), owner of CDG, also controls the second Paris Airport, Orly, which is also grim. Even after allegedly privatising the airport, the almighty state owns 52 per cent of ADP's shares.

C'EST COMME ÇA
PASSIVE AGGRESSION

This infuriating French expression is akin to 'whatever'. It means literally, 'that's how it is,' sub-textually can also mean, 'so, fuck off.' A French person tried this line on me at the airport in Kourou, French Guiana, trying to cut into the queue at the check-in desk. '*Non, c'est pas comme ça,*' I told him, blocking him with my suitcase. He pushed in front of me anyway. Being British, I avoided further confrontation.

CENTRALES NUCLÉAIRES
FRAGILE PROWESS

Une centrale is a nuclear power station. I am acutely aware that there are three of them within an uncomfortable distance from my house. All told, France has 58 nuclear fission reactors steaming away at 19 sites, generating 75 per cent of France's electricity supply. So far they have avoided a disaster (or have successfully covered up any that they might have had). But the French nuclear miracle is looking pretty fragile these days. The French nuclear champion, Areva, is a financial basket case and the heavy exposure of the French electricity grid to nuclear plants is looking less clever. The arrangements by which the nuclear estate has been financed and accounted for are opaque. The fundamental problem is that this glorious symbol of French technical achievement is not in the bloom of youth. Two stations are being expensively dismantled and the impossibly costly project for decommissioning the rest has been kicked into the long grass.

CHAMBRES DE COMMERCE
FETTERS OF THE ECONOMY

There are chambers of agriculture, trades, dentistry, lawyers - chambers of everything. They bear no relation to an American chamber of commerce, which sees its function as the promotion of commerce. French chambers often occupy themselves inhibiting commerce. The chamber is where you must go to get permission if you wish to start a business. And to get this, you will expose yourself to the full panoply of French rules that crush enterprise, punish investment, make it impossible to fire anyone and cost a fortune. These chambers must not only approve the business you intend to operate but must approve any change in the business. A farmer who wants to diversify by, for example, converting a redundant building to a livery stable, must obtain permission from the chamber of agriculture. Comparisons to the UK are always provocative but in England you can register a company online and go into business on the same day.

CHARLIE HEBDO
NATIONAL HYPOCRISY

Islamist massacre at this weekly magazine provoked a huge and ongoing display of French hypocrisy, from the streets of Paris to the Place de la République in my own village. In 2006 *Charlie Hebdo* provocatively republished contested Danish cartoons of Muhammad, adding more of its own. Its offices were firebombed in 2011 after the paper published a further drawing depicting him complaining that it was 'hard to be loved by CONS.' In January 2015, 10 members of staff and two policemen died after two terrorists penetrated the magazine's feeble security cordon. Eventually, 10 more people died after a chaotic pursuit of the gunmen brought much of France to a standstill. That it could have been worse is no comfort to any of the security authorities in Europe.

The affair exposed failure at every level. Nobody at *Charlie Hebdo* was properly guarded nor was their office. The entrance to the building was minimally protected. The cops on the scene were woefully vulnerable and unsupported. After the slaughter, the perpetrators casually killed one of the policemen, already wounded, before getting into their Citroën and driving away, eluding any police effort to stop them. It ended when the two brothers were cornered at a printing works and shot dead and a third gunman was killed in a Jewish supermarket in Paris after killing four people there.

CHASSE, LA
SHOOTING AT EVERYTHING THAT MOVES, INCLUDING CATS, CYCLISTS

French people who do not hunt say that while not all *cons* (variously translated as arseholes, cunts and dumbasses) are hunters, all hunters are *cons*. The hunt is either (a) a glorious man-ifestation of Republicanism in which anyone can participate, not just the nobility, or (b) a system, insanely regulated, that produces ongoing horror in the French countryside. I go with (b). In the royal *HEXAGONE* (France), hunting was the preserve of the aristocrats. After the revolution everyone else got the right to hunt, a right preserved to this day as each autumn, as soon as there is a brief stirring of revival in the local fauna, signs of the occasional bird, perhaps a rabbit, male villagers go out to slaughter it. Thus each autumn there is the scary sight of heavily armed men, who have paused at the village bar to tank up on *PASTIS* before setting off to terrorise the local wildlife, letting off their guns at anything with the temerity to crawl, fly or otherwise propel itself. Armed with shotguns and heavy caliber rifles, the hunters' bag included 57 people killed in the 2012-2013 season, with 89 wounded. Almost but not all of those killed are themselves hunters. Criminal sanctions for hunting accidents tend to be absurdly lenient.

'CHEESE-EATING SURRENDER MONKEYS'
NEVER ELEGANTLY TRANSLATED INTO FRENCH

Coined by the American TV series *The Simpsons*. In a 1995 episode, budget cuts at Springfield Elementary School force the

janitor, Groundskeeper Willie, to become a French teacher.
Expressing his disdain for the French people, he says to his
French class in a Scottish accent: 'Bonjoooouuuurrr, ya cheese-
eatin' surrender monkeys!' None of the efforts to translate this
into French are convincing. The literal gloss, *singes capitulards,*
bouffeurs de fromage, hardly does credit to the poetry of the original.
The French have never understood *Les Simpson* in any case
thinking it to be a rather ordinary cartoon for children and
entirely missing its sardonic parody of middle America, which
does not survive dubbing.

CHEVAUX
THE FRENCH BREED EXCELLENT HORSES, THE NOT-SO-EXCELLENT THEY EAT

French racehorses and competition horses (showjumping,
dressage, eventing) are among the best in the world and the *selle*
française (French sport horse) is celebrated everywhere. But where
the French truly excel is the *cheval de trait* (working horse). The
most magnificent are the Percheron horses of Normandy, where
the bloodlines are carefully conserved at the HARAS NATIONAL DU PIN
(national stud farm in le Pin-au-Haras), a temple to the breed with
its own chateau. It was constructed by LOUIS XIV to produce horses
for his army. ÉMILE ZOLA described the fate of many of these horses
in *LA DÉBÂCLE* (*The Downfall,* 1892) in passages that bring tears to the
eyes of all horse lovers. My own Percheron horses, Manet and
Rodin, weigh a tonne each. They are gentle but with an occasional
fiery disposition, a consequence of their Arab bloodlines. They
can be ridden, driven in harness, plough a field, haul timber from
the woods and Manet can even manage a little dressage.

France exports thousands of racehorses and working horses
all over the world. The Percheron thrives in America, where
Amish farmers continue to prize them for their steadiness and
appetite for hard work. The French have even re-imported
Percheron horses from Michigan and Ohio from stock originally

exported in the 19th century, to broaden the genetic diversity of their domestic breeding stock. Manet and Rodin share an American grandfather, Silver Shadow Sheik, born in Michigan (like Mrs Miller). I visited this magnificent black stallion in Normandy, where he was living in glorious retirement. The Comtois horse bred in eastern France is another exceptional working animal, equally versatile and now also becoming a major export with dozens starting to arrive in Britain where they are prized for their docility, power and compact size.

Fifty years ago there were 300 horses in my village, working in the vineyards. Only a couple are still employed this way, by a centenerian *vigneron* (wine grower) who manoeuvres his animals through the vines simply by talking to them. He is universally known as *le dernier des Mohicans* (the last of the Mohicans). I have visited other winemakers in Champagne who also use horses, but there can only be a few hundred vineyard horses left in France. Still, the French have been careful to preserve the heritage of their working horses, increasingly prized for carriage driving. Every few years, there is a spectacular relay between Boulogne and Paris, *La Route du Poisson* (Fish Race), in which working horses compete to transport fresh fish from France's leading northern fishing port to the fish market in the capital. Teams come from all over Europe to participate in the spectacle. I am not a sufficiently talented horseman to compete myself, but did join the British team as a translator. We rattled through French villages in the middle of the night, where thousands lined the streets to cheer us on.

The French, who eat anything, remain partial to horse meat, which has not always been labelled as such. Much of the frozen lasagne on sale in French supermarkets contained horse but claimed to be beef until the government belatedly cracked down on this deception. Some of this 'beef' was exported to Britain. A horse butcher comes to my village market every Friday and his cuts are especially prized by the old widows, who eat it raw, to give them strength. Appalling as the British find this, it does result in an exceptional advantage for French breeders. The French simply consume the lesser beasts, and breed from only the best.

But the lot of the horse in France can be unhappy. An explosion in French leisure-horse ownership has not been matched by universal aptitude in caring for them. A few months ago, a German neighbour came to my door in tears and begged me to accompany her to a small paddock next to a house on the outskirts of the village. Here she pointed out a stunted, crippled horse, evidently in pain, its leg fractured. She had reported the animal to the police three days earlier and they had done nothing. The animal was emaciated and had evidently been suffering for some time.

I knocked at the door of the family who were keeping the animal. They refused to acknowledge ownership or say where the animal had come from. It was clear they were lying. I told them that they must give me permission to take the animal or I would summon the GENDARMES. I had no idea if the gendarmes would even show up, but I put on my most menacing manner. Sullenly, they agreed. I phoned a vet on my mobile phone. She came almost immediately and agreed that the animal was beyond help. There was no alternative. I held the poor animal's head and stroked its neck, and she euthanised the creature. The vet said it was the worst thing she had ever seen. We wept.

CHIENS
DOGS HAVE RIGHTS, IN PRINCIPLE

Janet Langman, a British dog owner in France, says there are four types of French dogs. 'There are handbag dogs, hunting dogs, tied-up dogs and dogs on the loose.' Her taxonomy is incomplete. There are also howling dogs, starved dogs and dogs who foul the pavements. The handbag dogs are the privileged elite. Norman, an American who has many decades of experience dining in France, tells me of an evening at the upscale Maison du Caviar in Paris. A well-dressed lady arrived with her handbag dog, which installed itself on its own chair at her table, awaiting its dinner. Two women, evidently foreign, dining a few feet away, cast a dirty look at the dog, which, detecting their hostility, started barking at them. The women summoned the *maître d'hôtel*. He listened to their story without much apparent interest, offered a very Gallic shrug of the shoulders (shoulders elevated, arms outstretched, palms forward), and suggested that if they didn't like the dog, they could leave. 'The dog was obviously a regular customer,' observes Norman.

Walking my dog Ringo, formerly a dog on the loose and found abandoned at the side of the road, and who is correctly said by my French friends to have *bien tombé* (well fallen), I meet plenty of owners with well-nourished, clean and happy dogs, enjoying the freedom of the countryside as much as we do. Yet there seem to be many dogs in every French village who are ignored and abused and the further south you go, the worse it gets. The French say the English spell GOD backwards. But it's not just the British who are horrified.

Vast numbers are simply abandoned, usually without the legally required tattoo or microchip or even a collar with an identity disc, making them impossible to identify. Although animal abuse is technically a crime, it can be hard to prove and is not a priority for the police or the courts. Walk through any French village and listen to the dogs howling. In 2014 France adopted a new recognition of animals in the Civil Code as 'living and conscious beings' which in theory gives a better legal basis for animal protection in France. But little seems to have changed. The national animal rights group, *30 Millions d'Amis,* struggles to educate the public. Cats are more self-sufficient but still vulnerable. A friend's cat was shot by one of the madder local *chasseurs* (hunters) and it cost her 1,000 euros in vets' fees to save its life. The hunt offered a paltry 250 euros compensation, without admitting liability.

Ringo's favourite restaurants are the Louis XI steak house in Bourges, where the owner always presents him with a plate of raw beef, and Yumi Matsui's sushi restaurant in Pézenas, where he prefers a melange of tuna and salmon sashimi. He is never charged for these snacks; neither am I.

CHINE, LA
THE SUPER RICH

A Chinese businessman recently bought a house in the old quarter of our village. Another just bought a vineyard near Béziers. This has provoked tremendous excitement among those hoping to flog their decaying houses and exhausted vineyards to a rich Chinese. The Chinese are seduced by everything about France, from wine to luxury goods. Li Jinyuan, a Chinese billionaire, recently treated 6,400 of his employees to a holiday in France, booking 140 hotels in Paris and 4,700 rooms on the Côte d'Azur. Perhaps the solution to French economic malaise could be to simply sell the entire country to the Chinese as a job lot.

CHIRAC, JACQUES
SHADY PRESIDENT OF THE REPUBLIC, 1995-2007

Ethically compromised, nominally conservative French politician with unexplained wealth, a string of mistresses and a streak of chauvinism. Incredibly grand, famously priapic, before being elected President, Chirac was the holder of all of the great offices of state including prime minister. Nominally of the right but ideologically flexible or without a single political principle, depending on one's point of view. Notoriously presided over the *COHAbiTATION* government (in which the President and government are from different parties) of socialist Lionel Jospin in 1990, which introduced the disastrous *TRENTE-CiNQ HEURES* (35-hour week). Asked by the BBC's Jon Sopel, 'What do you stand for, Mr Chirac?' he replied, 'I stand for election.' To his credit, Chirac defied President George W. Bush by refusing to allow French participation in the second Iraq war, provoking an outbreak of FRENCH-bashing in the USA (French fries were removed from menu of the Senate restaurant and replaced by 'freedom fries'). Linked to shady business in five separate *affaires*, as mayor of Paris he was reported to have accepted suitcases full of cash. It was reported in 1996 that he had a secret Japanese bank account containing 300 million francs (roughly 40 million euros). Known to the French as the *super menteur* (super liar), he is a graduate of the École Nationale d'Administration, incubator of the French elite.

CHÔMAGE
FRANCE'S PLUGHOLE

The curse of France. In March 2015, *chômage* (unemployment) in France reached a new record high of 3,509,800. In April, it set another new record of 3,536,000. Youth unemployment increased 2.2 per cent between April 2014 and April 2015. The number of long-term unemployed was up 10.2 per cent in the same year. More than 2 million people have been looking for a job for more than 12 months. This count includes only those registered with the local *pôle emploi* (job centre). Unemployment in France is twice the level of Germany and the UK. Youth unemployment is more than 25 per cent and in the ghettos between 40-50 per cent. French politicians think unemployment will fall as the economy picks up but this is fantasy because even if it does, employers will do everything they can to avoid hiring workers, exposing themselves to punishing payroll taxes and employment laws. Innovations that could create employment, such as the authorisation of more Sunday shop openings, private hire care services and permission for dental hygienists, are obstructed so as not to offend unions and entrenched monopolies.

CINÉMA
FILM INDUSTRY THAT IS A FLAGSHIP OF FRENCH EXCEPTIONALISM

The art of projecting film was perfected in France and French cinematographers, directors and actors have strongly influenced the film industry throughout its history. France still reveres film and elevates directors to the status of *auteurs* (authors). The French love everything about film: the technical challenge, the artistry and of course the glamour. But despite protection for French films from barbaric American imports and heavy subsidies, and the glamour of the Cannes Film Festival, French cinema is in trouble, menaced by new technologies like Internet streaming. The industry's dependence on handouts has not promoted a culture of paying much attention to audiences.

Television channels pay 3.2 per cent of their profits and Canal+, the subscription TV monopoly, 12 per cent towards French film production. Yet it is in a slump, with increasing numbers of directors choosing to shoot their films in English and many of its most talented players leaving for Los Angeles. Many films that once would have been made in France are now being shot elsewhere. According to the *New York Times*, 22 per cent percent of filming for French movies was completed beyond its borders in the first nine months of 2014. In 2012, a particularly devastating year in terms of production flight, the rate was 50 percent for projects with budgets between 10 and 20 million euros, and 21 percent for films under 10 million euros, according to the French cinema industries federation. France has struggled to adapt to the new forms of cinema distribution such as Netflix streaming and has yet to fully adapt to the new long-form television formats. France has shown itself capable of producing internationally successful cinema-like TV series like *The Returned* (*Les Revenants*) and *Spiral* (*Engrenages*), which have found enthusiastic audiences in the anglophone world, even if the subtitles are often pretty dodgy. But these are exceptions.

In a blistering article in *Le Monde* in 2012, Vincent Maraval, a distributor, declared the year to have been a(nother) 'disaster.' French cinema, he complained, has structured itself around an economy of subsidies and even the greatest so-called successes produced by this system have lost money. Overpaid actors have consumed too much of the budget, leaving little space for innovation. Production costs are among the highest in the world. He blamed television for dragging down standards, illustrating that few in France seem to have recognised the platform revolution in audiovisual production. At least tax-payer subsidies continue to provide cosy insulation.

Does French cinema have a future? The French have taken perverse pride in boasting that their cinema is art. While superficially commendable, this is suicidal. The French government is dreaming of a so-called Google tax on end-users to keep the subsidies flowing once the old broadcast distribution network is supplanted by streaming. But in an age of media production - including some dramatic new successes from those money-grabbing Americans - French film will atrophy unless this industry, too, moves towards successful creative investments rather than politicised subsidies warranted by the elite.

CLIENTÉLISME
GOODS, SERVICES AND SUBSIDIES FOR POLITICAL SUPPORT

A malaise at the heart of French society, responsible for corruption and economic failure. *Clientélisme* and political corruption on the one hand, and normal political give and take on the other, are sometimes hard to tell apart. In France clientism is deeply embedded as a consequence of a political system in which the state provides a flow of subsidies to local government in return for the political support of local politicians, and awards government contracts to private enterprise with political *piston* (influence). The consequence is that politicians are dependent on their political superiors for finance of their projects, and that the private sector is often not as private as it looks (see *paraétatisme*). A third pillar of *clientélisme* is the relationship between the state and the *syndicats* (unions), to whom are delegated important governmental functions, and deferred to on reforms, in return for not making too much trouble.

CLOSER
MAGAZINE THAT GOES WHERE POLITICAL REPORTERS FEAR TO TREAD

Since French newspapers are so tame, French readers are turning to gossip magazines inspired by British tabloids, which they call the *presse people*. The most daring of these is *Closer*. Despised by the French journalism establishment, who believe that professional ethics prohibits investigating the private lusts of public figures, the British-founded *Closer* (circulation 350,000), although now run by Italians, has been treating the French elite with the contempt it deserves and paying the inevitable legal fines for invasion of privacy as a cost of doing business. The people's press is hardly virtuous. *Closer* revealed Kate Middleton topless and Carla Bruni in a swimsuit, but sometimes it produces genuine scoops, most notoriously pictures of President FRANÇOIS HOLLANDE on a motor scooter outside the actress JULIE GAYET's apartment. *Voici* and *Public* are other popular French titles. *Paris-Match*, akin to the now defunct *Life* magazine in the United States, is not strictly a people magazine since it also includes much serious reportage, but it is certainly interested in celebrity and has been the platform for the scorching revelations of President Hollande's erstwhile first lady, VALÉRIE TRIERWEILER.

COCORICO
THE CRY OF A CROWING COCKEREL AND A BOASTFUL FRENCHMAN

This is the triumphalist sound made by a Frenchman standing up to his ankles in shit. I merely pass on the definition proffered to me at a reception at the French embassy in Washington, by a senior diplomat.

CODE CIVIL
THE NATIONAL YOKE

The legal system under whose yoke the French are condemned to have every aspect of their lives regulated. The enduring legacy of NAPOLÉON BONAPARTE, there are in fact 60 separate codes and while they contain some enlightened revolutionary ideals, they are also in many respects today less flexible than the Anglo-Saxon tradition of common law that has come to dominate international business transactions, and resulted in the ascendance of English and American global law firms and the marginalisation of French law on the global stage (see *AVOCATS*).

CODE DU TRAVAIL
EMPLOYMENT LAW AGAINST EMPLOYMENT

Ludicrous, perverse compilation of employment laws, codified down to the tiniest detail. The code contains 196 pages of regulations just for hairdressers. Although called the employment code, it might as well be called the unemployment code. It is in every way a catalogue of restrictions that create obstacles for France to develop service industries. The regulations are enforced by *inspecteurs du travail* who have police powers and their rulings are subject to review by councils of *PRUD'HOMMES* (elected by, among others, the labour unions) who take months to make decisions and are not known for being employer-friendly.

The manifold restrictions and costs of the code, the imposition of inflexible contracts and conditions of employment that make it almost impossible to fire anyone, are more than enough to demotivate French businesses from hiring. The lethal cocktail of the code and sky-high *COTISATIONS* (social charges) is a job killer. In 1990, just 25 years ago, the *Code du Travail* was 1,000 pages in length and there were 1,000,000 unemployed. By the year 2000 the code had doubled in size to 2,000 pages, and so had unemployment, to 2,000,000. In 2010, following a perfectly symmetrical trajectory, the code stood at 3,000 pages and unemployment at 3,000,000. And in 2014-15 with more than 3,500 pages in the Code, unemployment is precisely on track at more than 3,500,000!

The *inspecteurs du travail* recently prosecuted Stéphane Cazenave, a master baker in Saint-Paul-lès-Dax, in southwest France, for his failure to close one day a week. The baker, who has 22 employees and has won a prize for the best baguette in France, says the judgement will cause him to let go some of his employees and lose hundreds of thousands in annual revenue. Other bakers had complained that Cazenave's energetic activities were unfair competition. A notorious perversity of the *Code du Travail* is that it is usual for companies to seek to remain under the plateau of 50 employees. At 50 or more, like it or not, an employer is required to involve social partners (unions), establish works councils with meetings, agendas, etc. and pay higher social charges. The result is that three times as many companies in France have 49 employees as have 50; another perverse triumph for French regulation.

COMMERÇANTS
A REAL NATION OF SHOPKEEPERS

NAPOLÉON BONAPARTE said the English were *une nation de boutiquiers* (derogatory term usually translated as a nation of shopkeepers), which was not an original sentiment as it had first been observed by Adam Smith. This is no longer true. Britain is now a nation of chain stores and Internet distribution and it is the French who are the *petits commerçants* (small shopkeepers). This is not all bad as there are still many family-owned *tabacs* (tobacconists) and *maisons de la presse* (newsagents), whereas in Britain these enterprises have long been transformed into a sterile branch of WH Smith or, in America, Hudson News. Family-owned businesses are advantaged in France because they can reduce their exposure to social charges and work-time rules. The *Daily Mail* says French shopkeepers are the surliest in Europe but in my village this is not true at all, although they do close for lunch.

CON, CONNARD, MERDE, PUTE
THE ART OF BEING VULGAR

The French curse liberally and creatively. *Con* is one of the great *polyvalent* (multipurpose) French insults. *Con* depending on context can be equivalent to asshole, jerk, imbecile or someone who is mentally deficient. It's a diminutive of *connard* (masculine) or *conne*, *connasse* or *connarde* (feminine). A *connerie* is a stupid or idiotic action. '*Casse-toi, pauv' con!*' (more or less, 'fuck off you pathetic asshole') was the phrase famously used by former president Nicolas Sarkozy during a walkabout in Paris after a man refused to shake his hand. The man told the president: 'Don't touch me, you'll make me dirty.' Sarko's riposte was considered below the dignity of a president. Although the French lack the word fuck, which is of Germanic origin, there are multiple ways to express this sentiment in French. '*Va te faire foutre,*' means go fuck yourself, in which the verb *foutre* (fuck) is freighted with the added insult of the familiar pronoun. *Dégage* is another way of telling someone to fuck off.

Merde (literally, shit) is another highly versatile French vulgarity. Can be used in combination with the particle '*de*' to form compound insults such as, *pute de merde de con* (literally 'asshole-shit-whore', lyrically 'holy fucking shit'). You can insult someone by saying *tu m'emmerdes* ('you're pissing me off', strengthened by using the familiar *tu* pronoun as an insult), or you can declare how pissed-off you are by declaring, *ça m'emmerde* ('that's pissing me off'). A *pute* or a *putain* (pronounced with a deep U - sounds like 'oo') is a whore but the word on its own can be used to express any negative emotion (reaction to a flat tyre) or to emphasise an imperative, *éteins cette putain de télévision* ('turn off the bloody TV'). A *bordel* is a whorehouse where you would find *putes* but the words can be combined with the ever versatile *merde* to produce *putain de bordel de merde* (roughly equivalent to 'fucking hell'). The masterwork on French swearing is *Merde! The Real French You Were Never Taught in School* (1998) by Genevieve, illustrated by my former newspaper colleague Michael Heath, although it is now rather dated.

The sentimental film *Le Dîner de cons* (Francis Veber, 1998) portrayed a club of arrogant Frenchmen who competed to invite the most awful *cons* to their dinners in order to mock them. The twist was that the supposed *con* turned out to be the only decent human being among them.

CONCURRENCE DÉLOYLE
UNFAIR (READ ANY) COMPETITION

The term refers not just to unfair competition but in practice to any economic activity that might force a market incumbent to compete. The French are very keen on monopolies, restraints of trade and inhibitions on market entry. In effect, any and all competition is *a priori* unfair to existing market players, hence there are tiers of regulation to protect established economic actors, no matter how inefficient, and to inhibit competitors, no matter how innovative. French booksellers were able to persuade the government to prohibit amazon.fr from offering free delivery, as this was considered unfair competition. Its scope to shake up the French book business is further handicapped by the price controls on the books themselves, forbidding discounting. Amazon does not function in France as it does in the UK or Germany; it can take days or weeks for goods to be delivered, if they are. See TAXIS.

CONSEIL CONSTITUTIONNEL
COUNCIL FOR GERIATRIC STATESMEN

Compromised arbiter of the constitution. The council is made up of former presidents of the Republic and nine other members, typically superannuated politicians at the end of their career in the

Senate and National Assembly. It decides whether new legislation is compatible with the French constitution. Riven with conflicts of interest, feuds and dubious appointments, the rulings are not supposed to be political even though they are made by people who are all politicians. The council struck down Hollande's first effort to impose a 75 per cent income tax as un-Republican and discriminatory. Since most members of the Conseil Constitutionnel can be fairly considered millionaires, this would be fair enough, except they have nothing to say about a tax code that is riddled with other exceptional privileges.

CONSEILLER MUNICIPAL
MUNICIPAL COUNCILLORS

Humblest *élu* (elected official) in France. I am one of these and have even been issued an official identity card to prove it. I have yet to discover what this card will do for me, other than reminding me of my weighty political responsibilities, should I forget. You do not need to be a French citizen to be a councillor - any EU citizenship will do - although before the election I did get a call from an official at the *PRÉFECTURE* to check me out. I suspect this may have been to verify that I could hold a telephone conversation in French. I have absolutely no power but I am allowed to speak at council meetings where I denounce villagers who let their dogs foul the sidewalks. Nepotism is taken for granted in local government and it is the relatives of the mayor and his close political allies who benefit. A nearby village recently hired a municipal police officer. Sixty candidates applied but nobody was surprised when the job went to the granddaughter of the deputy mayor. Some councillors are paid - the mayor and his *adjoints* (deputies). Not me. Much of the work is crushingly routine and largely to do with approving budgets in a form acceptable to the state, and voting to apply for subsidies to fix the sewers, etc. We also deliver copies of the municipal bulletin to our neighbours. Hence, I have gone from being a national newspaper journalist to a delivery boy. Sometimes the meetings get heated. One of our councillors demanded that we censor the contentious *tribune* (monthly political diatribe) of the ultra-left wing opposition councillors that is published in the municipal bulletin. This demand came immediately after the entire council had paraded in front of the town hall in a demonstration of solidarity with *CHARLIE HEBdo,* claiming to support liberty of expression. I spoke strongly against it, judging that the opposition was free to publish any drivel it wanted to. My intervention was approvingly reported in the *Midi-Libre* newspaper, after which I have gained a certain notoriety as a champion of free speech.

LA CORSE
VIOLENT PARADISE

The most beautiful part of France? No, the most beautiful place in the world, insists my Corsican friend. Corrupt, problematic but exquisite French island in the Mediterranean filled with offshore Frenchmen famous for murderous feuds, corruption and superb sausage. Although they are legally French, the Corsicans are really Italian. They are surrounded by water but they hardly fish; looking to their interior mountains for grazing, the surrounding sea tends to scare them. Like Albanians, Scots and other mountain men, Corsicans are celebrated for their multi-generational death feuds, settling old scores with their iconic Corsican vendetta knives. The reputation of Corsicans for random violence is satirised by René Goscinny and Albert Udezro in *Astérix in Corsica* (1973). Extreme violence remains endemic to Corsica. To take some 2014 reports more or less at random, a prominent lawyer was assassinated, a father was gunned down in front of his children and a woman was shot eight times in the back outside a shopping centre. In 1988, the prefect of Corse du-Sud, Claude Érignac, was shot dead by a Corsican nationalist.

Corsica is linked to the mainland by the ferries of *la Société nationale Corse Méditerranée* (SNCM), whose militant workers are represented by a hardline branch of the CGT union. SNCM has long been an example of gross inefficiencies, restrictive working practices and accusations of outright criminality. SNCM sailors work 200 days a year, although often less as they are frequently on strike. Although it loses roughly 40 million euros a year on revenue of 230 million euros, it remains in operation through gross applications of subsidies funded by French taxpayers.

Corsica is famously the birthplace of NAPOLÉON BONAPARTE, himself of Italian stock. Since the new style French *plaques d'im- matriculation* (licence plates) were introduced, many people with absolutely no connection to the island adorn their cars with Corsican plates. The subtext of this is, 'don't fuck with me.' (I have not bothered with this. My own car's licence plates are adorned with the departmental code 975, which baffles most French people until I explain that it represents the tiny French islands of St Pierre and Miquelon off the coast of Newfoundland, the closest department of France to Canada, where I was born.)

COTISATIONS
SOCIAL CHARGES TO FUND BUREAUCRACY

A couple recently moved to my village and bought the lease on the local café, to the delight of most of us. They'd scraped together their every last penny, started cleaning the place up after years of benign neglect, and worked every hour God gave them. Two weeks later, a demand dropped in their letterbox that they should immediately pay 10,000 euros in *cotisations* (social charges). They immediately protested. Their income was negligible, they had dedicated every penny of their savings to the project and there was much more to do. The response was hardly satisfacto- ry. If it turned out that the demand was excessive, they could claim a refund - in a year.

Cotisations are said to be the basis of the French social model, assuring medical care, social security and a comfortable retirement, but are an exorbitant tax on jobs and enterprise. They can add 80 per cent to the cost of employing someone (versus the average 13.8 per cent employer national insurance contribution and 3-5 per cent pension contribution levied in Britain), with the inevitable result that firms will do everything they can to avoid hiring anyone. My friend Bertrand, a talented and enterprising dentist (he is Swiss), had plans to open a new clinic in our village, employing 20 people. That's not going to happen now. He did hire a bright young graduate dentist to help him, whom he pays 3,000 euros per month. Then he discovered that the cotisations add 2,800 euros to his costs. His business plan became unviable. The local printer told me he now works on his own because after briefly hiring an assistant, he was working more and earning less. 'On my own, I work less and earn more,' he said. Social charges make French labour amongst the most expensive in the euro zone, which is itself much more expensive than the US, Japan or the UK. The social security system spends 40 per cent of the money it collects on its own administration.

CUISINE
THE REPUBLIC OF JUNK FOOD

The restaurants of France represent the national paradox, on a plate. There are the exquisite (rare, costly), the good (you have to look), and then the majority, which range from ordinary to mediocre to just awful. The glory of French cooking was most memorably celebrated in the magisterial tome *La Physiologie du goût* (*Physiology of Taste*, 1825) by Jean Anthelme Brillat-Savarin, celebrating the explosion of bourgeois cuisine following the French revolution. It's still in print. Ambrose Bierce celebrates him with the following story:

'I was in my drawing room, enjoying my dinner,' said Brillat-Savarin, beginning an anecdote. 'What!' interrupted Rochebriant, 'eating dinner in a drawing room?' 'I must beg you to observe, monsieur,' explained the great gastronome, 'that I did not say I was eating my dinner, but enjoying it. I had dined an hour before.'

Roland Barthes, the semiotician and phenomenologist, considered the phenomenological relationship of the Frenchman to his dinner in his famous essay *Le Bifteck et les frites* (*Steak and chips*, 1957). This amusing discourse goes beyond mere steak and chips to discuss, amongst other things, that great French variation on the dish, in which the beef is not cooked at all. *Steak tartare*, he says, is 'an operation by which a spell is cast against the romantic association of sensibility with sickliness; in this preparation are to be found all the germinative states of matter; the bloody pulp of beef and egg, a regular harmony of soft and living substances, a signifying compendium of images of parturition.' What might Barthes have made of a McDonald's hamburger?

You will never get a Frenchman to admit that the food is now better in England, except many of those who live there. France does not place in the top 10 of the top 50 restaurants in the world, scraping in at number 11 after establishments in Spain, Italy, Denmark, Peru, The United States, Japan, Brazil, the United Kingdom and Thailand. This ranking has predictably been denounced by French chefs. It is true that at the stratospheric end of the restaurant business where the bill can reach 500 euros a head, plus wine, there may be little difference between *El Celler de Can Roca* in Girona, Spain and the *Miramar* in Menton, France. The problem is not that it is impossible to eat superbly in France. If you pay enough, you can eat a meal that you will remember for 20 years. The difficulty is everyday dining.

There are still small family restaurants offering bourgeois cooking using local ingredients, serving lamb from the local shepherd, the fish landed that morning, seasonal fruit and vegetables from the *potager* (kitchen garden) out back. But these are increasingly hard to find and those who operate them are coshed by the stagnant economy, high labour costs, restrictive work-time flexibility and exorbitant COTISATIONS. There are probably 200 restaurants within 20 km of my village, but I tend to patronise only a tiny handful of them. The brutal truth is that the average restaurant is getting worse, even as the standards in other countries are rising. You are more likely to be offered a plate of boiled-in-the-bag duck *confit* at a restaurant in France than anything actually prepared in the kitchen. More than likely, this confection is produced in the industrial kitchens of Brake France, an assembly-line processor of ready meals, owned by Bain Capital, Mitt Romney's old outfit, headquartered in Boston, Massachusetts. Brake is the largest (but not the only large) supplier of frozen and *sous-vide* (vacuum-packed) meals supplied to tens of thousands of French restaurants. The French don't even know how to make pizza (outside of Nice, where they are really Italian), using the wrong flour, the wrong cheese (Emmental, for heaven's sake), and tinned tomatoes.

In 2012, Jacques Goldstein, a French filmmaker, produced an excoriating documentary on the decline of French kitchens, *République de la malbouffe* (Junk-food republic). The film, which can only be described as furious and heavy-handed, nevertheless exposed the degradation of French cooking, accusing then-president NicolAs SArkozy of collaborating with industrial catering companies at the expense of traditional restaurateurs. But the decline is nothing new. A. J. Leibling of the *New Yorker*, one of the world's greatest gourmets, was decrying the decline in French cooking in 1959.

Even the government timidly acknowledges that French cuisine is in crisis, recently introducing an official poster that can be displayed in restaurants guaranteeing that their dishes are *fait maison* (home made). However this scheme has rapidly proved to offer little meaningful advice to consumers. The best food in France is eaten at home. But French supermarkets are also often very mediocre and there is no equivalent in France to Waitrose. When I pointed out to an employee at the local Carrefour that there was a shattered jar of tomato sauce in one of the aisles, he shrugged his shoulders and said: 'That's not my job.' When I tried to complain at the service desk, I was told the manager was in a meeting and did not meet with customers in any case. The best bet for buying decent groceries in France remains the street market, which remain glorious although even these have been infiltrated by industrially-produced fruit and vegetables imported from Spain.

All this said, a terrific restaurant has just opened in our village, proudly declaring that everything is *faite maison, avec amour* (home made, with love). The chef is from Newcastle.

CULTURE
A SECULAR RELIGION

The French tend to be pretty snooty about their culture and they have some things to be snooty about. French culture is one of the unique selling propositions of France. In film, music, literature and fine art, the French have punched above their weight. *Chanson*, the tradition of French song, is glorious. But French artists no longer dominate as they did in the BELLE ÉPOQUE. And much of what currently passes for French culture in France is mediocre. The nation's favourite TV programme is *CSI* and a recent bestselling book was the translation of *50 Shades of Grey*. France's cultural establishment is enveloped in a cloak of protectionism, with subsidies flowing to politically connected producers producing films that sink without a trace, protected by quotas to restrict distribution of foreign films, music and television programmes. At a village fête in the south, you are as likely to see line dancers wearing cowboy hats as men playing the traditional *tambourin* (tambourine). French rock music has never made a huge impact and perhaps the liveliest contemporary music sector is rap, with its origins in the French ghettos where social conditions have given rise to some fierce energetic expression, not entirely approved of by the cultural establishment.

D

DAILYMOTION
FRANCE'S FEAR OF THE INTERNET

This video-sharing site was created in France at about the same time as YouTube and today counts 2.5 billion unique visitors per month, versus 4 billion a day for YouTube. Frédéric Filloux, a technically savvy French business journalist, has described how the government's protectionist industrial policy simultaneously prohibited foreign investment in DailyMotion and ensured its market failure. After a tortuous history, DailyMotion ended up being owned by Orange, the telecoms giant, which behaved like it hated the business and tried to get rid of it. But its efforts to sell to Yahoo were vetoed by the government, which retains golden shares in Orange. The company has now been turned over to Vivendi in a 'French solution' although there is not much evidence that Vivendi will know what to do with it, either. DailyMotion is an object lesson of what happens when a promising start-up is turned into a political football.

DEBORD, GUY
PROPHET OF 21ST CENTURY MEDIA CULTURE

Creator of *situationalisme*, which unlike its near-cognate, *existentialisme*, has proven a durable lens for viewing the world. A *soixante-huitard* (veteran of the Paris spring of 1968), a philosopher/ artist/ militant and an instigator of numerous amusing escapades with some of the wilder spirits of those times, he was among the first to notice the fabrication of narrative by interested economic parties. Authored counter-attacks using techniques of *détournement*, turning these narratives against those who had sought to control them. Author of *Société du Spectacle* (*The Society of Spectacle*

1967), director of numerous films. Born 1931. Shot himself aged 62, in 1994.

DE GAULLE, CHARLES
GREAT FRENCHMAN, NOT UNIVERSALLY LOVED

The arrogant Frenchman from central casting. Mistrusted by Roosevelt, Churchill and, at times, millions of his compatriots, a representative of the high Catholic caste of France. Charles André Joseph Marie de Gaulle (1890-1970) is today scored by opinion polls as the best-ever French president, in which role he served from 1959-69. After the French government capitulated to the Germans in 1940, he famously set up a government in exile in London and broadcast a speech of defiance on the French service of the BBC in which he declared, 'We have lost a battle, we have not yet lost the war.' He never liked the British. British historian Anthony Beevor teases de Gaulle for having written an entire history of the French army without ever mentioning Waterloo. Churchill supposedly said he looked like a female llama surprised in her bath.

De Gaulle had a visceral hostility to the Nazis. He also had a daughter with *trisomie 21* (Down's Syndrome) and, as military attaché in Berlin before the war, had witnessed Hitler's persecution of the intellectually handicapped. While many in the upper echelons of the French establishment were prepared to treat with the Nazis, it was his daughter who inspired his refusal to accept the inevitability of Nazi conquest. This is my personal theory anyway, de Gaulle never wrote about the subject.

A physically imposing man, de Gaulle looked as if he had been created to represent France. 196cm, 6'5", and even more commanding in his habitual *képi* (military hat with a flat, circular top and visor), he was determined that France should be represented at the top table after Hitler's defeat. He also first set France on the path of bilateralism with the then West Germans, a course that has been followed by every French president since. He never forgave the British or the Americans for their snubs during the war and directed France to become a nuclear power, another policy continued by every subsequent president. In 1966, he withdrew France from the NATO military command structure and ordered American armed forces out of France. The American Secretary of State, Dean Rusk, asked de Gaulle if that was to include the bodies of 60,000 American soldiers buried in France. De Gaulle, embarrassed, got up and left the room, without answering. De Gaulle withdrew from Algeria against strong armed opposition from hardcore integrationists who attempted to assassinate him.

De Gaulle's austere retirement office is still preserved in Paris. On a pilgrimage to the *maison particulière* (town house) owned by the de Gaulle foundation, I made friends with the curator who let me sit at his desk in his plain wooden chair. I imagined him walking in at any moment and demanding to know what on earth I was doing there.

There are still plenty of French people who do not revere his memory. At a village fête in Limousin I was engaged by an aged veteran of the French war in Indochina who spoke bitterly of how the General had betrayed his comrades. And he remains unforgiven by many for his retreat from Algeria.

DÉFENSE, LA
EUROPE'S 'LARGEST' OFFICE PARK

Claims to be the largest office park in Europe. Soulless, modernist, a jungle of steel and concrete even worse than London's Canary Wharf. *La Grande Arche*, a modernist reinterpretation of the *Arc de Triomphe*, is its symbol. Headquarters of many leading French *PARAÉTATIQUE* (semi-governmental) companies, *La Défense* has lurched from crisis to crisis throughout its existence. Many of its 1970s-80s era buildings are obsolete.

DÉLOCALISATION
THE FLIGHT OF EMPLOYERS

Poland is the number one destination for French companies exporting their activities in search of lower labour costs, with 153,000 jobs created there. Among the French companies who have gone elsewhere in search of lower labour costs are: Airbus, Renault, PSA Citröen and Groupe Seb (Tefal, Rowenta, Calor, Moulinex, Krups). When I was in Poznan, Poland my hotel was filled with French executives hunting for Polish subcontractors. Many young French people delocalise themselves in search of work. See LONDRES.

DENTISTES
NOTHING TO SMILE ABOUT

Ambrose Bierce defined a dentist as a 'prestidigitator who, putting metal into your mouth, pulls coins out of your pocket.' In France, dentists are a protected profession and dental care can be pretty unimpressive. I go to London to get my teeth cleaned because dental hygienists are illegal in France, as they are considered CONCURRENCE déloyale (unfair competition) to actual dentists. It is evident to even a casual observer that many thousand dental hygienists could be usefully employed in France, earning a decent living, contributing to the economy, and clearing up the miasma of halitosis. According to VALÉRIE TRIERWEILER, FRANÇOIS HOLLANDE's former girlfriend, the President of the Republic refers to poor people as the sans dents (toothless ones). Hollande's friends have denied he said this, but it seems hard to believe she invented it. And French teeth are pretty awful, so he had a point in any case. As with food, it always used to be the English who were mocked for their mouths.

DÉPARTEMENTS
LAVISH JOBS FOR THE BOYS AND GIRLS

In my *départment* of Hérault in May 2015, the newly elected socialist-dominated departmental council at its very first meeting shamelessly increased its pay by 8 per cent to 5,512 euros per month for its president, 3,458 euros for its 15 (!) vice-presidents (if one vice-president is good, then 15 must be better) and 2,718 euros for its 34 ordinary members - virtually all of them already drawing salaries as mayors and deputy mayors of their various communes. Hérault is one of the poorest departments in France. Oddly, the Socialist party candidate who won the election in our own canton never made mention of this intention to self-enrich when he visited us to proclaim his commitment to fighting for our interests. Not that there seems a good reason for the departmental council even to exist since there is also a regional council, even more lavishly compensated. There are 96 departments in France excluding the overseas territories. French children are expected to be able to memorise the entire list, from 01 (Ain, Rhône-Alpes) to 95 (Val-d'Oise, Île-de-France). There is no Number 20 but 2A and 2B indicate Corse-du-Sud and Haute-Corse (southern and upper Corsica). Vast re-organisations of French regions are underway, which will inevitably involve hiring even more civil servants, and it is expected that these may eventually include reorganisations in the departments themselves, but for the time being, every department will also have a *Préfet* and a *PRÉFECTURE,* representing the central government. See *GOUVERNANCE TERRITORIALE.*

DETTE PUBLIQUE
97.5 PER CENT OF GROSS NATIONAL PRODUCT

By the summer of 2015, the French national debt exceeded two trillion euros, up 1.9 per cent in six months. The debt of the state was 1.6 trillion, that of the social security administration 232 billion, local government owed 188 billion and diverse public debts were 22 billion. French debt is accelerating despite President FRANÇOIS HOLLANDE's promise to reduce it (it has increased by 220 billion euros since he took office). Hollande, meanwhile, lectures the Greeks that they must reduce their own debt while his left-wing friends splutter against government austerity (of which there is little evidence). Hollande has told Brussels that French debt will be reduced by 2017, but this depends on achieving growth of 1.5 per cent, which is hardly likely. If the current trend continues and Hollande cannot rekindle growth, debt will soon break the symbolically important barrier of 100 per cent of GDP, putting France outside its commitments to the EU and putting beyond doubt its status as a sick man of Europe.

DIEUDONNÉ
COMEDIAN AND DR EVIL

In a nation that professes to venerate Voltaire, liberty of expression sometimes means just the freedom to say the same thing as everyone else. This seems especially to be the case with Dieudonné M'bala M'bala (born 1966) who has become a symbol of defiance to the conventions of the state. The name means literally a 'Gift of God' but to many French establishment figures, he is a devil. Allied with JEAN-MARIE LE PEN and a friend of Mahmoud Ahmadinejad, former president of Iran, both of them notorious Holocaust deniers. His shows, wildly popular among young immigrants in the ghettos, have been banned by the government. Whether he is anti-semitic or not is by now a purely academic question since he has become a hate figure for those who believe that he is, and a symbol of defiance for many in the ghettos, some of whom do not mind if he is. Ironically, he began his career as a performer in partnership with his boyhood friend Élie Semoun, a Jew. In 2012, Semoun said the Dieudonné with whom he once collaborated and the Dieudonné of today are completely different people.

Repeatedly charged by prosecutors with incitement to racial

hatred, Dieudonné has been physically attacked by Jewish militants. Yet all efforts to marginalise Dieudonné, ban his concerts, and attack him in the courts have done little to suppress his popularity and he is much admired by many young people who identify with his defiance of the French establishment. Many young French people simply do not understand why *Charlie Hebdo* is fêted for exercising its right to free speech, whereas Dieudonné is repeatedly condemned and prosecuted for doing the same thing.

DIRIGISME
FRANCE'S CHAIN AND BALL

Flaubert said the French like to be ruled by the sword and this is the traditional explanation of *dirigisme* in which *l'État* (the State) takes for itself the role of directing rather than merely regulating the economy and all other aspects of French social and cultural life. *Dirigisme* is most pernicious in the state's management of the economy. Chronic unemployment and lack of investment, directly attributable to incompetent economic regulation, has not stopped the state remaining in control in every key decision, exasperating managers at large French companies who are not allowed to make decisions in the best interest of their firms, but are required to take into account the demands of the state. Yet there are many, like my friend Jacques, in Paris, who argue that the state has the exclusive democratic authority to make the ultimate economic decisions.

DJIHADISME
ISLAMIC HOLY WAR

With the largest Muslim population in Europe, Islamism is a gigantic challenge to the Republic, being ineptly addressed. The French seem bemused if not paralysed by the phenomenon. At least 1,200 French Islamists are estimated by King's College,

London's International Centre for the Study of Radicalisation, to have made their way to Syria and Iraq to fight for the Islamic State. France's ghettos, full of angry and unemployed young men, are a fertile recruiting ground. At least 17 men from the small southern French town of Lunel, population 27,500, were reported in 2015 to be fighting for the Islamic state; at least six have been killed. A jihadist interviewed by *Paris-Match* in March 2015 said there are so many French recruits in ISIS, 'I couldn't even count them all.' MANUEL VALLS, the prime minister, has spoken of thousands of people in France who need to be actively surveilled. This Islamist fifth column has emerged under the government's nose and it has had mixed results countering it.

After the massacres at a Toulouse Jewish school, at *CHARLIE HEBDO* and at a Jewish supermarket in Paris, President FRANÇOIS HOLLANDE announced a two-pronged approach, transparently hopeless: more and more heavily armed police, and more money for schools for instruction in Republican values and *LAÏCITÉ* (secularism). How giving pistols to our three municipal policemen is going to help is not easy to see. I further suspect that the young men in the ghettos might be more impressed with the prospect of employment than instruction on civic values. But these issues were not addressed by the President. Farhad Khosrokhavar, a sociologist at the *École des Hautes Études en Sciences Sociales* in Paris, writing in the *New York Times* in January 2015, offered a succinct *précis* of the path to radicalisation: 'The typical trajectory of most French Islamist terrorists follows four steps: alienation from the dominant culture, thanks partly to joblessness and discrimination in blighted neighbourhoods; a turn to petty crime, which leads to prison, and then more crime and more prison; religious awakening and radicalisation; and an initiatory journey to a Muslim country like Syria, Afghanistan or Yemen to train for jihad.' Should these recruits return to France it is inevitable there will be more trouble.

DOM-TOMS
OVERSEAS FRANCE

La France d'outre-mer describes overseas France. There are French departments, territories and *collectivités* in North and South America, the Caribbean, and in the Indian and Pacific oceans. They are considered an integral part of France itself and the currency is the Euro. Some of them are little more than promontories, others are more substantial. Most of them constitute a bottomless pit into which the French pour subsidies for benefits that are debatable.

Napoléon Bonaparte sold Louisiana and much of the midwest to the United States, after the French were kicked out of Quebec by General Wolfe. Hence the North American empire today is reduced to the tiny *collectivité* (administrative district) of St Pierre et Miquelon, off the coast of Nova Scotia (population 8,000), subsisting from a bit of fishing, a bit of tourism but mainly off subsidies from the mother lode. Closer to Montreal than Paris, St Pierre et Miquelon boasts a detachment of gendarmes, a prefect, and must send its most seriously ill people to Canada for medical care.

In South America, France still rules in jungly Guyane (Guyana), wedged between Brazil and Surinam, with its rapacious mosquitos, poisonous giant moths and the French space agency's satellite-launching centre. Just off the coast is the Devil's Island penal colony (*le bagne*) where Dreyfus was imprisoned and from which Henri Charrière (*Papillon*) famously escaped. There are amusing bars in Kourou, the administrative capital, populated by French Foreign Legionnaires who appear to be engaged in murky operations on the border with Surinam in the north and in the jungle to the south near the border with Brazil. Cayenne is where the eponymous peppers come from. On a visit to the space centre I once made the mistake of eating one of these, raw.

Martinique and Guadeloupe, islands heavily dependent on tourism and with little depth to their economies, soak up more French taxpayer largesse in the Caribbean. Away from the resorts there is plenty of poverty and social instability. St Martin, the French half of an island shared with the Dutch, is more prosperous but the embarrassing jewel in the crown is the hyper exclusive island of St Barthélémy, where a bowl of soup at the beach restaurant of the Eden Rock hotel can cost 100 euros (admittedly with a fabulous view of topless Russian girls disporting themselves on the sand). Too expensive for mere millionaires, it is the preserve of plutocrats with yachts and private helicopters. Russian oligarch Roman Abramovich has an estate there and his yacht has two helipads, one for his own helicopter, the other presumably for the pizza delivery helicopter. St Barth is entirely exempt from French taxation under a treaty signed with the Swedish during the Napoleonic war, when the French took possession of the island. When French tax inspectors visited the island to discuss a change to the status, they were run off by outraged locals.

In the Indian Ocean the French rule Réunion, with 850,000 people, southwest of Mauritius, another troubled dependency with 60 per cent youth unemployment and recurrent outbreaks of chikungunya, a paralysing disease. Mayotte, with a population of just over 200,000, is another headache. There were violent demonstrations there in 2011, which went largely unreported in France. The French Southern and Antarctic Lands, comprising a slice of Antarctica and several scattered islands, must not be overlooked either, despite a population of just 140 people and countless penguins. (The Southern and Antarctic Lands do have their own prefect, be assured).

The Pacific boasts French Polynesia, with the unique status of an overseas country within the French Republic, and where there is continued political turmoil and calls for independence among elements of the population of 250,000. Next on the tour of non-hexagonal France is New Caledonia, with a population of around 250,000, and an economy that on paper looks much better with a GDP per capita comparable to New Zealand, although with huge income disparities. Next to last is Wallis and Futuna which comprises three kingdoms (there were four, but those owing their allegiance to the fourth tribe were eaten by the other three) but whose president is FRANÇOIS HOLLANDE. Clipperton Island (Île de Clipperton or Île de la Passion), is the final piece - an uninhabited nine-square-kilometre coral atoll located 1,280 kilometres south-west of Acapulco, Mexico, in the Pacific Ocean. France clings onto this because of the possibility that minerals may be found in its territorial waters. The sun never sets on the French empire.

DSK
SEXUALLY INCONTINENT SOCIALIST POLITICIAN

Economist, lawyer, Socialist politician, Dominique Strauss-Kahn is apparently convinced he can resume his political career even after a series of sex scandals. He has tested to the limit French tolerance for private misbehaviour by public figures and described attending a dozen orgies in three years as 'recreation.' He referred to women in emails as 'material.' He engaged in what was described in court as 'rough sex' with prostitutes who subsequently wept on the witness stand describing brutal behaviour. He paid off a chambermaid in New York who accused him of forcing her to fellate him. And yet many French people seem ready to forgive him and many French journalists continue to insist this is none of anyone's business. After the incident in New York, any hope he had of contesting the Socialist party primary for the presidency (which fell eventually to the uninspiring FRANÇOIS HOLLANDE) was destroyed. Many in France doubted that the events in America were entirely coincidental and asked who benefited. Well, Hollande, obviously. Would Hollande have been capable of masterminding such a conspiracy to bring down his rival? Many French people think so. Given Hollande's general competence, I doubt it.

Strauss-Kahn is an arrogant, deeply unpleasant man who has been entirely the author of his own downfall. After the debacle in New York, he seemed ready to rapidly resume his political career until he was accused of *proxénétisme* (pimping, basically) involving lurid libertine affairs at the drab Carlton Hotel in Lille and other venues, at which large contingents of prostitutes were supposedly imported for orgies involving politicians, businessmen and journalists. We have never been told the identities of the journalists involved. Strauss-Kahn denies knowing anything about the girls being prostitutes and even the prosecutor admitted he couldn't prove it. Richard Nixon famously said, 'I am not a crook.' Strauss-Kahn essentially said, 'I am not a pimp.' He was acquitted but while I thought it impossible to imagine him returning to front line politics, he has emerged from his bunker and remains seemingly protected by journalistic *omertà* (silence).

The case of Strauss-Kahn shames French journalists who have for years turned a blind eye to such conduct on the grounds that it is a matter of personal privacy of no interest to the public. Until we know the identity of the French journalists who were also involved in Strauss-Kahn's orgies, it is unlikely that answers will be forthcoming.

E

ÉCOLE NATIONALE D'ADMINISTRATION
ELITE SCHOOL CREATING MEDIOCRITY

'Ireland has the IRA, Spain has ETA, Italy the Mafia, and France the ENA,' former finance minister Alain Madelin once said of this elite institution, responsible for generations of sometimes corrupt politicians. Founded after the Second World War by Charles de Gaulle, supposedly to replace France's collaborationist administrative class with a rigorously trained meritocracy schooled in Republican virtue, the *École Nationale d'Administration* is the ultimate finishing school for the French political elite. Most of its students are drawn from highly privileged backgrounds.

With numerous top jobs in the French administration reserved for its graduates, termed *Énarques*, the ENA diploma is a meal ticket for life. Despite all the emphasis on academic rigour, the quality of the graduates is highly questionable. President François Hollande graduated at the top of his class. With graduates including former prime ministers Alain Juppé, Edouard Balladur, Michel Rocard and Laurent Fabius, Philippe Seguin, former speaker of the National Assembly, and former presidents Valéry Giscard-d'Estaing (VGE) and Jacques Chirac, ENA has provided almost all the politicians who have presided over the country's economic decline in the past 40 years. There is supposed to be a shake-up with the appointment of a new director, Nathalie Loiseau, unusually not herself an *Énarque* but a graduate of the Sciences Po university in Paris and a student of Chinese. A high-flyer in the French foreign office, she was press officer at the embassy in Washington during the 2003 Iraq war. ENA recently announced that competence in English would in the future become a requirement of graduation from the school, which is surprising only because one might have thought this should have already been a requirement.

ÉCOLE NORMALE SUPÉRIEURE
ELITE INSTITUTION TRAINING TEACHERS

Normal/e is a *faux ami* (a false friend - a similar word with a different meaning in English and French). *Normale* in French means a given standard, and *supérieur* means above ordinary, hence the *École Normale* is a school that claims elevated standards, i.e., higher than a bog-standard school. Established during the French revolution and reorganised by NAPOLÉON, it stands alongside *ENA* and *X* as one of the elite schools of the French establishment. Tony Judt, who spent a year there and was later awarded an honorary doctorate, described it as an 'elite humanist academy… distilling the status and distinction of Harvard, Yale, Princeton, Columbia, Stanford, Chicago, and Berkeley.' An enormously long list of notorious and celebrated alumni includes Samuel Beckett, JEAN-PAUL SARTRE, Louis Pasteur and Michel Foucault. The college was intended to train an elite corps of educators thoroughly indoctrinated in Republican values, tasked with the creation of a national education system itself designed to coin Republicans. It recruits 200 students annually, half in sciences, the rest in humanities, and students are considered to be trainee civil servants. Recently ranked between 18-33 in world university rankings, so maybe not today as impressive as it likes to believe or its history deserves. Students and graduates are called *Normaliens*.

ÉCONOMIE
NOT A FRENCH STRONG POINT

Marxism is the basis for much economic thinking in France. France's star economist, THOMAS PIKETTY, is characteristic of the breed. He is the scion of a well-to-do family of leftists. Adam Smith's *The Wealth of Nations* never seems to have made it onto French student reading lists. Economics is seen mainly as the challenge of redistributing existing wealth, rather than creating it. Not that the French economic model lacks admirers. Paul Krugman, the Princeton professor and *New York Times* columnist, has declared: 'News reports consistently portray the French economy as a dysfunctional mess, crippled by high taxes and government regulation. So it comes as something of a shock when you look at the actual numbers, which don't match that story at all.' What 'actual numbers' has he been looking at? France has been in a state of near-recession for 15 years. See PRODUCTIV-ITÉ.

ÉCONOMIE ET FINANCE, MINISTÈRE DE
LALA LAND

House of dreams, cooking the books since 1975, which was the last time France balanced its budget. France has a remarkably successful, open and reformed economy, according to 'The Economy of France' page on Wikipedia, which it can be assumed is authored by the Ministry of Economy and Finance, since it reads like a press release for an imaginary country, one that exists solely in the fantasies of the Ministry of Economy and Finance. Not even the department's own ministers believe the official line.

ÉCOTAXE
RUINOUS RED-BARET DEBACLE

A couple of years ago great steel gantries began to appear on the A9 motorway near my house and Dalek-like kiosks sprouted on the edges of minor roads. This was repeated throughout France. All were bristling with cameras linked to automatic number-plate recognition systems. A few months later the government was preparing to pay 800 million euros to dismantle them. The idea was that trucks could be tracked wherever they went and made to pay for their environmental impact. But truck drivers in Brittany, wearing red bonnets and styling themselves *les bonnets rouges*, attacked the equipment and blockaded the highways. The tax was 'suspended' (forever) by SÉGOLÈNE ROYAL, President Hollande's environment minister and former partner. She claimed she would collect the money from the autoroute operators instead, whom she accuses of excessive profits, but this hasn't happened. Taxpayers are still paying 10 million euros a week to the Italian consortium hired to collect the *écotaxe* and these payments are expected to continue for several years. The total bill for this project is expected to reach 1.2 billion euros.

ÉDUCATION NATIONALE
LIKE THE NHS
The Republic promises all of its students access to an equal education from which anyone, from no matter how humble an origin, may ascend to the very top. That's the theory, anyway. The delivery of this Republican ideal is more complicated. The mission is entrusted to the system of *Éducation Nationale*, words which are as engrained in the consciousness of the French as, for example, the National Health Service in Britain. The words encompass every element of the French education system. Yet there is an ideological component to this and it could also be termed *endoctrinement national* (national indoctrination).

The nation's education is centrally directed from the Ministry of Education in Paris. But the Prime Minister and President of the Republic are also deeply involved in a subject which is so politically sensitive and that accounts for spending of more than 150 billion euros a year. *Éducation Nationale* is a pillar of the Republic, charged above all with the assembly-line production of loyal Republicans. But how is it holding up? 'It's on its knees,' says one teacher I know. And, say many, has been for some time. Jean-Paul Brighelli in his book *La Fabrique du crétin* (The making of idiots, 2005) was exaggerating, but perhaps not too much, when he declared, 'Our children can't read, can't count, can't think.' He alleged that 30 years of good intentions, badly managed, had turned the French education system from one of the best in the world to one responsible for the collapse of social mobility.

The more cynical might say that the more teachers that have been hired, and the more money spent, the greater the apparent deficiencies of national education, but this is not entirely fair. Even though there are a fair number of ultra-left teachers and unfit teachers on the job, there are serious professors too and some well disciplined schools, yet in various league tables the educational achievements produced by this investment have been rather middling.

National education begins at three at *maternelle* (infants school), continues from 6 to 11 at *primaire* (primary school), then *collège* (middle school) from 11-15 and finally *lycée* from 15-18 (secondary school). Instruction is compulsory in France to age 16, but this does not mean it is compulsory to attend school, only to be educated. I have *altermondialiste* friends who withdrew their children from school and said they could learn more working on their farm and would learn to read when they wanted to, but this is rare. In supposedly egalitarian France, schools are not equal, especially the *lycées*. The rich who have sufficient PISTON (clout) and who live in the best postcodes, have access to the handful of elite *lycées,* a disproportionate share of whose graduates move on to the *Grandes Écoles* (elite higher-education establishments). These high schools are known to all as the entry point into the French establishment and include Lycée Henri IV, Louis-le-Grand, Stanislas, Thiers, and Le Parc. Throughout France, ambitious parents, few of them devoutly religious, take their children out of the state *lycées* and into private, mainly subsidised Catholic schools, to avoid the perceived inconsistency and mediocrity of *Éducation Nationale*. These Catholic schools charge fees of 100-1,000 euros a year, and are subsidised by the state, which pays the salaries of the teachers.

EDF
FRENCH ELECTRICITY MONOPOLY

Gigantic bureaucratic French energy company, largest generator of electricity in the world. Like many French industrial giants, PARAÉTATIQUE (semi-governmental), nearly indistinguishable from an arm of the state. Électricité de France was partly privatised in 1999, being floated on the stock exchange, although the French government continues to hold de facto control of the group. EDF has used the monopoly profits of its activities in France to buy electricity generators abroad and is now active throughout America, Africa, Asia and Europe, Britain. Under EU rules, it is now possible to buy electricity from competitor companies but these have made little impact and the market dominance of EDF is unchallenged. In 2011, EDF was fined 1.5 million euros and two executives were jailed for spying on Greenpeace. EDF's corporate culture was comprehensively skewered by CORRINE MAIER in her book *Bonjour Paresse* (*Hello Laziness*, 2004).

ÉLECTIONS
DEMOCRATIC THEATRE

Healthy turnouts in French elections seem to affirm the legitimacy of the political system. It's common to have 80 per cent turnout in presidential elections and even municipal elections draw 75 per cent of the voters. But whether the votes mean anything is another matter, as the French discovered in 2005 when they voted 55-45 per cent to reject the proposed European constitution, which was nonetheless imposed essentially intact in any case, re-labelled as a treaty.

Most elected offices in France are filled from party lists. This keeps the politicians safely remote from being directly accountable to voters. Those at the top of the lists are always likely to be elected, while the lower the candidate is listed, the chances of election decrease. Thus it is the party, not the voter, who really gets to choose who will be elected. The voter is required to vote for the entire list or none of it, there is no crossing out of names that displease individual electors, as was once permitted.

Presidential elections and elections to the National Assembly are conducted differently, over two rounds. In the first round, any number of candidates can present themselves and there are typically candidates from the *Chasse, Pêche, Nature et Traditions* (hunting, fishing, nature and tradition) party as well as monarchists, Esperanto speakers, etc., but after the first-round votes are counted, only the top two go through to the next round, when it is a straight choice. The French joke that in the first round you vote for the candidate you like and in the second you vote against the candidate you hate the most.

Senators are elected by *les grands électeurs*, an electoral college comprised of parliamentary deputies, already-elected senators, regional councillors and delegates from municipal councils. In other words, politicians elected by other politicians.

France has a vast number of officials elected in this way: 620,000 or one for every 100 people.

ELYSÉE
INFLATED PRESIDENTIAL PALACE

If Buckingham Palace is more shabby than chic and the White House rather suburban, the principal palace of the French Republic represents the gilded extremity of interior design. Only the princes of Araby can return home to more splendid apartments. It is so grand, so ornate, so over-the-top, it is doubtful that anyone who lives there can have any idea whatsoever of reality. It would probably help restore the French presidency to reality (and help balance the budget) by moving to the grimly modernist office district of La Défense or maybe Clichy-sous-Bois, one of the worst French ghettos, and flogging the Elysée to the Chinese.

EMBOURGEOISEMENT
GENTRIFICATION

A tendency to be heartily decried at leftish dinner parties, even if those doing the decrying are the self-same bourgeoisie. Gentrification is nothing new and modern Paris itself is the consequence of Haussmann's brutal displacement of poor people driven to the suburbs by rising rents, with the new *quartiers* repopulated with bourgeois. The archetypal gentrified suburb of Paris is Montreuil, equivalent of Brooklyn or Hackney and home to journalists, artists and gallerists, where they talk about house prices as if it was London.

EMPLOIS D'AVENIR
FANTASY JOBS FOR THE FUTURE

An old idea, re-launched by President François Hollande but never delivered. The only plentiful jobs of the future for most French young people seem to be wiping old peoples' bottoms in care homes, which are the only institutions in France constantly recruiting staff, although at the minimum wage. Real jobs for the future seem to be elsewhere, like the UK where 27,884 French citizens were issued national insurance numbers in 2014, up 25 per cent in a year.

ENGIE
FORMERLY KNOWN AS GDF SUEZ

The new name for what was once called *Gaz de France*, like EDF, a state monopoly, partially privatised but still under the thumb of the almighty state. GDF was merged with Suez, the water and energy company, in 2006 with the objective of creating the world's largest liquified natural gas company and has 215,000 staff in 70 countries. The French state continues to hold 35 per cent of the shares and has an effective veto over all strategic decisions. As with EDF, the electricity generator, alternative suppliers are available but have hardly eroded Engie's dominant position. It is the 6th largest company in the world.

ENGRENAGES
HYPER-GRITTY COP SHOW ON FRENCH TV

As close as French TV has got to *The Wire*. Rare export success sold to more than 70 countries. Perhaps the first feminist cop show. Basic story is about Parisian criminal investigator Laure Berthaud, running a serious crime squad in waters infested with dangerous criminals and scheming superiors. In some ways she is the opposite of the semi-autistic Sarah Lund in the Danish show *Forbrydelsen* (*The Killing*). Laure is almost too emotional but like Lund, her life is shit. A literal translation of *Engrenages* is 'gears'; it is called *Spiral* in England where it is broadcast by the BBC, though I would have thought helix a better title. The series has a noirish visual palette and scripts rich with contemporary *parigot* (the street slang of the capital city). Bravura performances by Caroline Proust as Captain Berthaud and Audrey Fleurot as Joséphine Karlsson, a brilliant but ethically compromised criminal lawyer. One of the two directors is also female, Alexandra Clert. One could accuse the series of being utterly implausible except at the real-life headquarters of the judicial police, the truth is even stranger than the fiction. See *36 Quai des Orfèvres*.

ENTENTE CORDIALE
THE FREQUENTLY GLACIAL ALLIANCE BETWEEN BRITAIN AND FRANCE

Opening the channel tunnel, then-president François Mitterrand evoked the famous *Entente Cordiale* of 1904 establishing the Franco-British alliance against Germany and Austria-Hungary. He added that indeed relations between the two countries were indeed cordial and then he paused, adding: '*presque toujours*' (almost all the time, not always). This caused SA GRACIEUSE MAJESTÉ (Her Majesty Queen Elizabeth II), who is fluently francophone, to laugh. She knows that in the sweep of history France and England are more comfortably at war than peace with a state of almost continual conflict that goes back for 1,000 years. Since 1945 there has been no special *entente* between Britain and France, indeed the French kept Britain out of the earliest institutions of Europe and turned to the Germans as their new best friends.

ENTREPRISES FANTÔMES
PRETEND COMPANIES WHERE THE UNEMPLOYED PRETEND TO WORK

The Candela web site is right up to date, offering special offers on its catalog of office furniture, gifts for mother's day, and more. But do not click on anything because Candela is not a real business but a government-financed pretend business where unemployed people can pretend to work. The idea is that by exposing the unemployed to a simulated work environment, they might be able to move on to real jobs. More than 100 pretend companies are operating in France where the long-term unemployed are exposed to all the experiences of employment, so that they might be prepared to take a real job, should one ever materialise. Workers at Axisco, a pretend virtual payment centre in Val d'Oise, north of Paris, recently staged a pretend strike.

ENTREPRENEUR
ALIEN CONCEPT

'The problem with the French is that they have no word for entrepreneur.' President George Bush supposedly said this to British prime minister Tony Blair, but whether he said it or Blair invented the story, it is both funny and true. Funny because *entrepreneur* is a French word (from the verb *entreprendre*) and true because it is a *faux ami* (false friend) whose meaning is markedly different in

English and French. In France an *entrepreneur* is a builder. The Anglo-Saxon meaning of the word is not readily available in French.

ÉOLIENNES
WIND FARMS

France produces 3 per cent of its electricity using wind turbines at a cost per kilowatt hour double that of traditional energy sources. The main operator of these wind farms is a subsidiary of EDF. Consumers thus pay more for their electricity, and the shareholders of EDF profit. This is justified because it is *durable* (sustainable).

ESCARGOTS
GASTROPODS PREPARED WITH GARLIC; ROAD BLOCKAGES TO PROTEST PROPOSED REFORMS

The most delicate snails are harvested after rain, from locations where they will have feasted naturally on fennel, thyme, rosemary and other wild herbs. The old ladies in my village emerge after a shower with their *paniers* (baskets), pluck the fattest specimens off the wild fennel, take them home and put them in a shoe box where they are starved to allow their intestinal tubes to empty completely, then cooked with olive oil and garlic or tomato sauce. They are delicious. *Escargot* is also a disruptive action mounted by taxi and truck drivers intended to reduce autoroutes to the speed of a snail and inconvenience as many of their compatriots as possible, all while calling for *solidARITÉ*. See *TAXIS*.

ESPAGNE
SPAIN, FOR BUYING CIGARETTES, MELONS, HASHISH AND TOXIC CHEMICALS

For millions of French people living within 100km of the border,

Spain is a tobacconist, drug store, source of cheap groceries and agricultural chemicals banned in France. A pack of 20 Marlboro cigarettes in France costs 7 euros versus typically 5 euros in Spain. The A9 motorway from the Spanish border is also Europe's biggest conduit for Moroccan hashish and more legitimately much of the melon and citrus sold in French supermarkets. The French *douaniers* (customs agents) keep the motorway under video surveillance and mount barricades at the *péages* (toll booths) where they search suspect cars, often with spectacular results. Imports of cheap Spanish wine into France have provoked road blockages and destruction of Spanish tanker trucks. An Aldi supermarket in Pézenas selling Spanish plonk was actually bombed by infuriated French *vignerons* (wine growers).

ESPIONS
SPIES

There are eight principal intelligence agencies but it is not clear that quantity equals quality. The *Direction générale de la sécurité extérieure* is the foreign intelligence agency responsible for the RAINBOW WARRIOR debacle; the *Direction générale de la sécurité intérieure* is responsible for internal security and counter espionage, a task at which they have been caught flat-footed, failing to prevent attacks by Islamist extremists including the CHARLIE HEBDO massacre. The security services failed again to prevent a known Islamist militant from beheading his employer and attempting to bomb a chemical factory in Isère in June 2015. President François Hollande has given the *espions* unprecedented new powers to intercept the private communications of French people. But all recent attacks have been perpetrated by persons already on the radar of Hollande's spooks.

Faith in the competence of French security was further shaken with the revelation by Wikileaks that the Americans have been systematically intercepting the communications of French presidents for years. What the Americans will have made of

Hollande's voicemails is intriguing. If they may have learned few state secrets, perhaps they gleaned a reasonable understanding of the president's complicated sex life. French outrage over this business seems to me in any case overblown. When I worked in Washington and occasionally flew for work on the Air France Concorde to French Guyana I was warned by an American security official to watch what I said, since 'every seat was bugged.' Was he joking? Absolutely not.

ESPRIT
NASTY WIT

The *bel esprit* was always thought to be the best possible social passport in France. If the English are understated, ironic and perhaps falsely modest, and the Americans oversharing and sometimes loud, the tradition of *esprit* in France is wit that is razor-sharp, wounding, often cruel, seasoned with unabashed one-up-manship and linguistic pyrotechnics, wrapped in a veneer of phony *politesse*. Those without this *trait d'esprit*, even the very rich, such as many of Molière's characters, are simply laughed at. This is social death by mockery. The film *Ridicule*, (Patrice Leconte, 1996), set in the court of Louis XVI, exposes the viciousness of the courtiers, vying with their *esprit* to humiliate others. *Esprit* lives on in France, but is fading in a culture under increasing Anglo-Saxon influence, especially the importation of notions of what is considered POLITIQUEMENT CORRECT (political correctness).

L'ÉTAT
STATE WORSHIP

'A people accustomed to live under a Prince, should they by some eventuality become free, will with difficulty maintain their freedom,' observed Niccolo Machiavelli. In secular France, the state has become practically a religion and its citizens required to practice a form of *statolâtrie* (state-idolatry). The French state is a mighty apparatus with its own secular articles of faith, even its own trinity - *LIBERTÉ, EGALITÉ, FRATERNITÉ*. Since 2004, the state's share of GDP has risen from 44 to 58 per cent, despite the privatisation of numerous state enterprises, although in effect they have become merely *PARAÉTATIQUE* (semi-governmental). The modern French state is a not-so benign growth from the administrative machinery conceived by the dictator NAPOLÉON BONAPARTE, and indeed from the monarchy that preceded him.

While the precise geometry and competences of the state have shifted through the numerous kingdoms, empires and Republics, the tendency towards *DIRIGISME* (centralised state power) has never waned. The state serves not only to control all aspects of French life but also to fund jobs in an effort to pretend that the government has a strategy to address chronic unemployment. President FRANÇOIS HOLLANDE was elected after promising to hire 60,000 new teachers - although nobody thought more teachers was the real answer to the crisis in the national education system. He might have done better to fire 60,000 under-performing ones.

The omnipotence and omnipresence of the state remains the default grandiose pretension of the French, the delusion being that there is no problem for which the state does not have an answer. The state remains enduringly attached to the vainglorious symbolic bling of the Sun King. Presiding at the head of the modern state is a *de facto* elected emperor, the President of the Republic, housed in the glittering ELYSÉE palace, a fleet of Dassault and Airbus jets at his beck and call, a vast entourage of uniformed flunkies at hand and a female retinue to service his sexual demands.

The state, from the immense ministries in Paris to its *PRÉFECTURE* outposts in every department, is omnipresent and omnipotent. It has influence in every town hall, with its daily bulletins and circulars. Its 5.6 million *FONCTIONNAIRES* (civil servants) staff every school, whose curriculum is decided at the Ministry of Education, in Paris. All of the departmental, regional and local governments depend on central government for subsidies and transfer payments. Decentralisation is an unimaginable concept for the French, who remain firmly attached to the idea of *une République unique et indivisible* (a singular and indivisible state).

ÉTUDIANTS
REBELS AGAINST CHANGE

Chatting with the president of an important French regional university, I asked him why his institution couldn't do better. His answer was blunt. 'Because we can't select our students and we can't make them pay.' Students are curiously conservative and resistant to change. They demonstrate against any proposed reform, not just of the universities, but of France generally. Writing in 2015 for the *Huffington Post* French edition, William Martinet, president of the French national union of students, denounced the government's efforts to reform the labour market (feeble though they are) as a capitulation to the demands of the bosses and an attack on the young. 25 per cent youth unemployment might suggest some need for a more flexibility, but it is safe to say that Mr Martinet will never work a day in his life outside the political bubble that he inhabits as a professional student leader.

It is an oddity that many university students in France appear to be studying commerce although there is very little actual commerce occurring in France. There are no fees, or at most charges of just a few hundred euros to attend universities in France hence no real economic value has to be put on getting one degree or another. When former president NicolAs SarkoZy timidly suggested increasing the role of partnerships between universities and the private sector, university students declared a strike. Lycée students are equally reactionary and are represented by their own union, invariably led by a left-winger from one of the elite Paris high schools. They practise for adulthood by organising strikes at which privileged students from smart arrondissements demonstrate against reform, while taking selfies with their latest iPhones on Instagram.

L'EURO
FRANCE'S TROJAN HORSE

The euro is mostly hated by ordinary French people, and for good reason. But their opinion doesn't count, as no mainstream political party ever questions this supreme manifestation of French economic self-delusion. The currency was introduced with a barrage of propaganda. 'It's simple,' said the signs at every French petrol pump, *boulangerie* and post office in 1998. 'One euro is 6.55957 francs' - five decimal places.

In the absence of meaningful structural reform, the euro has sealed France's only remaining escape hatch to prosperity, preventing the French from devaluing their currency to make themselves at least more competitive on price. The euro was promised to be the launchpad for growth but it is not the case that the average French family feels any better off today than it did in 2008. House prices have barely moved or have fallen, except in Paris where many of the best apartments are bought by foreigners. Wages have not greatly increased; energy and food have risen. France's share of world trade has fallen. Economic growth is stagnant. There has been no job creation. So whatever promises might have been made about the euro as a ticket to prosperity have not been fulfilled. In theory, membership of the euro ought to force structural reforms on members unable to devalue their currency and hence inflate away their debts. This is what the Germans think, and they have prospered. That's not been how the French govern and the price has been paid in a stalled economy where private dynamism is harshly punished. President FRANÇOIS HOLLANDE believes France can escape the euro straightjacket by creating a new economic government for the euro zone complete with a high commissioner and its own parliament. That would mean more jobs for his friends, but the Germans see the idea as ridiculous.

EUROPEAN UNION
ARTICLE OF FAITH

Pay no attention to the EU flags flying outside every government building in France. The European Union is as unloved as its money, except by the elite, who profit handsomely from its patronage. The left hates Europe for its alleged responsibility for the policy of austerity. The right hates it for diminishing national sovereignty. Ordinary people hate it because since its introduction the cost of living, taxes and unemployment have all increased. But as they found out after voting against Valéry Giscard-d'Estaing's (VGE) proposed European constitution, which was imposed anyway by treaty, their opinion does not count. The European Union is an article of faith for the French political and media establishment and opinions to the contrary are not considered respectable. The French political elite is a winner with their sinecures in Brussels, Luxembourg and Strasbourg, the rest of France is a loser and many voters are turning to a dead-end nationalism in frustration. The many promises made for Europe, not least that the single market would stimulate another TRENTE GLORIEUSES (30 glorious years) of prosperity in France, have proved hollow. MARINE LE PEN'S FRONT NATIONAL (National Front) is openly anti-European, protectionist and nationalistic. So are many on the extreme left.

EXCEPTION FRANÇAISE
ALIBI FOR IGNORING REALITY

All-purpose excuse why France is entitled to ignore economic reality. A central policy supporting the psychotic French belief that they are capable of withdrawing from the world into a contented bubble of their own. It is a guiding principle of French economic diplomacy that the French are exceptional and are entitled to exempt themselves from international trade agreements in order to protect the French language and culture and even yoghurt (see *YAOURT*). Numerous other countries also claim to be exceptional including the United States and Russia but while the Americans claim their exceptionalism represents a manifest destiny to alter the world in its own image, and the Russian claim their exceptional destiny is to reclaim its shattered empire, the French adopt exceptionalism to mean the ability to erect trade barriers.

EXISTENTIALISME
FRANCE'S ENIGMA MACHINE

Philosophy identified with JEAN-PAUL SARTRE, re-invented as term used in international diplomacy to describe threats to existence, i.e., existential threat. France faces plenty of existential threats: political, economic and social, but existentialism itself has never been straightforward to define (Sartre's book on it was titled *L'être et le néant: Essai d'ontologie phénoménologique* (*Being and Nothingness: An Essay on Phenomenological Ontology*) and argued that 'existence precedes essence.' Perhaps it is unfair to describe this dense work as highly seasoned drivel but it is easy to parody. I doubt Flaubert would take it very seriously and it conspicuously lacks any significant modern following. Ambrose Bierce defined philosophy as 'a route of many roads leading from nowhere to nothing,' which perfectly sums up existentialism. See *SURRÉALISME*.

F

FACEBOOK
WILDLY POPULAR IN FRANCE

One third of French people use Facebook, roughly 22 million. But Facebook has never employed more than a few dozen marketing people in France. In June 2015 I received enthusiastic tweets from the industry minister EMMANUEL MACRON and the mayor of Paris ANNE HIDALGO announcing that Facebook was to open an artificial intelligence laboratory in Paris. Perhaps it was time to re-evaluate my thesis that France was uncompetitive in terms of the new information economy. But then I looked into the story and discovered the number of researchers to be employed was, er, six. And that the number was to expected grow to, er, 12, by the end of the year. So only 3.5 million unemployed people to go.

FEMMES
A FORTY-YEAR LAG

In the land that claims to have invented feminism, women have noticeable second-class status, compared to their British and American sisters. Simone de Beauvoir (partner of SARTRE) wrote a foundation text of feminism, *Le Deuxième sexe* (*The Second Sex*). Feminist politics in France is largely one of gesture. The French government has banned skinny fashion models as inappropriate role models for young girls. There are some female politicians and even a handful of women *patrons* (bosses). But in terms of women represented at the top, French institutions look like British ones in about 1985 and French women are still celebrated for their look and style more than for their brains. The average salary of a female engineer in France is 47,850 euros, compared to 59,000 euros for men. The French cartoonist Jean-Jacques Sempé once drew a whimsical cover for *The New Yorker* magazine titled 'The Secret Shame of Paris,' depicting a predawn police roundup of portly women. It was a dig at the then-current wave of books by British and American authors obsessed with French women. Those would be the French women who don't get fat, raise perfectly disciplined children and always wear matching underwear. Female bosses like the Englishwoman Linda Jackson, chief executive of Citroën, Martine Jourdren, boss of Brittany Ferries, and Nathalie Loiseau, director of the *École Nationale d'Administration* (ENA) are highly exceptional.

FÊTE DE LA MUSIQUE
A GREAT AMERICAN IDEA
In 1981 the minister of culture, Jack Lang, decreed that the first day of summer should be a national festival of music and since then it has become a joyous global phenomenon, now celebrated in 700 cities in 120 countries. The idea originated with Joel Cohen, an American who was a producer for France Musique, one of the French national radio stations, roughly equivalent to BBC Radio Three. The festival is celebrated in almost every town and city in France on June 21, and often in even very small villages, as hundreds of thousands of amateur and professional musicians perform in the streets. All performances are free and all performers play for nothing. Subsequently, the idea has been extended and in many cities during the summer including Montpellier, Pézenas and Sainte-Maxime there are now weekly *estivales* (summer evenings) featuring performances, street food and, of course, wine. These events pass without the vandalism and random aggression so typical in British cities on weekend evenings. Perhaps because the combination of wine, food and street music, with a massive presence of families and people of all generations, promotes nothing other than *bonhomie* (geniality). British binge-drinking

culture, fuelled largely by beer, is entirely different. The *Fête de la musique,* the *estivales* and similar summer festivities throughout France represent fraternity at its very best.

FINKIELKRAUT, ALAIN
PUBLIC INTELLECTUAL

Philosopher, republican, Zionist, member of the ACADÉMIE FRANÇAISE, started out as a Maoist before breaking with his friends over the 1973 Yom Kippur war when he supported Israel. Glorious academic career including spell at University of California teaching French literature, returned to Paris where he has published on numerous subjects but especially anti-semitism and, recently, the barbarism of money.

FLAUBERT, GUSTAVE
SNUBBED BY THE ACADÉMIE FRANÇAISE

Still the indispensable French writer, full of insights that explain ancient and modern France. Nowhere near as prolix as such contemporaries as ÉMILE ZOLA, or as long-winded as Marcel Proust (*À la recherche du temps perdu*) or VICTOR HUGO. But never mind the width, feel the quality. Inspired Franz Kafka, among numerous others. Understood just what strange, conceited animals humans can be. Among many great French writers never elected to the ACADÉMIE FRANÇAISE. A worldview informed by spells in England, where he learned the language in the best of all possible ways (in bed). Was a law student, hated it and quit. Lived in Paris, hated it and left. Creator of *Madame Bovary*, the classic tale of adultery and provincial banality, and *L'Éducation sentimentale*, alongside VICTOR HUGO's *Les Misérables*, in which he tells the story of the Paris commune through the story of a young man and his love for an older woman.

FONCTIONNAIRES
PINNACLE OF FRENCH SUCCESS

In France, the height of professional achievement is not to be a successful business person, or professional, but an official of the Republic, a *fonctionnaire*. There are 5.6 million functionaries of the state from the elite *hauts fonctionnaires* (senior officials) who are graduates of the *grandes écoles,* to every other servant of the state including school teachers, GENDARMES, officers of *lA police NATioNAlE*, and the clerks who intermittently attend to the customer service windows at the motor vehicle registration department, in between cigarette breaks. For all functionaries there are generous pensions and a near-impossibility of ever being fired. The retirement age is between 60 and 62, depending on the official's date of birth but for those deemed to have physically demanding jobs, it is possible to retire at 55. For the grandest there are additionally all sorts of unpublicised perks such as *appartements de fonction* (official residences), for which occupants are charged peppercorn rents. At the bottom of the totem pole are the territorial functionaries, employed by the town halls and regional governments, who may pick up your garbage, or answer the phone at the *MAiRiE*. There are especially spectacular allowances for those working in the overseas departments who get hardship pay in the form of tax-free *indemnités* (allowances), extended paid home leaves and free housing.

FOOT
FOOTBALL

Football in France is corrupt, racist and under the influence of deeply dubious personalities. In May 2015, the French football federation actually voted to keep FIFA boss Sepp Blatter in his job after the FBI and Swiss police swooped on the global football organisation accusing it of deep-seated corruption. The then secretary general of Fifa, Blatter's right-hand man, is Jérôme Valcke, a French former journalist, accused by the FBI of implication in a $10 million bribe to three FIFA executive committee members to support South Africa's bid to host the 2010 World Cup. The FBI suggests bribes were paid in the run-up to the selection of France as World Cup host in 1998, but doesn't say to whom or by whom.

The French football federation was instrumental in helping Qatar win the rights to the world cup in 2022, allegedly on orders from former president Nicolas Sarkozy, who was sucking up to Qatar at the time. Immediately following the decision, Qatar ordered 50 Airbus A350 jets and later was to buy French-made Rafale fighter jets in a 6.3 billion euro contract concluded by President François Hollande. According to the magazine *France Football*, former president Nicolas Sarkozy held a lunch at the Elysée in November 2010 at which the guests were then crown prince (now Emir) of Qatar, Tami bin Hamad al-Thani and Michel Platini, president of UEFA. Following this lunch, Platini switched his support for the 2022 cup from the United States to Qatar, and Qatar bought PSG, the Paris football club. Qatar also got the rights to launch four sports channels in France to compete against Canal+, which Sarkozy loathed. The Qatari channels have the rights to major football tournaments in France and the UEFA champions league. Platini denies any wrongdoing and is presenting himself as a clean-hands candidate to replace Blatter. Platini's son Laurent, FIFA executive committee member for France, was subsequently employed by Burrda, a Qatar-owned sports company.

At club level, French football was deeply compromised by a torrid *affaire* involving Marseille football club, which continues to resonate today. In 1993 Marseille owner Bernard Tapie was accused of match fixing. In 1995 he was sentenced to two years in prison. He was subsequently prosecuted for tax fraud. Tapie later supported Sarkozy's bid for the presidency (although Tapie was ostensibly a socialist at the time), allegedly because Sarkozy had promised to help him with his legal difficulties. The French state paid Tapie 400 million euros in an *affaire* that implicated

CHRISTINE LAGARDE when she was finance minister and which continues to rumble on. The state is now asking for it to be repaid. Fat chance. Further accusations of match-fixing were made in 2014 when police arrested the presidents of *Stade Malherbe Caen* and *Nîmes Olympique* while in the same year three directors of Olympique Marseille were accused of misusing club finds.

The most outlandish accusation against French football relates to the nation's World Cup victory in 1998 against a lacklustre Brazilian squad stricken with food poisoning. While food poisoning is not unheard of in France, conspiracy theorists in Brazil wondered whether this was merely unfortunate, or something more sinister. From a nation with a secret service capable of bombing a Greenpeace vessel moored in a harbour in New Zealand, an ostensible ally, it is not inconceivable that the French were leaving nothing to chance, although it will forever be impossible to prove.

Racism is a constant feature in French football despite many of their best players being black, including Thierry Henry and Patrick Viera. Willy Sagnol, the Bordeaux coach, was quoted accusing African players of lacking intelligence. The French world cup team in South Africa essentially went on strike over the expulsion of Nicolas Anelka after a row with white coach Raymond Domenech, who had then to physically separate the player Patrice Evra, who is black, and fitness coach Robert Duverne, who is white. The managing director of the French football federation quit in disgust. See ZIDANE.

FORCE DE FRAPPE
THE FRENCH NUCLEAR DETERRENT

The French first tested nuclear weapons in the Algerian desert in 1960. France today has an estimated 300 nuclear warheads including ballistic missiles launched from submarines and guided bombs launched from Mirage and Rafale fighter jets. It's evident that there are no immediate scenarios in which the French would nuke anybody, nor that this would even be a practical response to any conceivable security threat. Nevertheless, the bomb lets France keep its seat at the top table as a permanent member of the United Nations Security Council.

FOX NEWS
HATED AMERICAN TV NETWORK

After the *Charlie Hebdo* shootings, Fox News, the punchy, conservative, American TV network, reported that there were 'no-go' zones in French cities. This provoked a storm of protest from Anne Hidalgo, the Mayor of Paris, and *Le Petit Journal*, the closest thing in France to *The Daily Show* (formerly presented by Jon Stewart). Fox was made to look foolish but it is still a mystery why they ever apologised since there are definitely neighbourhoods in many French cities where it would be most unwise for outsiders to venture unaccompanied. Hidalgo absurdly threatened to sue Fox News (she never did) but since the prime minister Manuel Valls has himself subsequently described the grim French suburbs as 'ghettos' and more honesty would go a long way. Whether you call them no-go zones or something more tasteful, the biggest victims are those condemned to live in these places.

FRANCE, LA
THE 'INDIVISIBLE' NATION

What does France mean, what does it mean to be French? Republican certainty on this question (to be French is to be a Republican) is hardly supported by the historical background. The Republic says that everyone is equal and the nation is indivisible, but an ideology cannot make everyone the same. Graham Robb, an English writer and historian, cycled through France to produce a masterful biography of the French people, *The Discovery of France* (2007). It shreds the French mythology comprehensively, demonstrating that Frenchness is a recently invented construct. Needless to say, Robb's excellent book was ill-received in its French translation.

More or less everything about France's modern identity has been created in the service of Republican ideology and much of it rather recently. France has been going through an identity crisis that began even before the turn of the century, and has since been exacerbated by the ugly mood in the ghettos of major French cities. The French believed that their Republican model would integrate everyone and sneered at the multiculturalism practised in Britain. But it has turned out that neither appeals to *laïcité* (secularism) in France nor celebrations of difference in Britain have turned out to be fit for purpose. One reason is that in neither Britain nor France is it entirely clear what it means to be British, or French. Or English, or Catalan. Or Scottish or Alsatian.

Robb reminds us that identity has local origins - certainly in France. French conscripts during the Great War, the *poilus*, were not even able to communicate with each other, since their dialects were so strikingly different. As Robert Louis Stevenson observed in *Travels with a Donkey in the Cévennes* (1879), French people living on opposite sides of the same valley were often literally at war with one another.

The French agrarian tradition celebrated today is as mythical as the rest. Agronomists, dispatched from Paris, of course, in the 19th century despaired at the peasantry's refusal to cultivate the land, holding to their pastures and the animals who kept them warm. Only the invention of the internal combustion engine and the tractor persuaded French men to till the land – when they had machines to drive around in. Modern France is therefore largely invented, a construct of Republicanism and the ideologically-driven imposition of national education.

Today, France is a nation united, perhaps, only by its hatred of tax collectors and officials. But it is still not one nation but several, cohabiting often uneasily. An intensely local identity, bound up in town or village life, concerns itself with buying only organic *chèvre* cheese from the local goat farmer, and playing football with the village squad. Yet this exists in contradiction with a new social media identity which crashes through localism and has created entirely new horizontal communities, sometimes more interested in their Facebook friends than their regional roots, and often reaching far beyond France itself.

FRANÇAIS, LE
THE FRENCH LANGUAGE

Charles V, the Holy Roman Emperor, supposedly spoke French to his wife, Italian to his mistress and German to his horse. So, it has long been true that you can only get so far speaking just French. 'Why would you want to learn French?' an expatriate Frenchman once asked me at a *Sciences Po* alumni club meeting to which I had been invited in London. 'Just so you can talk to French people?' Well yes, actually. While true that French ranks well down the list of global languages, the language of Molière still offers what a cultivated anglophone would recognise as a certain refinement as well as access to some of the world's greatest literature. Miss Piggy was a francophone (Pretentious? *Moi?*) All kinds of interesting people speak French including The Queen, Mick Jagger and the actress Julia Robert-Dreyfus (distantly related to Alfred Dreyfus), as well as 275 million Francophones on five continents. People who are not French seem to enjoy learning French for the pure pleasure of it. French is an accessible language for native English speakers because it shares so many words with English (and a few *faux amis,* or misleading cognates). Culturally, French is a fabulous brand, carrying with it the suggestion of earnest conversations in Parisian cafés, fresh baguettes, runny cheese and a delicious glass of something with or without bubbles.

Yet despite all that it has going for it, the French themselves have taken a highly defensive posture. Even if Fleur Pellerin, the culture minister, said in 2015 she is relaxed about English, the government continues to lavish money on *francophonie* and there are still laws on the books (lA loi TouboN) regulating the use of English in legal documents and advertising. (Although an exception has been made so British motorists caught speeding in France can receive their *procès-verbal* (summons) in English.) There is no evidence that this regulation is inhibiting the use of English in its entirety and in parts, nor that French itself is in anything other than rude good health, with an important foothold in Africa, and a continuing cohort of support from the same people who read the *New York* or *London Reviews of Books*. French today is more dynamic than ever, careless of the rules made by the old men at the ACADÉMIE FRANÇAISE in Paris.

FRANÇAISE, ACADÉMIE
MALEVOLENT GUARDS OF THE FRENCH LANGUAGE

'Mock it, but try to become a member if you can,' was GUSTAVE FLAUBERT's advice. He was never a member. The 40 members of the Academy, known as Immortals, wear the *habit vert,* a long black coat and black-feathered 18th century *bicorne* (two-cornered) hat, the robe and hat both richly embroidered with green leafy motifs. They are also issued a sword, presumably to enforce their decrees on the correct use of the French language. Spends its days debating such vital questions as whether it is correct to address a female government minister as *madame la ministre* or *madame le ministre*. A *ministre* (government minister) is a masculine noun; feminists object. The French language is evolving at break-neck speed in spite of all the efforts of the Academy to control it, and has been thoroughly contaminated by anglicisms (e.g. the *selfie).* Other than running through transgressors with their swords, *les académiciens* might be seen as powerless to do much about this. It is unkind but not entirely untrue to say that the *Académie* has become gloriously irrelevant, even ludicrous.

Of 726 Immortals, eight have been women. Members have

included various rogues, politicians and Nazi collaborators (including Marshal PÉTAIN). Excluded have been such greats as Marcel Proust, Honoré de Balzac, Jules Verne and ÉMILE ZOLA. The Academy has taken a reactionary stand against official recognition of regional languages (Alsatian, Basque, Breton, Catalan, Corsican, Occitan and Provençal). Its official dictionary of the French language can be defined with exactitude by reference to the inspiring American journalist Ambrose Bierce, who defined a dictionary as 'a malevolent literary device for cramping the growth of a language and making it hard and inelastic,' although he wrote one of his own. Sir Michael Edwards OBE, a literary scholar and poet, became the first British member of the *Académie* in 2014, confessing that he was 'worse than a foreigner - an Englishman.' Sir Michael believes that English should have a similar institution to defend itself against Americanisms, proving that for other-worldliness, he lacks nothing in comparison with his native colleagues. Sir Michael's views are contestable in any case, as he has applied for and been granted naturalisation as a French citizen, although holding onto his British passport and his royal gongs. I suppose one must admire someone who is capable of carrying royal honours and being a republican at the same time.

FRANÇAIS DE SOUCHE
BORN IN FRANCE OF FRENCH HERITAGE

Literally, French by roots. Controversial expression with racist and anti-Republican subtext used to distinguish 'real' French people from immigrants and their families. In my village, where half the population has Spanish surnames (Lopez, Sanchez, Martinez, etc.) and there are also plenty of English, Germans, Swedes and even a Brazilian, the *Français de souche* are probably in a minority.

FRANCE INTER
ORGAN OF THE LEFT

Like BBC Radio Four, with added Marxism. Programmes are often beautifully produced and presented. Listening to France Inter is a very good way of learning French. The announcers pronounce the language with exceptional clarity and elegance. But as is often the case in media content analysis, you miss the point if you analyse only the content. It's what's missing that matters. And in the case of France Inter, it is any kind of critique of what is really going on in France. That's not surprising because France Inter is itself part of the state, as embedded within the establishment as it is possible to be, dependent on the state for its budget, its frequencies and its licences. France Inter is not interested in the economic functionality of France. It broadcasts many beautiful programmes about the arts, and natural science, some highly amusing talk shows featuring many of the most brilliant Parisian talkers, as well as a lesser diet of quiz shows and call-ins. These are interspersed with anodyne news bulletins, in which government spokesmen are rarely challenged. France Inter announces repeatedly that it is a 'public service,' but in its failure to challenge state power, it is really a public disservice. France Inter is at its best when the journalists are on strike, which is frequent, sparing listeners the dull repetition of its narrow-minded view of the world. France Inter does play a varied and engaging range of music, which it stitches between its talkier segments.

Like public broadcasters everywhere, its primary goal is self-preservation. Spokespersons for the right-wing parties are allowed perfunctory participation, though the centre-point of debate is always *gauchiste*. But it is not so much the ideology paraded by France Inter that makes it pretty unreliable, it is the radio station's seeming absolute indifference to questions that challenge the elite French consensus. France Inter is not remotely interested in business, capitalism, jobs, innovation, wealth creation, or really anything outside its tight circle of arts and letters. A lens to an ordered France of ministerial announcements, it is a plush platform for a commentariat of *la gauche caviar* (caviar-eating leftists) who circulate between Inter and the editorial rooms of *Le Monde*.

FRANCOPHONIE
THE COMMONWEALTH OF FRENCH SPEAKERS

In terms of absolute number of speakers, measured globally, French is the 18th most important global language after *Basa Jawa, Wu* and *Telugu*, among others. The *Organisation internationale de la francophonie*, financed largely by France, is supposed to act as a fulcrum of solidarity among Francophone countries. Naturally, this is a considerable operation with much opportunity for high-flying jollies and many lavishly-compensated make-work jobs, including an executive secretariat in Paris, summits and ministerial conferences, all sustained by a parliamentary council and, as if this was not enough, a parliamentary assembly.

'FRENCH-BASHING'
ANGLO-AMERICAN PASSTIME

Term used by the French to describe any foreign criticism, especially that emanating from Britain. It is true that French-bashing is fun and also easy, since there is plenty to bash. Nothing lights up the countenance of a grumpy English newspaper editor like a slashing story ridiculing the French. It is also true, firstly, that there are plenty of stories in British newspapers that admire the French (e.g., 'Thank goodness I gave birth in France,' Gillian Harvey, *Daily Telegraph*, June 2015) and second, that many of the most celebrated examples of French-bashing are pretty historic and much of what is condemned here as French-bashing might otherwise simply be considered journalism that dares to note that France is not exactly without problems. French-bashing has indeed lately been pretty tame, in comparison with its antecedents. C. S. Forester wrote a classic novel of the Peninsular War which he titled, simply, *Death to the French* (1932).

The most notorious practitioner of French-bashing was the former editor of *The Sun*, Kelvin MacKenzie. 'Hop off you frogs' was his classic headline in 1984, during the so-called lamb war with France, when French farmers hijacked British sheep exports to France. In response, MacKenzie sent a detachment of Page 3 girls to France to plant a union flag on the Place d'Angleterre in Calais. 'Up yours Delors,' was his headline on 1 November 1990, urging the paper's 'patriotic family of readers' to tell 'the French fool' Jacques Delors, president of the European Commission, 'where to stuff his ECU' (predecessor to the Euro). MacKenzie again mobilised Page 3 girls, this time to the French embassy in London, after declaring the French to be the filthiest people in Europe. (He had read somewhere they didn't buy much soap, which may be true, but they do use a lot of shampoo.) MacKenzie, it might be noted, bought a holiday home in France in 2004. He insisted, 'Look, I don't mind the French, but when I'm there I don't spend any time talking to them.' French newspapers are rarely as creatively offensive in writing *rosbif*-bashing stories, tending instead to embittered diatribes condemning Anglo-Saxon *ultra-libéralisme*. But *Le Monde* did well in June 2015 with an article, in English, warning that 'Britain beware, Brexit [UK withdrawal from the EU] could be your Waterloo.' It was published on the 200th anniversary of the famous battle.

FROMAGE
GLORY OF FRANCE

'Fetch hither *le fromage de la belle France*,' demanded Mousebender (John Cleese), vainly trying to order Camembert in the cheese-shop sketch in *Monty Python's Flying Circus*. 'I don't care how fucking runny it is. Hand it over with all speed.' Replies Wensleydale, the shop assistant: 'The cat's eaten it.'

When I visited England with a French winemaking friend (his first visit), he was astonished to visit the Neal's Yard cheese shop in London's Borough Market, specialising in British and Irish cheese, which must be one of the finest in the world. Astonished because he had no idea that this food of the gods could possibly exist outside France. But if cheese in Britain is just food, it is a French national sacrament and must be treated with reverence. At a French dinner party I reached for the brie and witlessly, instead of cutting a radius, crudely lopped off a piece from its apex. A deadly silence fell around the table. A greater *faux pas* could hardly be imagined. Had there ever been need of further proof of the crassness of the British, this had just been supplied, declared one of the guests, sparing me the hint of a wink. It is a lesson I will never forget.

Cheese is part of the culinary trinity of the French diet, alongside *pain* (bread) and *vin* (wine). With these simple rations, and the correct ritual (not barbarously cleaving the brie), a sort of Republican transubstantiation occurs at each meal time. When I worked briefly at the French embassy in Washington as a consultant to the science attaché, the highlight of the week was the arrival of the diplomatic bag (actually, a sealed air freight container), flown to Washington each week by the French air force, containing the unpasteurised cheese that is otherwise unavailable in the United States. The work of the embassy would grind to a halt as everyone trooped to the loading dock to collect their rations.

French people say a meal without cheese is like a night without a woman. Even more colourfully, Flaubert said it was akin to a beautiful woman with a missing eye. It is not true that there are 246 varieties of cheese in France, as famously stated by General de Gaulle, who wondered how a country with such diversity could be governed. I suspect there are thousands. Nobody agrees exactly how many there are but some of the best never travel more than a few kilometres from the dairies, and are often sold by the producer personally at local markets. I recommend the *chèvre* from Mas Rolland, just up the road from my village.

FRONDEURS
POLITICAL REBELS

The inept administration of PRESIDENT FRANÇOIS HOLLANDE has provoked dissidence in the Socialist party, most notably led by MARTINE AUBRY, the mayor of Lille, and the former industry minister Arnaud Montebourg (famous for insulting MAURICE TAYLOR, the American boss of Titan Tyres who objected to saving an ailing factory in northern France because the communist trade union was refusing to work more than three hours a day). Mounteboug interrupted the party congress in June 2015 by declaring that the president was leading the country to disaster on a path of austerity. In truth, his analysis of the consequences of Hollande is resonant - more than 60,000 business failures and more than 600,000 more unemployed in three years. He also called for lowering taxes on the middle class, but did not explain how these prescriptions would downsize the gargantuan state, speculating instead that French debt, 97.5 per cent of GDP, could be reduced as a consequence of the growth that would be unleashed by abandoning austerity.

FRONT NATIONAL, LE
SOCIALIST/NATIONALIST PARTY

Not at all a party of the extreme right, as portrayed by the *Guardian*, LE MONDE, the *New York Times* and practically all other media, but much more a party of the confirmist left, where all French political parties congregate, with added nationalism. The brand has been partly detoxified by MARINE LE PEN, daughter of party founder JEAN MARIE LE PEN, who remains a thorn in her side with his unreconstructed views on, e.g. the Holocaust ('a detail' of history, he says). Marine cosies up to gays and Jews and never speaks directly of other races but instead emphasises the FN project of Frenchness, which is a code that can be interpreted rather broadly although it is frequently taken to mean anti-Arab. One poll says 14 per cent of Jews in France are likely to vote FN. Le Pen is certainly one of very few contemporary French politicians who knows how to hold a crowd when she gives a speech. It may be a hollow project but to many French people, some of them former communists, it sounds better than the *blanc-manger* (blancmange) on offer from the two other parties, so she is getting a lot of support.

The pretence of the left-wing media that Marine Le Pen's party is of the extreme right is presumably designed to confuse voters into imagining there is a centimetre of difference between the protectionist, isolationist and *clientéliste* policies of the National Front and those of, for example, the *Front de gauche* (Left Front) a coalition of the Communist party and a variety of other extreme leftist parties. There is no reason to imagine the FN is remotely close to having a clue how to manage the French economy. Indeed, the evidence is they will make matters worse, being even more unreconstructed interventionists than the socialists.

The difference between the National Front and Communists is not economic policy. The differentiator is nationalism, with a whiff of *Vichysme* and a *soupçon* of the reactionary social movement MANIF POUR TOUS. There should be an implausibility about the idea of the National Front ever forming a government. That it has borrowed 10 million euros from a Russian bank to finance its political campaigns verges on corruption. But it is not impossible that the party could advance further given the clue-lessness of the mainstream parties and the disillusion of so many voters.

FUITE DES CERVAUX
BRAIN DRAIN

More than a million French people have left the country in the past 10 years, most of them to other countries in the European Union, and the rate is accelerating. They are often the most talented and ambitious. Twenty per cent of them have started their own businesses elsewhere. Among skilled engineers who have left, 40 per cent say they are not contemplating returning. One of my colleagues on the municipal council recently told me that her son was leaving London. 'Is he coming back to France?' I asked. 'No,' she replied, 'he's moving to New York'.

G

GARDE À VUE
POLICE DETENTION CONDEMNED AS TORTURE

Police detention. Avoid if at all possible. France has been condemned by European courts for abusive police detentions but such detentions remain widely available to the police under French laws, despite some modest reforms. Under French law, a police officer can put you in custody for, in principle, 24 hours but longer under many exceptions, while possible crimes you may have committed are investigated, to stop you from interfering with evidence, merely to present you to a magistrate so he or she may question you, or for any of several other reasons. Suspects are routinely strip-searched and kept in primitive conditions. The committee for the prevention of torture of the Council of Europe has visited *garde à vue* cells in numerous police commissariats through France and found minuscule cells, filthy conditions and glacial temperatures.

GARE DU NORD
DECREPIT PARIS RAILWAY STATION

Andy Street, managing director of John Lewis, was forced to apologise after calling this once great Paris railway terminus 'the squalor pit of Europe' but although the French were duly outraged, the Gare du Nord is pretty decrepit and menacing. Despite efforts to spruce it up the station has a reputation for muggings, pickpockets and filth, especially on the platforms connecting the station to the volatile northern suburbs. One must have a certain sympathy for Andy Street since the Gare du Nord bears no comparison with the expensively renovated and rather magnificent St Pancras station in London, where there is at least a convenient branch of John Lewis. The French seem to have been shamed by Mr Street since they have announced that they will spend more than a billion euros improving the station - by 2024. ANNE HIDALGO, mayor of Paris, makes a speciality of professing outrage when foreigners say things about her city that are true.

GAYET, JULIE
PRESIDENTIAL SQUEEZE

An actress and Socialist party activist, aged 43 in 2015, who sued *Closer* magazine for revealing to the French public what the entire political and media class of Paris already knew: that she was having a sexual affair with President FRANÇOIS HOLLANDE who was living with someone else at the time. She was duly awarded 15,000 euros in damages against the magazine, which had published a picture of Hollande, looking characteristically gormless, arriving at her apartment on the back of a motor scooter driven by one of his bodyguards. A parade of French journalists appeared on France Inter and in the pages of *LE MONDE* to denounce *Closer* for having disclosed the liaison, which they claimed was a private affair of which the public deserved no knowledge. Meanwhile, the line between private lust and public trust appeared already to have been violated as Gayet had been nominated by the minister of culture to a position with the Academy of France in Rome which, although unpaid, would have involved jolly expenses-paid trips to Italy. This nomination was subsequently withdrawn. Gayet in summer 2015 was reported to be spending four nights a week with Hollande, entering through the garden gate of the Elysée to avoid paparazzi. Ms Gayet is said to refer to herself as Hollande's *fiancée* but the Paris rumour mill says she has competition as the President is believed to have grown increasingly close once more to SÉGOLÈNE ROYAL, the environment minister. She is mother of his four acknowledged children and was the presidential squeeze before she was displaced by Trierweiler, who was in turn displaced by Gayet. But of course this is none of anybody's business, according to the Paris media elite.

GAZ DE SCHISTE
FRACKING

France has some of the biggest shale gas reserves in the world with 4 trillion cubic metres estimated to lie deep beneath the Paris basin, so maybe could power itself for decades and export plenty of gas, too. However there is an absolute ban on fracking and lower oil prices have taken the heat out of the argument in any case. Green movements in Europe have seized on the idea of shale gas as a uniquely dangerous form of energy and would certainly physically contest any attempt to frack in France. In the meantime, France will continue to import most of its gas, mainly from north Africa and Russia. It is all somewhat ironic because Total, the French petrol giant, was among the first to master the techniques of extracting gas from deep rocks. I tease my friends at the organic café in Pézenas by demanding genetically modified coffee roasted with *gaz de schiste*.

GENDARMES
ARMED COLLECTORS OF FINES

Despite the glamorous image of the anti-terrorist intervention teams abseiling from helicopters, the *gendarmerie* is also more prosaically a fine-farming wing of the state, mounting checkpoints at which motorists are stopped and issued on-the-spot fines for the most minute infractions. Keeping farmers and angry trade unionists from closing motorways is not so much their thing. Catching actual criminals also often proves much more difficult. A friend in my village who is a recently retired gendarme (we meet at the local café when I walk Ringo) tells me that as a young officer, he was able to stop in the villages on his rural beat, chat with the notables and locals, and help people with their problems. At the end of his career, he said, much of this had been swept away by a target culture, in which officers were expected to write tickets. By tradition the 100,000 Gendarmes are part of the military and provide the splendidly uniformed Republican Guard and other ceremonial elements on state occasions, including a mounted detachment, but their policing responsibilities are supervised by the Ministry of the Interior.

Gendarmes live in gated subdivisions called *casernes* (barracks) and carry 9mm pistols. Although they have lost some ground to the *police nationale* (national police) in the expanding cities, and many of the towns in their jurisdiction are establishing their own municipal police services, they still have ultimate authority in the smaller towns and the countryside, and they control most of the motorway speed cameras. Many *gendarmes* (there were honourable exceptions) were collaborators in the Second World War, rounding up Jews, resisters and other troublemakers and providing intelligence to the Gestapo, but they remained in the job after the invasion.

The motorways and many national roads are now covered with cameras and number-plate recognition systems. These systems generate thousands of penalty notices daily. The new big police administration centre at Rennes where the penalty notices are generated mints a tidy sum for the government and has created exciting new employment opportunities for fortunate gendarmes who can do all of their law enforcing from a desk with a computer screen, without ever getting their boots wet.

GHETTOS
ALSO CALLED BANLIEUES, CITÉS

To the Mosson stadium in northwest Montpellier to watch my beloved Arsenal play the local team, Montpellier Hérault Sporting Club. The stadium is slummy (it has subsequently been condemned) and is located on the edge of a neighbourhood that could easily be mistaken for a city in north Africa. It is early evening and no women are visible on the streets. Young men loiter aimlessly on corners. Grim tenements festooned with satellite dishes loom over scuzzy-looking kebab shops. France might deny that it has no-go zones, but this wouldn't be the place to walk down the street wearing a *kippa*. Before and after the game, scores of cops huddle next to the tram station, protecting each other, letting the arriving fans fend for themselves. Mosson is not special at all but similar to dozens of ghettos on the outskirts of every French city. Its inhabitants lead a life utterly separate from the rest of French people. There are essentially no jobs, other than crime. There is no reason for outsiders to come here, other than to watch a game of football, following which they will quickly depart. When you've seen one ghetto, you've seen them all, said Spiro Agnew, but in France they range from the merely dreary and impoverished to drug-ganglands.

These estates had their origins, believe it or not, in good intentions, although these were wrapped in a theory of supposedly benevolent social engineering that has proved hopeless in practice. The ambition was to clear the old urban slums (*les bidonvilles*) and put in their place a new type of housing, in the fresh air and open spaces of the suburbs, to be fit for workers.

In 1954, l'Abbé Pierre, the famous social activist priest, was among those goading the government into the rapid construction of these massive suburban housing estates. The projects were even celebrated at the time. Charles-Édouard Jeanneret-Gris Corbusier, the celebrated Swiss modernist architect (and fascist), created the two most celebrated of these human warehouses, safely located on the outskirts of cities so their inhabitants might not perturb the bourgeoisie: *La Cité radieuse* in Marseille, and *La Cité radieuse de Briey*, in Lorraine. At first these concrete estates were occupied by poorer native French people decanted from the bulldozed slums, but as the estates matured, they became increasingly populated by immigrants from Algeria and other African countries. See *MUSULMANS*.

GO-FAST
DRUGS SMUGGLING TECHNIQUE

A French neologism formed from two English words. It involves the high-speed transport of drugs, weapons or other contraband on France's motorway network. Insane as this would seem as a viable criminal strategy, the *go-fast* is a real thing, according to the GENDARMES, who have equipped themselves with speedy Subaru motorcars to give chase.

The *go-fast* involves using two high-powered vehicles, one travelling ahead, keeping an eye out for the cops and roving customs controls, the other, with the actual contraband, laying back just a little. This technique, which has captured the imagination of French journalists and film and TV directors, itself would seem to illustrate that French criminals are as delusional as everyone else in France, since there are radars and cameras with automatic number plate recognition covering practically the entirety of the motorway network and nothing is so likely to attract official attention as two flashy motors full of home boys moving at 200 km/h. If I were in this business I would have my merchandise transported in camping vans driven annoyingly slowly by old people. Soon after I had this insight, reports appeared in the media suggesting that some criminals are doing exactly that. This latest technique has been dubbed by journalists, in another neologism imported from English roots, as the *go-slow*.

GOOGLE
LOATHED BY THE FRENCH GOVERNMENT

Used daily by tens of millions of French people, condemned by government ministers as an example of American information imperialism. Google in France is increasingly compelled to censor its search results by the *Commission nationale de l'informatique et des libertés* (national commission on information technology and liberty). The French government indeed claims the right to censor Google worldwide, demanding it remove listings from its entire global search database if they are 'inaccurate, inadequate, irrelevant or excessive.' Among those exploiting this ruling have been a British call girl jailed in France for running a ring of 600 prostitutes, suspected terrorists and a priest who stood naked at his window and shouted abuse at children. This censorship of reality, which originated with the European Union, has been enthusiastically gold-plated by the privacy-obsessed French, who have discovered that canny users can bypass google.fr and click directly to google.com in America, where they might come across non-conforming data.

But this is hardly the only problem raised by Google. The larger issue is why is there no viable French competitor? For a country that once had pretensions to be a leader in information technology, state subsidies of technologies and market participants have produced mainly failure. Axelle Lemaire, a Socialist party deputy (representing London's expatriate French, among others), and a minister of state, claimed the reason is because the American Google is too big and powerful. She believes Google should provide links to its competitors - which is like asking the Socialist party to add a line to their election manifestos advising voters that they also have the choice of voting for other parties. It's typical of the French elite's belief that citizens are infants who cannot be trusted to make their own decisions. It seems not to have occurred to her that the reason there are no French successes like Google is because it is impossible to launch such an enterprise, or indeed any enterprise, in France.

Google, naïvely, thought it could buy off its opponents in France, giving millions to legacy French media to reinvent themselves for the digital world. These enterprises, showing no gratitude, are now suing Google before the European courts, claiming unfair competition. Google may or may not be guilty of uncompetitive practices, or perhaps it is guilty simply of being more effective than anyone else. But because everyone in France depends on Google every day, Google is an in-the-face reminder of how France has failed on the Internet. Therefore, Google is depended upon but hated at the same time. Perhaps it is hard to be sympathetic to such a giant enterprise, but Google's real crime is that it is a success.

GOUVERNANCE TERRITORIALE
FRANCE'S MOST EXPENSIVE PASTRY

Local government (*gouvernance territoriale*) in France resembles the *mille feuilles*. This pastry otherwise known as a *Napoléon* is a creamy patisserie made up of a 'thousand leaves' of ultra-fine pastry with lots of cream and a sugary top. A perfect metaphor for the model on which France has constructed its system of local government. That is to say there are many layers, a squishy centre, and it is very fattening. The *mairie*, or *hôtel de ville* (town hall) is the first stop for many government services. The *mairies* are ruled by an elected mayor and a municipal council and are part of a larger *canton*, comprising numerous villages or a town or two, whose representatives go to the *Conseil départemental* to govern the *département*, which is itself subsidiary to the *région* (e.g. Languedoc-Roussillon), although these regions are currently being reorganised and some are being consolidated.

Entwined amongst all this are 200 *communautés d'agglomerations* (metropolitan councils) and thousands of *syndicats intercommunaux* (inter-communal syndicates), established to provide services to local government customers (avoiding privatising them). These include syndicates for water and sewage services, trash collection, animal control, graffiti-removal and promotion of tourism. A local council meeting in France looks like a pretty good example of local democracy in action, although they are greatly constrained in what they can do by the overseeing eye of the state. If proximity is a virtue in local government, the French system delivers it, with around 40,000 elected mayors and councils. As for economy and efficiency, that is another question. Some of these organisms undoubtedly deliver good services but many are stuffed with relatives, friends and allies of local politicians.

GRÈVES
STRIKES

The French strike 10 times more often than the Germans. Often in an industrial dispute the strike is the first resort, not the last. Anyone can strike, even if they are not employed. Students strike. Even the pharmacist in the village went on strike for a day. I asked her to explain who she was striking against since she owns the business and is apparently prosperous. She was striking, she explained, to protest a scheme for reforming the retail pharmaceutical market, including the revolutionary possibility that consumers might be able to buy a packet of aspirin in the supermarket. Air Traffic Controllers, when they strike, tend to ground first flights of airlines which they consider unfair competition to Air France. Doubtless for most people the inconvenience of Dominique the chemist being on strike for the day was pretty minimal. Simply withholding labour is not enough for French strikers who do not hesitate to impose misery on their innocent fellow citizens. Tactics used by strikers include blocking motorways and railway lines, factory occupations and holding managers hostage. The police are generally passive observers of these events.

GROSSESSE
PREGNANCY - FRENCH EMPLOYERS' DISASTER

A friend who runs a small business tells me he got four weeks' work out of one of his secretaries in four years. Are women really benefiting from such a regime? An *enceinte* (pregnant) French woman will benefit from the most generous maternity regime in the world. She needs to have worked for an employer for only 60 hours (less than two weeks, since the maximum working week is

35 hours) to be entitled to receive two years' paid maternity leave after *accouchement* (delivery). France is the most fertile country in the European Union, although seeing its lowest population growth in a decade in 2013, with the birth rate per woman falling to 1.99, from 2.03 in 2010. But who will hire a fertile woman?

GUERRE DE CENT ANS
HAS IT EVER ENDED?

One Hundred Years' War, 1337-1453, which was not precisely 100 years but 116 and in some respects never has ended in terms of shifting dispositions on the ground. Land fought over on the Dordogne in the 14th century is now largely occupied by colonies of anglophones in their *résidences secondaires* (holiday homes). As for the actual war, the competing claims of the Plantagenets and Valois for the throne of France morphed into an almost impossibly complicated series of conflicts, taught rather differently in England and in France and has left confused memories all around. It can be argued that the war left Britain, cut off from its continental possessions, in search of another empire, and above all, looking west and globally, whereas the outcome cemented France as a caged continental power, uncomfortable for its neighbours. Although supposedly this conflict ended more than 700 years ago, there is an argument that manoeuvres remain ongoing.

GUERRES DE RELIGION
FRANCE'S INVENTION OF THE HOLOCAUST

The French have been killing one another for religious reasons for a long time and, in the sweep of history, only recently ceased to do so, if they have. Recent killings of French Jews by French Muslims suggest the habit is not entirely extinguished. The various wars of religion were largely won by the Catholics who pushed Protestantism into a pretty marginal place in France. The consequences of this have been grave. A large number of the most motivated members of the French mercantile class, who were Protestant, relocated elsewhere, to the benefit of the economies of e.g. England, the Netherlands and the United States. The Catholic caste who were left behind, with their horror of commerce, consolidated France's embedded suspicion of business, to its eternal cost.

GUIGNOLS DE L'INFO, LES
TV PROGRAMME COPIED FROM SPITTING IMAGE

Satiric puppet show modelled on Britain's *Spitting Image*, on Canal+ since 1988. *Les Guignols* in 2015 broadcast a sketch of President FRANÇOIS HOLLANDE in bed with JULIE GAYET and SÉGOLÈNE ROYAL watching a replay of a press conference in which he had condemned Vladimir Putin. 'Was I firm?' he asked. 'More or less,' replied Gayet. 'It was perfect,' said Royal. Although there are still occasional moments of brilliance like this, the show is pretty tired. The *patron* (boss) of Canal+, VINCENT BOLLORÉ, would like to cancel it; he fired the writers instead.

GUILLOTINE
THE NATIONAL RAZOR

A machine which makes a Frenchman shrug his shoulders with good reason, *pace* Ambrose Bierce. MARINE LE PEN, leader of the National Front, wishes to re-introduce this. Perfected by the French although early versions were used in England from 1280. As many as 40,000 French people were guillotined in France after the revolution under the direction of Maximilien Robespierre ('pity is treason'), who met his own fate on the national razor in 1794. The guillotine was a popular mass entertainment. More than 50,000 spectators came from as far away as Montpellier to witness the guillotining of my village's most notorious highwayman, Jean Pomarèdes, in 1843, on the site of what is now a car park.

H

HAÏTI
PRODUCT OF FRENCH GREED

France's terrible behaviour led to the establishment of the first black republic, in 1804, which in turn destabilised the institution of slavery throughout the western hemisphere. Amy Wilentz, professor of literary journalism at the University of California, Irvine, is author of *Farewell, Fred Voodoo* (2013), a love letter to Haïti and Haïtian *créole* and a scorching account of the shameful, corrupt, catastrophic international aid efforts following the Haïtian earthquake in 2010. She says France, with the brutal slavery it imposed before Haïti's revolution, and the vicious financial strictures it imposed after it, almost destroyed Haïti, leaving it with a legacy of enduring poverty and political dysfunction. Wilentz explains: 'They managed to bring over so many Africans that the ratio at the time of the revolution was something like 10:1, and the country was ripe for revolution. The French treated their slaves so badly that they were always having to bring in new ones from *Mère Afrique* (mother Africa) because so many died, and they needed so many more to work to death. These new recruits were the angriest, the least willing to bow to the yoke and the whip.' These were the slaves rallied by Toussaint Louverture, whose revolution finally overthrew the French although he was himself betrayed by Napoléon Bonaparte who invited him to treat, broke his word and imprisoned him. Louverture died a miserable death in French captivity.

The French left Haïti with crippling debt, intense class snobbery, a politics of pointlessness, Christianity, and also, though not with any benevolence, the extraordinary Haïtian *créole* language, a fabulous *macédoine* (mixture) of French and African tongues, in which French is simplified and the African languages reach an apogee of purity, wit, and clarity, notes Wilentz. An odd sidebar: the Haïtian revolution in 1946 followed a visit to the island by the French surrealist ANDRÉ BRETON at a time when children were eating tadpoles from the sewers and labourers were working for one American cent per day. Breton condemned 'the imperialisms that the war's end had in no way averted,' remarks reported approvingly by the reformist journal *La Ruche*. The subsequent suppression of the newspaper led to student unrest and then a general strike, which ultimately led to regime change.

The progressive nature of the revolution was sadly short lived. Breton said later that the Haïtian spirit, 'miraculously continues to draw its vigour from the French revolution' and that 'the striking outline of Haïtian history shows us man's most moving efforts to break away from slavery and into freedom.' This may itself have been a somewhat Franco-centric analysis, as Haïti's subsequent history has not provided any enduring democracy or freedom for people who remain among the poorest in the world. The country was ruled from 1957 to 1986 first by François Duvalier (Papa Doc) and then by his son, Jean-Claude (Baby Doc). Papa Doc killed 30,000 of his opponents, sometimes watching as his Tonton Macoute secret police immersed them in baths of acid. Baby Doc amassed a fortune estimated at $800 million and after he was deposed, hid out in France. Haïti shares the motto *LIBERTÉ, EGALITÉ, FRATERNITÉ* with France and is equally remote from delivering on this promise.

Haïti's art, drawn from Voodoo animism, remains influenced by a formality and composition drawn from French art of the 18th and 19th centuries. And then there is the food. In Haïtian cuisine, thyme, wild mushroom, garlic and onions are fundamental. And their home-grown, home-roasted coffee is outstanding and idiosyncratic. I would suggest, though Wilentz does not, that among the most enduring legacies of the French are the Haïtians themselves, some of the most handsome people anywhere - Africans, with a Gallic twist.

HAUTE ÉCOLE DE COMMERCE
ELITE 'BUSINESS SCHOOL FOR CIVIL SERVANTS

HEC is a business school that makes future administrators rub shoulders with the idea of business, with little impact. The usual elite selection and rigorous exams have produced no French equivalent to Bill Gates or Steve Jobs (neither of whom even graduated from university). Its primary role seems to be to produce managers for the giant *PARAÉTATIQUE* (semi-governmental) enterprises that pass for private industry in France. It ranks 16th in the *Financial Times* list of the best global MBA factories.

HEXAGONE
THE VERY APPROXIMATE SHAPE OF FRANCE

One of the certain ideas the French have about themselves is the geographically dubious notion that they inhabit a space called *L'Hexagone* (the Hexagon). This is supposedly the geometric form most closely resembling what would more accurately described as Contiguous France. I've never been entirely convinced. The *Hexagone* is also sometimes even less convincingly referred to as the *métropole*.

HIDALGO, ANNE
GLAMOROUS, SPANISH-BORN MAYOR OF PARIS

Boasts that London is a suburb of Paris but nobody believes this and if she believes it herself, she is plainly psychotic. Threatened to sue Fox News for reporting that there are no-go areas in Paris. Her meteoric rise through the Socialist party is sometimes attributed to her extremely close working relationship with President François Hollande. She has angrily denied published reports that he fathered one of her children. Has a degree in trade unionism and spent years working on party business while being paid as an *inspecteur du travail* (an employment inspector and civil servant). She subsequently traded her inspectorship in for a mega-money job with VIVENDI while remaining active in Paris socialist politics, rising to first deputy mayor before being elected mayor at the head of the Socialist party list in 2014. Tweets boastfully practically every day.

HOLLANDE, FRANÇOIS
'MONSIEUR NORMAL' - PRESIDENT

Catastrophic choice of French voters as President of the Republic in 2012. No charm or style but plenty of entitlement and ego. Claimed he would reduce unemployment and inequality yet unemployment has risen, and social disharmony has worsened. Hollande claims to be *monsieur Normal*, a product of the French meritocracy who rose from a humble background, but he is in fact the privileged son of a bourgeois family, born in Rouen in 1954. His father was an ear, nose and throat consultant, his mother a social worker. He graduated top of his class at the *École nationale d'administration*. Like an increasing number of top politicians in Britain, Hollande has never had a real job outside politics.

His colourlessness and invisible political talent, wrapped in infinite self-regard (he dyes his hair), made him an unlikely choice to stand for president until the economically literate DOMINIQUE STRAUSS-KAHN (DSK) was eliminated by scandal. Since his erstwhile companion and fellow socialist politician SÉGOLÈNE ROYAL had already lost her own presidential campaign against NICOLAS SARKOZY, Hollande became candidate by default. He ran against the not enormously popular incumbent Sarkozy and still nearly lost. Hollande began his mandate in coalition with the greens, which caused further catastrophic economic results and sent Hollande sinking in the polls. He has subsequently claimed to be a reformer but little reform has actually been delivered, and the president has concerned himself increasingly in foreign affairs, especially in Africa.

Hollande enjoys a surprisingly diverse and entertaining love life for a flabby middle-aged political hack. He is famous for deferring making decisions and his indecision carries into his private life where he flits from one companion to another, never committing: presidential contender SÉGOLÈNE ROYAL; a journalist on *Paris Match*, VALÉRIE TRIERWEILER; a B-list actress, JULIE GAYET; and there is a rumour about the now socialist mayor of Paris, ANNE HIDALGO. According to France's political journalists the private life of the president and other senior politicians is nobody's business, a point of view fortified by the fact that often politicians are having their affairs with journalists. Many French people think differently. Hollande has left either four or five children in his wake, depending on who you believe.

Perhaps the most perspicacious account of François Hollande's absence of character is contained in the kiss-and-tell memoir of Trierweiler, who employs a literary style that is tabloid but that nevertheless has a ring of authenticity. In private, Hollande has led a double or even triple life and deception is second nature to him, not just in his complicated sex life. In his political life he also says whatever he thinks he can get away with, and when he is caught in an inconsistency, just lies again and denies it, according to Trierweiler. Hollande was elected declaring that he didn't like the rich but in private is said to have contempt for the poor, whom he described as the *sans dents*, (without teeth), according to Trierweiler. It is hard to know when he last paid for his own ample lunches; his nickname on Twitter channel #*radiolondres*, a withering testament to his multiple chins, is #flanby. This is a sugary pudding for children sold in French supermarkets. ANGELA MERKEL, the German chancellor, apparently cannot stand him.

When the diminutive Hollande visited London and inspected the guard of honour, Prime Minister David Cameron had him escorted by a towering Guards officer, who reduced Hollande to the stature of a dwarf. He photographs poorly. In 2013, Agence France-Presse, the French news agency, withdrew a photograph of a gurning Hollande visiting a school in northern France, implausibly denying that the decision was to protect the president's dignity. AFP receives officially no subsidies from the French government but the state is also AFP's biggest customer, so make of its so-called independence what you will.

Apparently, Hollande ranks his ministers by the number of laws they have pushed through and decrees they have published, no matter how meaningless or feeble. As if France needs more of either.

HOUELLEBECQ, MICHEL
DYSPEPTIC AUTHOR

Pronounced 'well-beck.' French novelist, notorious for *Les Particules élémentaires* (*Atomised*, 1988), a dystopian meditation on the pointlessness of human existence, feted by some, savaged by the *New York Times* as 'deeply repugnant.' Author of *Soumission* (*Submission*, 2014), another miserabilist tome positing an Islamic takeover of France. His own mother has condemned him as a liar, imposter and parasite. Houellebecq launched his promotional tour for *Soumission* by announcing that the Fifth Republic was 'already dead' and he might have developed this theme before cutting his tour short after the massacre at Charlie Hebdo in 2015. He is hated by many of the French literati because he sells so many books. Houellebecq says: 'They hate me more than I hate them.' Contemptuous of the French establishment, hippies, new-agers and *soixante-huitards* (veterans of the Paris student revolts in 1968). Born in Réunion in 1956, ravaged by his lifestyle, he looks much older, . See BHL.

HUGO, VICTOR
PROLIX AUTHOR

Les Miserables is not quite as long as *À la recherche du temps perdu*, perhaps merely the second-longest novel ever in French. Poorly reviewed when it was published in 1862: Baudelaire called it tasteless, Flaubert said it was neither true nor great. Hugo's opus of the Paris Commune in 1871 subsequently inspired 14 films, numerous television treatments and musical versions in English and French. Epic, dazzling, gigantic cast of characters, highly digressive text, the novel is today highly regarded although few can honestly claim to have read all of it. It has been suggested that if the song from the *Les Miserables* musical *À la volonté du peuple* (transcribed into English as *Do You Hear the People Sing?)* had been written at the time of the actual barricades, the Paris uprising would have succeeded and there would have been no need for the second half of the book. The song has subsequently been sung, *inter alia*, in Cantonese by democracy protesters in Hong Kong in 2014 and by demonstrators opposing the opening of a McDonald's restaurant in Sydney, Australia, in 2013.

HUISSIERS
OVER-PAID BAILIFFS
A highly-specialised type of French lawyer resembling a bailiff who holds the monopoly right to serve and enforce orders of the courts. Reforms to open the profession to competition from normal lawyers are described as cinematic, changing nothing. The average *huissier* makes 8,000 euros per month. I repeatedly asked the *huissiers'* trade association to explain why they deserve protection from competition. Answers came there none. This could be because they are too lazy to respond to questions, or have no good answers. I suspect both might be true.

HUMOUR
YES, THE FRENCH ARE FUNNY
Contrary to received wisdom, the French have a sense of humour although they tend towards wit (*esprit*) and word games (*jeux de mots*) rather than Anglo-Saxon irony, understatement and

slapstick. The French love to talk dirty and they are often cruel and mocking. Relying on puns that can require a sophisticated knowledge of French to understand, many French jokes are fundamentally untranslatable. I note that the French often laugh at my jokes, or perhaps they are just laughing at me. It is also very easy to laugh at the French, as when the English comedian David Lowe set up a stand at the weekly market in the southern French market town of Castelnaudary to sell *Cassoulet*, a French version of pork and beans, proclaiming it to be a British invention, imagining that the French would get the joke. Instead, it provoked a near riot that ended with his bowler hat being unceremoniously knocked from his head.

IMMOBILIER

REAL ESTATE: NOT REALLY A RESPECTABLE SUBJECT OF DINNER PARTY CONVERSATION

Property is 'the base of society, more sacred than religion,' pronounced Flaubert. But that was the Second Empire and since the restoration of the Republic, this is not so true. If the best house in the village has been painted, it is probably owned by foreigners. The French like to conceal their wealth from the taxman: behind the shabby exteriors there is often magnificence inside. Few French characteristics offend the British so profoundly as the general indifference to property values, an obsession that is bred into British people from birth.

Why does so much of France's housing stock look so dilapidated? Away from the centres of the cities visited by tourists, 2.5 million houses are empty and many of them are crumbling. In my own village, houses are literally rotting and falling down because their owners refuse to sell them, or cannot. It is too difficult to sell them because of Napoleonic laws of succession, which can turn transactions into protracted nightmares as generations of inheritors fight over the spoils. And it is too expensive to renovate them. Selling property in France requires the employment of a NOTAIRE, the navigation of numerous archaic procedures and a great deal of taxation. Estate agents are frequently lazy and unimaginative and charge three times as much as they do in Britain. If most of France is blessedly free of the insane property-price inflation common in the UK (Paris is an exception), it has the opposite problem that prices have actually been falling.

All *notaires* have stories of clients who price their properties ridiculously above any conceivable market value. The French often prefer to hold onto their old houses, leaving them vacant, and move into ghastly *lotissements* where there is a place to park the car, a small garden, and somewhere for children to play. These may not be the most beautiful solution to the demand for housing. *Lotissement* houses, especially in the south, are typically surrounded by towering walls made of cinderblock, which many French people never bother to roughcast. A country that claims cultural exceptionalism and boasts a magnificent architectural heritage seems broadly indifferent to the appalling quality of its new settlements.

IMMOBILISME
THE INABILITY TO CHANGE

The French have not always resisted change and indeed have at times embraced the modern, but as an unintended consequence of *clientélisme*, weak governments terrified of unions and social unrest have cut and run from reforms at the first sign of trouble. Although the government announces reforms, it is extremely difficult to identify many that have been implemented, and easy to draw up a list of those that have been abandoned, delayed or watered down beyond all recognition. The headline reforms in 2015 include allowing shops to open on Sundays - but only 12 times a year; allowing intercity bus services (but with limitations); and reducing the maximum amount of compensation that can be demanded from people who have been fired. None of these are going to re-launch the French economy.

IMPÔTS
SQUEEZING UNTIL THE PIPS SQUEAK

Taxes have risen since President François Hollande's election by an average of 1,517 euros for the middle class and 3,851 euros for the better off. In 2013, 8,000 households paid more than 100 per cent of their income in taxes, 12,000 paid more than 75 per cent.

The administration has now generously decided that nobody should pay more than 75 per cent of their income in taxes. Innovation in France may be generally lacking but the tax collectors are never short of ideas. There is a tax called a *taxe foncière* on property and then another one, called a *taxe d'habitation* for occupying it. To this is added a *redevance audiovisuelle* (TV and radio tax) of 136 euros. There is a professional tax on business activities, payable even when the business is not profitable, a tax on income, numerous payroll taxes and that's not including deductions (*COTISATIONS*) for social security. Efforts by President Hollande to increase income taxes on the wealthiest to 75 per cent eventually petered out, but France remains assiduous in taxing its rich while not sparing the middle class.

Wealth tax is officially known as the *Impôt de solidarité sur la fortune* (ISF) and was introduced in 1981 during the presidency of FRANÇOIS MITTERRAND. Solidarity in this case means a tax avoided by the truly wealthy, who can put their money into antiques and fine art, which are exempt, ignored by politicians who undervalue their own villas, yet that hits hard professional people in their retirement who may have accumulated assets but who have limited incomes. The politics of envy play well in France.

President Hollande entered office saying he hated the rich but is of course comfortable himself, the issue of a bourgeois family, with a bijou vacation property in Mougins, a smart suburb of Cannes, co-owned with his former consort SÉGOLÈNE ROYAL. This property in one of the swankiest villages of the Côte d'Azur (a 'modest villa', according to Hollande), convenient to some of the best restaurants in France, is nevertheless surely worth more than 1m euros. He has apparently declared it to be worth just one third of this amount. Then there is the flat in Paris worth a million euros, which he has reportedly declared to be worth half that, and then there is another property in northern France which has been put into a holding company, to avoid ISF altogether. Hollande has been estimated by critics to pay 1/10th of the tax he should pay if his properties were correctly valued. It is impossible to verify these claims but neither has Hollande provided any transparency.

While the rich avoid wealth tax buying works of art and antiques, those who live in houses that have sharply appreciated in value (even if their income has not) have faced draconian demands. The worst stricken are small farmers in smart areas such as the vacation island Île de Ré. The latter have cultivated potatoes on land the value of which has sharply increased, and some face ISF bills of more than 100 per cent of their income. There is no evidence that wealth tax is contributing any meaningful sum to the French treasury, indeed its effect is counter-productive as it is estimated that 1,000 people a year subject to wealth tax are leaving the country. Not even Nicolas Sarkozy dared scrap this tax; Hollande increased it.

INTERMITTENTS DU SPECTACLE
SEASONAL CULTURAL WORKERS

An attractive status for cultural workers who have chosen to engage in seasonal work, mostly in the many festivals, concerts and *animations* (spectacles) put on in France during the summer. When they declare themselves 'unemployed' during the winter, their social benefits continue, at the expense of other taxpayers. Unionised *intermittents* have disrupted numerous expensive cultural productions including international festivals in Montpellier, Orange and Aix-en-Provence. The *intermittent* regime is so attractive that it now claims 254,000 *adherents* (qualified participants), a number that has grown tenfold in 10 years.

INTERNET
INVENTED BY THE FRENCH BUT NOT QUITE

The French claim (not entirely implausibly) to have invented the idea of the Internet or at least the idea of consumer-level data communication. They did pioneer in the field but then bungled the execution in a classic demonstration of how dirigisme turns out to have unintended consequences. Far from positioning France in the fast lane of the information superhighway, the poorly architected Minitel system administered by the French post office became an anchor and the United States raced ahead in what became a digital free-for-all. If there is any comfort for the French in the depressing failure of even one French firm to become a top Internet company, it is that Britain is not ranked either (nor Germany, or any other EU member).

The French paid a high price for the failure of the Minitel and still have a relatively undeveloped Internet culture, not helped by the disproportionate exodus of the best French coders to London and California (the French consulate in San Francisco apparently knows of 40,000 French citizens working in Silicon Valley).

ITALIE
PLACE LIBERATED FOR ITS PIZZA

Pizza is, alongside McDonald's, the French national dish. There are two pizza parlours in our village of 2,500 people, as well as a pizza van, which visits regularly. Pizza in France is often not very good, except in Nice, where they are really Italians. Some French people believe pizza should be made with Emmental cheese rather than Mozzarella. And they use the wrong flour. The French are comforted that Italy's economy is even more of a basket-case than their own, and possibly equally un-reformable, although the current prime minister, Matteo Renzi, seems at least to be making an effort. The French believe that NAPOLÉON BONAPARTE liberated Italy. He crowned himself emperor in 1805. The French lost control of the country in 1870 after the disastrous Franco-Prussian war but held onto Nice and the *Savoie* (Savoy).

J

JARDINS
THE IMPOSITION OF GEOMETRY ON NATURE

The French revere highly formalised gardens like that at Versailles, created by André Le Nôtre, Louis XIV's gardener. Le Nôtre's extension of the *Tuileries* gardens in Paris eventually became the axis of the Champs Elysées. The French garden is completely different from the English garden, which valorises nature above all. The great English gardeners, like Capability Brown, prized the romantic and natural, expressed in such iconic invented landscapes as Sheffield Park, an imagined England, the enormous country house perched above its lake, bridge, meadow and woodland. The French don't need to invent this because their immense countryside provides plenty of nature, with no shovel work.

JEUNES, LES
YOUNG PEOPLE, BETRAYED BY THE REPUBLIC

With an education system that is crumbling and bland universities that are absent from the top tier of international league tables, only a tiny elite of young French people secure well-paid, stable employment. Official unemployment among young people is 23 per cent and in the ghettos it is double this. One in five young people subsists at the official poverty level. Despite France's vaunted social protections, 58 per cent of young people are hired on short-term CDD contracts, usually at the minimum wage (which has become de facto practically a maximum wage, given the surplus of labour). This contrasts with 14.7 per cent hired this way in the UK, and 25 per cent on average in the OECD. Twenty per cent of French young people are not in education, employment or training, twice the rate in Germany. FRANÇOIS HOLLANDE promised in his election campaign a 'sole objective' of ensuring that young people do better. France is still waiting..

JOURNALISME, JOURNAUX
COMPROMISED PROFESSION

Journalists in France have historically been divided between the impossibly brave French correspondents and photographers on the front lines of war zones, returning with narratives that were too good to check, and the whiners, as brilliantly satirised by Evelyn Waugh in *Scoop*, grumpily complaining whenever they are beaten on a story, which is frequently. But the modern French journalist tends towards the pompous, the dull and the compliant. New web and app platforms are trying to challenge the established journals, which will be hard to dislodge, since they are massively privileged by the state.

Astute journalists like the Belgian-born Florence Aubenas of the weekly *Le Nouvel Observateur* have noticed that news is now routinely fabricated, that the 'makers' of news are well able to manipulate it, and that the media is itself complicit in all of this. The freedom of the press, she notes, is the freedom to say the same thing as everyone else. The compliance of the press to a manufactured agenda is a process especially advanced in France as a consequence of numerous subsidies and privileges, which makes the very politicians the journalists are attacking the ones who are in a position to turn on, or off, their salaries at will. So while individual French journalists may be brave, newspapers and broadcasters are largely timid, pompous, introverted and mediocre and governed above all by their dependency on others to pay the bills.

To be recognised as a journalist in France one must hold a press card issued by a commission established by the state, a form of state licensing. The claims of French journalists to independence are consequentially implausible. Those with press cards get a special tax break, making them even more dependent on the largesse of the state. The most rarefied journalists of all are those embedded with the President of the Republic in the Elysée Palace. They're very grand, perhaps even grander than the White House press pool, or certainly very similar, with their own motorcades, chefs, etc. They are mostly poodles.

Professional political journalists don't inform their readers of the private lives of public figures, on the grounds that this is a violation of the *déontologie* (ethics) of the profession. The assertion that the French have 'no interest' in the private conduct of their leaders is nonsense judging from my conversations with ordinary French people.

Liberty of the press, supposedly a bedrock of the French constitution, is compromised from the outset by the press having become habituated to feeding at the trough of subsidies. The privileged tax regime for recognised journalists sees the first 7,650 euros of income tax free, because it allows publishers (bless them) to pay journalists less! Scandalously, the government in addition hands 300 million euros a year in direct subsidies to the press, with the biggest handouts for *Le Monde* and *Le Figaro* (16 million euros each), 11 million euros for *Le Parisien/Aujourd'hui en France*, and tailing down to 7 million euros for the communist paper *l'Humanité* which sells fewer than 50,000 copies (and which also has benefited from the government forgiving it 4m euros of debt). Even the *International New York Times* (formerly the *International Herald Tribune*), published in Paris, is listed among the organisations receiving subsidies (not much by comparison: 356,000 euros in 2014, though perhaps sufficient to cover the expenses claims for the paper's Paris correspondents). These figures have only just emerged after being kept confidential for years.

All these media insist that the subsidies have no impact at all on their outlook and coverage. Do not look to the local and regional press for courage, either. They not only receive state subsidies directly, but are stuffed with advertising placed by local and regional governments. In 15 years I cannot recall a single article in the *Midi Libre*, our local journal in the Languedoc, that could even vaguely be characterised as investigative reporting, or holding power to account. Indeed, the only newspaper that I have noticed to concern itself with demanding investigation is the sports daily, *L'Équipe,* whose pursuit of dope-cheat cyclist Lance Armstrong was more impressive than anything produced by the supposedly serious press. *L'Équipe* outsells both LE MONDE and *Le Figaro.*

The effects of these subsidies are not limited to the production of timid journalism. They have produced a French media landscape that is largely moribund, with unsubsidised innovators forced to compete against subsidised rivals. The very small circulations of these supposedly serious papers are partly due to an antiquated and anti-competitive printing and distribution infrastructure that's expensive, inflexible, inefficient and apparently irreformable. Wapping never happened in France, printing of newspapers remains controlled by unions. The argument for the subsidies is to preserve the diversity of the press but in fact it does the very opposite, privileging established players against newcomers and excluding digital publishers altogether.

JUIFS, LES
JEWS, UNDER ATTACK FROM A NEW DIRECTION

At a wine tasting, I was chatting with a local *vigneron* (wine grower) and mentioned that I'd recently tasted an excellent wine made by a recent arrival in the village. I hazarded that I thought he might be a Belgian. 'No,' he replied, 'I think he's a Jew.' I was taken aback that he would even think of making such a remark, although arguably I'd started it with a reference to him possibly being Belgian. While this was hardly an example of extreme anti-semitism, I found it curious nonetheless.

Anti-semitism is deeply embedded in France yet the country continues to have the largest Jewish community in Europe. The

Marais neighbourhood in Paris is where you can see young Jewish men dressed like Polish aristocrats of the mid 16th century. One gets the feeling they are posing mainly for the benefit of tourists from Great Neck, New York. You can even queue up at a restaurant called L'As du Fallafel. It's very colourful, but one can't overlook the presence of soldiers carrying machine guns.

Jews have been disproportionately victims of violence in France for a very long time. The Dreyfus affair, in which a Jewish army officer was falsely accused of treason and imprisoned on Devil's Island in French Guyana, remains notorious (see ZOLA). By 1937, the fascist, anti-semitic Parti Social Français had 700,000 members. The great French writer Céline was a virulent anti-semite and wartime collaborationist. During the war, the French government and police enthusiastically deported Jews to concentration camps. For more than 40 years the government denied the responsibility of French authorities for the murders. Only in 1995 did President Jacques Chirac acknowledge the crimes.

But it is no longer the state that persecutes the Jews, but young Muslim Frenchmen who present the danger. Half of all racist attacks in France are directed against Jews, who constitute but 1 per cent of the country's population. Soldiers now patrol every street where there is a Jewish institution. An Israeli journalist walked across Paris wearing a *kippa* in 2015 as a companion covertly filmed him. The videotape shows him being constantly harassed and threatened. Jewish graves are routinely desecrated (300 so far in 2015) and four Jewish schoolchildren were gunned down by an Islamist in 2012 in front of their school in Toulouse. Following the *Charlie Hebdo* massacre, an Islamist gunman attacked a kosher supermarket and slaughtered four Jews.

The Jewish Agency claims 7,500 Jews left for Israel in 2014, 1.5 per cent of the estimated French Jewish population. But many others are determined to stay put. When Israeli Prime Minister Benjamin Netanyahu went to the Grande Synagogue in Paris, the congregation sang the *Marseillaise*.

JUPPÉ, ALAIN
PRETENDER TO THE PRESIDENCY

Contesting the nomination of the *Républicains* (the right-of-centre political party, formerly the UMP) for the 2017 presidential election. Polls of voters in 2015 showed that among conservative voters he is in a strong position against the other leading candidate, former president Nicolas Sarkozy, although amongst inscribed party members, Sarkozy remains more popular. The candidate will eventually be selected in a primary and so it could be a toss-up. A graduate of the *École Nationale d'Administration*, he is the mayor of Bordeaux and was prime minister under Jacques Chirac. Although personable and intelligent, there are more skeletons in his closet than in a ghost house. He was convicted in 2004 for abuse of public funds for using public employees for political purposes. He was nevertheless re-elected as mayor of Bordeaux in 2006. In 2008 he was named in a Rwandan government report on the alleged French complicity in genocide. Although he has talked of reducing the burden of social taxes on business, his political strategy seems to be centrist and to appeal to disaffected voters on the left. Like all French politicians, he is hardly a reformer.

K

KINÉSITHÉRAPIE
THERAPEUTIC MASSAGE

Physical therapy of an intimacy that can shock sensitive ANGLO-SAXONS. My neighbour the novelist Helena Frith-Powell had a baby in France and was afterwards urged by her doctor to see a *kinésithérapeute* (practitioner of *kinésithérapie*), since after all it would be paid for by the state. Imagine her surprise when after he told her to remove her skirt and knickers, he inserted two fingers into her vagina and asked her to squeeze. In France this is called perineal re-education although it is possible in America or Britain that it might be termed sexual assault. 'He seemed very disappointed when I asked him to stop,' Helena reported afterwards. She swears this is true.

L

LAGARDE, CHRISTINE
MOST SUCCESSFUL FRENCHWOMAN

Mistrusted French political figure suspected of having gone native in Washington. Sometimes talked about as a future presidential candidate although she told Arianna Huffington there is absolutely no chance of this. Since she is a politician, this might not be a definitive denial. It would be a pity if she was telling the truth since on economics, she is head and shoulders above every other politician in France. A fluent English speaker, a former Baker & McKenzie partner, a technocrat, she was parachuted in by President NicoLas SarKozy to serve for four years as France's finance minister from 2007-2011 before she segued to America as director of the IMF. Her taste for reform exceeded Sarkozy's political courage. She was dragged into the Crédit Lyonnais *affaire* when she authorised 400 million euros compensation to the businessman Bernard Tapie, a convicted criminal and football club owner (see *foot*) who was defrauded by the rogue bank (see *banques*). At one point she was herself under criminal investigation and although this seemed politically motivated, it damaged her standing.

She has apparently put this behind her, emerging as a major voice in global economic policymaking. To the right of the traditional French economic consensus, she described the 35-hour week as a symbol of the right to be lazy, 'the ultimate expression of this historic tendency to consider work as a form of servitude.' She took a tough line on Greece's debt crisis, and seems almost more German than French in her disciplined approach to economics. She has also urged her nation to stop philosophising, stop dithering and simply roll up its sleeves. '*Il faut cesser de penser et se retrousser les manches.*' Forbes magazine says she is the fifth most powerful woman in the world, and is the top-ranked Frenchwoman on the list.

LAÏCITÉ
BRITTLE BACKBONE OF THE REPUBLIC

This is a French constitutional term describing the separation of the state and religion. In fact, it is a word that carries heavy freight partly because, the Republic having declared this frontier between belief and the state, *laïcité* has itself become national dogma.

President FRANÇOIS HOLLANDE, at his press conference in February 2015 following the *CHARLIE HEBDO* massacre, made it clear that any deviation from the principle of *laïcité* is itself heretical. He began his two-hour sermon, delivered from the pulpit of the gilded *Salle des Fêtes* at the Elysée Palace, by lecturing the respectfully assembled ministers, diplomats, journalists and guests on the right of the Republic to defend and even fight for *laïcité*, defining it as an unchallengeable state ideology. In effect, he was proclaiming himself a crusader for a secular *intégrisme*, a French term originally applied to reactionary Catholic defenders of sacred tradition against the forces of modernism. No one in the French media challenged this point of view.

When school resumed in the autumn of 2015, every French student and their parents was required to sign a pledge of allegiance to *laïcité*, which if nothing else suggests that Hollande is the last existentialist. What exactly does *laïcité* mean? There are every day a thousand confusions. The state pays the cost of restoring France's religious structures, claiming they are historic monuments and saving the Catholic church the cost of keeping its own roofs repaired. The French army operates its own Catholic seminary, training priests to provide spiritual support to its soldiers. Paris Mayor Anne Hidalgo made city hall available to celebrate Ramadan, but offers no such support for Easter or Passover. Schools exclude Muslim girls for wearing headscarves and long skirts to school, while closing schools entirely for the

Christian festivals of Christmas, Easter, Ascension and Whitsun. Veiled Muslim women have been banned from taking their children to amusement parks or chaperoning children on class trips. National Front mayors have threatened to offer Muslim children no choice but to eat pork for their school lunch, or go hungry, citing *laïcité*. Efforts to establish Muslim schools are fiercely resisted by the state, which subsidises private Catholic schools. Politicians compete with each other to make these restrictions ever more harsh, demanding measures to deny veiled women access to jobs, education and community facilities. This isn't religious tolerance, it is racism.

Laïcité is an idea born of enlightenment-era anti-clericalism, in a country that had suffered from centuries of religious strife. The entire population of Béziers, including Christians, was burned alive in 1209, just to be sure they had killed every last heretic. '*Tuez-les tous, Dieu reconnaîtra les siens*,' (kill them all, God will know his own), declared Arnaud Amaury, the Cistercian abbot and papal legate. In 1572 France achieved a new plateau of religious violence with the betrayal and massacre of St Bartholomew's day, killing probably 20,000, but happily resulting in the installation of numerous Huguenots in London, immeasurably strengthening England's trading position against the French. There was little wrong with establishing a separation of church and state, particularly in a country with a tradition of religious slaughter.

Laïcité is sometimes compared to the American first constitutional amendment, which guarantees free speech, freedom of assembly, the right to petition the government and prohibits the state from 'respecting an establishment of religion (or) impeding the free exercise of religion.' But the French seem to have dropped off the last clause.

If Hollande's embrace of *laïcité* is cynical, other French people seem merely confused. I found myself in the foyer of the town hall after the *Charlie Hebdo* attacks arguing with the deputy mayor. I alleged that the *Charlie Hebdo* attacks had been politically hijacked and exploited by the socialist government. He replied:

'But Jonathan, in this country we believe in *laïcité*.' 'So what is that?' I replied, pointing to the crèche of the baby Jesus in a display cabinet. 'But that's been there for years,' he replied, failing to see any contradiction. As much as it is taboo to question the idea, it was obligatory to agree with the I Am Charlie campaign, see CHARLIE HEBDO.

LAIT UHT
DISGUSTING MILK-LIKE LIQUID

Ultra-Haute Température (ultra-high temperature) processing of milk produces a product with a shelf life (unopened) of 6-9 months and although it tastes burnt and frankly foul, is by far the most popular choice of French consumers, accounting for 95 per cent of milk consumption in France. Fresh milk is available in the chiller counters of most larger supermarkets. But it is typically far inferior in quality and freshness to milk sold in the UK, which is crazy because UK supermarket milk often itself comes from France. The French even make ice cream from UHT milk. For a nation that prides itself on the finest unpasturised cheeses on earth, why does France tolerate such horrid milk?

LANGUE DE BOIS
HOW POLITICIANS SPEAK

Wooden language is a stock in trade of politicians everywhere, not just France, but the suspicion is that when French politicians speak drivel, they actually believe their own rhetoric. *Langue de bois* is the French term for the 'Newspeak' described by George Orwell in *1984*, a language used to eradicate undesirable concepts by cloaking them in approved terminology. In 2013 *The Economist* produced a compact guide to the wooden doublespeak employed by François Hollande and his team, and to those words banned by the government, as potentially upsetting. A few examples:

Flexibilité (flexibility): word prompting grim visions of

unregulated Anglo-Saxon free-for-all (see *Libéral*).

Laissez-faire: iffy Anglo-Saxon phrase with no place in French.

Redressement des comptes publics (putting right the public finances): budget cuts and tax increases, never combined with *austérité* or *rigueur* (banned words).

Minable (pathetic): departure of French national who considers taxes too high (e.g. the actor Gérard Depardieu).

Ultra-libéral (ultra-liberal): beyond the pale, e.g. *The Economist*.

LÉGION D'HONNEUR
HYPOCRITICAL SYSTEM OF GONGS

'You call these baubles, well, it is with baubles that men are led,' declared NAPOLÉON BONAPARTE as first consul in the last phase of the French revolution in 1803. (Presumably he got the idea from the English.) Flaubert said: 'Joke about it until you get it and always say you never asked for it.' Advice not followed by the economist THOMAS PIKETTY, author of 2014's most fashionable tome on inequality. The French claim the British are obsessed with status but in supposedly egalitarian France the honours system is thriving and those honoured are much more blatant about it than the British. A miniature bauble called a rosette is worn on the lapel to ensure everyone knows who has been anointed. Who gets honours? Senior politicians of course anoint one another. Senior civil servants get honoured for showing up to work. Captains of nationalised industries, university presidents, diplomats and soldiers are always well represented. Sometimes, it seems that those who have achieved the least ascend to the highest ranks. The system is a lot like Britain's. For a nation that claims to prize equality, the legion of honour comes in a bewildering number of varieties including special (lesser) honours for school teachers, a second-division order of 'Merit,' proving the point that some are less equal than others. There are even awards for Hollywood figures (Steven Spielberg, Clint Eastwood) although Bob Dylan was famously snubbed.

LIBERTÉ, EGALITÉ, FRATERNITÉ
THE UNDELIVERABLE PROMISE OF THE REPUBLIC

Easily translated as liberty, equality, fraternity but the problem is that the meaning of these words is ever disputable and the incompatibility of the three taken together has never been in much doubt. The *devise*, the motto of France since the second Republic (with various interruptions), the slogan *Liberté, Egalité, Fraternité* continues today to decorate every town hall, every official document and every rubber stamp. So what does it really mean?

Liberty is a word with which the French have a troubled relationship. In ancient French it included rights but these came with laws and taxes. Since 1836, Liberty has been represented in Paris by the *Génie de la liberté* at the Place de la Bastille, a gilded male angel clutching the torch of liberty in one hand, and the broken chains of oppression in the other.

Liberty may strike a pose in Paris, but other than his halo he is strikingly naked in France. The cognate of *liberté*, *libéralisme* (liberalism, see *ultra-libéralisme*) is actually a dirty word to the establishment. (There is further confusion with the word *libertinage*, which refers to uninhibited sexual practices). Liberty to make a lot of money? Not so much. Liberty to seize opportunities and break the mould? Not in France. French liberty at its most expansive seems to go no further than the right to do those things that are not otherwise forbidden. Liberty comes down to an obligation to obey the law, the source of liberty being the law itself. French attachment to the idea of liberty is in any event tenuous. When France recently changed the law to allow its intelligence agencies virtually unfettered freedom to spy on private communications, 66 per cent of French people polled said they were happy to accept reduced individual liberty in the fight against terrorism. Ultimately, French liberty equals obedience.

Which leads onwards to the second part of the *devise*, which is equality. There's an interesting quote in *Sapiens* (2014), a history of humanity by the Israeli social historian Yuval Noah Harari: 'Ever since the French Revolution, people throughout the world have gradually come to see both equality and individual freedom as fundamental values. Yet the two values contradict each other. Equality can be ensured only by curtailing the freedoms of those who are better off. Guaranteeing that every individual will be free to do as he wishes inevitably short-changes equality. The entire political history of the world since 1789 can be seen as a series of attempts to reconcile this contradiction.' The French themselves, still Catholics at heart and adept at simultaneously believing in two contradictory ideas, do not speak much of this contradiction, they merely repeat the trope.

And then we come to the odd one out: *Fraternité* seems to have been added to the slogan perhaps because things sound better in threes. Fraternity is founded in the much more ancient traditions of fellowship. The French are actually good in practical terms at being quite fraternal and friendly, even if all the kissing might make them vulnerable to viruses. But when it comes to solidarity beyond everyday politesse, maybe not so much. The French don't give a great deal to charity. They can be pretty squalid in how they treat public spaces. A YouGov poll found 85 per cent of Parisians doubt that anyone would come to their aid if they were attacked on the Metro. And the unions don't show much fraternal respect for their fellow French citizens when they blockade motorways.

The French are good company but do they really have liberty, equality and fraternity? Not a lot of the first two although in *la France profonde*, (rural France) where they still look you in the eye and say good day as if they mean it, maybe still some of the third.

LIBERTINAGE
PROMISCUITY

On the outskirts of many French cities (and even some smaller towns and villages), are not necessarily immediately attractive establishments proclaiming themselves to be a *Club échangiste* (sex-partner swapping club) or *Sauna coed mixte* (mixed sauna). There is one in the next village, next to a truck stop and a car-body repair shop. I have not been there so cannot offer a first-hand report. In any case, apparently the form is to patronise a sex club far from home, to avoid running into neighbours. I am told that these sex clubs are not at all the same as the mega-brothels you see when you cross the border from France into Spain, or from Germany into Poland for that matter. Libertinage is about sexual liberation and partner swapping, not necessarily PROSTITUTION at all, although there may be professionals in the clientele. These establishments operate with apparent official tolerance and one supposes they pay their social charges and the attendants work no more than 35 hours per week. Because there are of course no reliable data, it is hard to say how many swingers there are in France but they evidently include some high in society, judging from the orgies organised to entertain DOMINIQUE STRAUSS-KAHN. That the French are any more *libertine* than anyone else may be questioned but those who practise it are increasingly open about it.

LIVRET A
UNDER-PERFORMING INVESTMENT

A financial instrument little better than putting your money under the mattress, this is the flagship financial instrument in France. Paying in 2015 just 0.75 per cent interest, free of tax, the Livret A sold by all banks and financial institutions is by far the most popular savings vehicle for French families of modest means. French households have invested more than 260 billion euros in the Livret A. In theory, the deposits of the Livret A are supposed to finance social housing, although it is not clear that social housing greatly needs or benefits from Livret A, and there is criticism that it distorts French savings by diverting money from where it is needed (private investments, higher risks, consumption) to where it is not (social housing, which would have no trouble borrowing money on the markets).

LOI TOUBON
THE WAR ON ANGLICISMS

A 1994 law sponsored by Jacques Toubon (a literal translation of his name is 'all good') mandating that French must be used in all government publications, contracts, schools and advertising. Widely ignored in French academia where innumerable papers are published in English. In advertising, any use of an English word or phrase must be accompanied by a translation, hence McDonald's 'I'm lovin' it' was translated as, *c'est tout ce que j'aime* (it's everything I love). Avis car rental accompanies its slogan 'unlock the world' with the not exactly similar *offrez-vous le monde* (offer yourself the world). Of course there is a regulatory authority to ensure conformity and the *Autorité de régulation professionnelle de la publicité* (advertising standards regulator) has been active, cracking down on such terms as 'eyewear,' 'make believe' and 'must have.' An unintended consequence is that international contracts are invariably executed outside France - a boost for London law firms.

LONDRES
FIFTH OR SIXTH FRENCH CITY IN EUROPE

A city on the river *Tamise* (French pronunciation of Thames). Destination number one for French exiles, now and for hundreds of years. Many great French writers hid out in London to avoid difficulties with French censorship and oppression including Victor Hugo, Voltaire and Émile Zola. Enterprising Huguenots fleeing France helped make London into a financial powerhouse (and deprived France of much of its mercantile class). Later, London was to become the base of General de Gaulle and the Free French. The opening of the *Tunnel sous la Manche* (Channel Tunnel) in 1994 and the stagnant economy in France seems to have kicked off a much larger and more sustained northward migration. It is hard to be absolutely sure but there may be 400,000 French people living in London with at least 500 more arriving every week. Boris Johnson, the mayor of London, boasted in 2015 that he had more French constituents than the mayor of Bordeaux but this seems a highly conservative estimate. It is true there is also a vast number of British people in France: the British retire to France, the French go to England to seek work they can't find in France.

In 2007, Hamid Senni, a young Frenchman of north African extraction wrote a moving book, *De la cité a la City*, 2007 (*From the Ghetto to the City of London*), describing his own move to London, provoking widespread commentary in France. Senni tells of the constant discouragement he encountered in France where he was unable to obtain more than precarious employment and was the victim of constant discrimination, to his experience in London, where he immediately found employment and was judged on his ability, not his background. Perhaps this was a little rose-tinted but the book provoked vocal agreement from contemporaries describing their similar experiences.

The modern French exile community is having a strong and positive social influence on London and is so numerous as to have spilled out of their traditional south Kensington ghetto, to invade Fulham, Battersea and Clapham with Tufnell Park and Islington in North London rapidly being colonised. The cultural influence of the French has always been strong in London but never so ubiquitous. On the South Bank of the Thames there are classic Citroën HV 'tube' vans converted into food trucks. The Lycée Français Charles de Gaulle in South Kensington is bursting, the network of French feeder schools in London is expanding rapidly, and the French community is soon to open a second lycée in Brent, north London, the Lycée Winston Churchill. London has a French-language radio station, numerous French magazines and websites. The French in London deserve more political representation in the French national assembly. In population terms, they should be entitled to 8-10 seats, but have only one, which they share with French expatriates elsewhere in Europe.

LOTISSEMENTS
GROTESQUE OUTSKIRTS OF FRENCH VILLAGES

The traditional French village is one of the world's most exquisite forms of settlement, yet for the past half century, the French have seemed determined to achieve another superlative by building some of the world's most hideous. They appear to have been inspired by the American subdivision, memorialised by Pete Seeger in the song *Little Boxes:* 'Little boxes made of ticky tacky… There's a pink one and a blue one and a yellow one and they all look just the same.' These sprawling sub-divisions, called *lotissements*, are constructed out breeze blocks and each dwelling is surrounded by a wall made of the same material. Often these walls are left unfinished, sometimes they are sprayed with a *monocouche* (render), typically in garish colours unknown to nature. *Lotissements* have no centre, no marketplace, no dwellings crafted from local stone with roofs of clay tiles or slate. They are, above all, cheap and can be built with semi-skilled labour. In my village, a modest amount will buy one. For a country that prides itself on its culture and aesthetics, the *lotissements* are monuments to the greed of developers and the indifference of planners to the nation's heritage. Meanwhile, many of the traditional village houses are crumbling because it costs more to restore them than to buy a new house in a *lotissement*.

LUNDI
A DAY OF REST

Monday was the last day of the weekend in much of France even before the 35-hour week was imposed. Many banks and restaurants are closed.

M

MACARON
MYTHIC FRENCH GÂTEAU

In English, a macaroon. Iconic French circular cake composed of almond base filled with ganache, buttercream or jam. Paris *macaron* specialist, Pâtisserie Ladurée, adored by tourists, has leveraged the little cake (which it cheekily claims to have invented) into an international network of shops and in recent years macarons have become a phenomenon. My friends in Lorraine say Ladurée is a con; the treat was invented in Nancy long before the Parisian upstart claimed credit for it. And far from being an intimate family business, it is part of the giant conglomerate that also owns the global chain of Paul bread shops (see *PAIN*).

MACRON, EMMANUEL
BANKER COOPTED AS MINISTER

Rich politician, former member of socialist party, now independent who in 2014 threw in his lot with the government of Prime Minister MANUEL VALLS. The Minister for the Economy and a former Rothschild banker, Macron is regarded as the most reformist minister France has seen in a while but is a member of a government so weak that he will not be allowed to upset too many of the social partners and clients who President FRANÇOIS HOLLANDE wants to keep quiet. His reforms seem more theatrical than efficacious. 'Cinema,' snorted one lawyer when I asked what he thought of the supposed reforms.

Hollande declared early in his mandate that he dislikes the rich (*Je n'aime pas les riches*), and Macron is rich. There is a suspicion that Macron exists mainly as window dressing - a man with a decent suit who can talk to any foreign investors who might turn up.

Macron is also probably not greatly loved by his boss, Prime Minister MANUEL VALLS. Although both are reformers, they are putative rivals. Macron famously declared that economically 'France is sick' and deplored a culture of 'mistrust, complexity and corporatism' as 'three diseases' throttling the economy. A fair enough analysis. He wants to lift restrictions on Sunday trading, open intercity-bus transport to competition and sweep away protections for professionals in the health and legal sectors. Good luck to him.

MAGISTRATS
LEGAL AND POLITICAL OFFICIALS
Not to be confused with English magistrates. The amazingly convoluted French system of justice is one in which lots of people have a claim to be magistrate. Mayors are technically the *premier magistrats* of their communes. Some magistrates in France are akin to prosecutors while all judges are also automatically magistrates. A *juge d'instruction* is a magistrate (like Judge Roban, in *ENGRENAGES*) directing a criminal investigation at the request of prosecutors or civil parties. There are several highly politicised magistrates and it is routine that former presidents who have absolute immunity in office are pursued into retirement with cases that sometimes seem to involve actual corruption but seem more like political vendettas. Former president NICOLAS SARKOZY proposed suppressing the post of *juge d'instruction* but without success and has been hounded by them ever since he left office. See *MUR DES CONS*.

MAIER, CORINNE
ZEN IN BUSINESS
Author of *Bonjour Paresse* (*Hello Laziness*, 2004), titled in homage to Françoise Sagan's *Bonjour Tristesse* (*Hello Sadness*, 1954). Hilarious best-selling survival guide to employment in a giant

French corporation, translated into 25 languages. Maier was a middle manager at ÉLECTRICITÉ DE FRANCE before committing corporate suicide with her tract. She skewers its corporate culture, ridiculing the gibberish of its internal communications, exposing the idiocy of her bosses and explaining how it is possible to thrive in a corporate environment while doing absolutely nothing of value. She asserts that what you do is pointless as you can be replaced from one day to the next by any cretin and that you are not judged on merit but whether you look and sound the part. Never accept operational roles but make a beeline for research, strategy and business development where it is impossible to assess your contribution to the company, she advises. The only people who do any work are those on short-term contracts so be nice to them, she says. Includes a magnificent guide translating the American-English business speak of the corporation into French, e.g. 'downsizing' - *vous virez des gens* (fire people). She would undoubtedly still be there but her book embarrassed EDF, which finally fired her. Maier is a true *situationiste* (anarcho-Marxist), even starting her book with a quote from GUY DEBORD: *'Ne travaillez jamais'* (never work). I read this book when it was published and re-read it recently and it is spot-on. She is currently a self-employed psychotherapist and will be my first choice should I find myself in need of ludic analysis.

MAIRE, LE
GATEWAY TO HIGHER OFFICE

Being a mayor in France can be a thankless task of endless work for little remuneration, but can also be the stepping stone to further and more lucrative political offices. A politician can use the visibility and prestige of office to seek election to the Regional Council, the National Assembly, the Senate or even the Presidency. Hence, starting as a mayor, an ambitious French politician can start his career of collecting multiple mandates, multiple salaries, multiple allowances and multiple pensions. The mayor has huge influence over planning, which makes him a key figure in every village. The performance of mayors varies dramatically and there are examples of dynamic mayors who have delivered major projects but others have little imagination or behave with either languor or mischief.

LA MAIRIE
BLACK HOLE

Ground zero in French local politics. Sometimes called the *Hôtel de Ville*, the *mairie* is the headquarters of municipal government. Superficially appealing because of its proximity to citizens, but often a nest of clientelism with the *équipe municipale* (the team of paid local government employees) stuffed with the relatives of the mayor and his principal allies. The *mairie* acts as an agent of the state, the department and of all the other local government syndicates and agglomerations that make up the *mille-feuilles* (multiple layers) of local government in France, hence there is often very little scope for local initiatives, major projects being driven by subsidies granted on the basis of priorities decided elsewhere. There are dynamic mayors in France but mostly the *mairies* are deeply conservative, way behind in the electronic delivery of services, and not really subject to much scrutiny, despite occasional prosecutions of the most blatantly corrupt.

MANIF POUR TOUS
CONSERVATIVE SOCIAL MOVEMENT

Led by Madame Frigide Barjot (this is not a typo), a comedian turned self-appointed guardian of traditional values, this is a reactionary social movement upholding Catholic values against the *laxisme* (social liberalism) of the French state. Launched to protest the movement for MARIAGE POUR TOUS, it is ignored with a shrug by the government which has pressed ahead with gay marriage and explicit sex education in schools, despite the howls of protest from Frigide. Everyone else who holds a demonstration seems to get their way, but the government's calculus is that the *manif pour tous* crowd people will never ever vote for them. Poor Frigide, meanwhile, has been ejected from her rent-controlled Paris flat by the vengeful Paris social bureaucracy in classic punishment for doing what is not *comme il faut*.

MARIAGE POUR TOUS
GAY MARRIAGE
'Marriage for everyone legislation' in 2013 legalising gay marriage. Marriage for everyone, it is joked, except the President of the Republic, who remains a confirmed bachelor, though not in the British sense - more like a heterosexual rabbit in heat.

MARSEILLAISE
BLOODY NATIONAL ANTHEM
A stirring revolutionary march taught to every child in France, as part of their instruction in being Republicans. While it has a great, catchy tune, the controversial verses, with sanguinary lyrics, disgust the more sensitive, such as my friend Yvette, a teacher, who describes the 14th of July, when she and her classmates were made to sing the secular hymn, as the worst day of the school year:

> Do you hear, in the countryside,
> The roar of those ferocious soldiers?
> They're coming right into your arms
> To cut the throats of your sons and women!

So that's definitely one for a trigger warning, as are lyrics like

> Tremble tyrants and traitors...
> vile despots...

your patricidal schemes…

bloodthirsty tigers who mercilessly rip their mother's breast… etc.

All of them designed to get the blood up in 11-year-olds.

Numerous attempts to rewrite the lyrics to make them less bloodthirsty have failed. Overlooking the lyrics, the tune is better than the gloomy dirges adopted elsewhere. The scene in *Casablanca* (Michael Curtiz, 1942) when Rick (Humphrey Bogart) orders the band to play it remains one of the greatest scenes in one of the most fabulous movies of all time. Indeed the film quotes the anthem throughout. It is quoted musically by The Beatles (*All You Need is Love*), Shostakovich in the score for *Новый Вавилон* (The New Babylon, Grigori Kozinstev and Leonid Trauberg, 1929) and Edward Elgar. Only the Americans and Russians even come close. The Simpsons have parodied the *Marseillaise*, including the following line:

There's a few things they do well.
Like making love, wine, and cheese.

Which is still better than any of the previously attempted rewrites.

MARIANNE
GODDESS OF LIBERTY

Ubiquitous allegorical icon, signifying democracy and opposition to monarchy, personifying the authority of the state. Often portrayed wearing the Phrygian bonnet, a conical cap associated with Phrygia in Anatolia. Marianne has played greater and lesser roles during the various republics. She has been represented by various models including Brigitte Bardot (BB) and Catherine Deneuve. The most celebrated image of Marianne is in the painting *La Liberté guidant le peuple* (Liberty

Leading the People) by Eugéne Delacroix, celebrating the July revolution, portraying a bare-breasted Marianne leading revolutionaries into battle.

MAYLE, PETER
AUTHOR, A YEAR IN PROVENCE (1989)

A man bought a house, hired some builders, ate some meals, drank a lot of wine and sold 6m books. Then he moved to Long Island, New York, before returning to France to write several further versions of the same book, selling millions more. You will learn virtually nothing about France from any of them although there is plenty about what Mayle ate and drank, and the often-annoying habits of French builders.

MCDONALD'S
FRANCE'S NATIONAL DISH

French dietary staple, always known as McDo (pronounced Mac-dough). McDonald's is the number one restaurant chain in France, with 1,285 sites, serving one million meals per day. Were Marie-Antoinette to live today, she might, having been advised that the people had no bread, have proposed, 'Let them eat McDo.' The restaurant chain proclaims itself to be *Le Monde de Happy* (a play on words, meaning a happy world and happy people). Its operations in France are said to be the most successful and innovative in its worldwide portfolio. They offer a *croque McDo*. To be condemned outright by all right-thinking French people even if everyone is forced to stop there every once in a while for a cleanish loo (see *TOILETTES*) and free wifi. That McDonald's should conquer republican France with a hamburger called a *Royal* is one of numerous French culinary paradoxes.

MÉDECINS
DOCTORS

You really wonder why anyone bothers to do this job. Doctors in France are theoretically independent of the state but must work within a minutely regulated framework. Doctors do not enjoy an income or standard of living remotely equivalent to their British counterparts, never mind the Americans. They often work out of quite grubby premises, lacking capital to invest in modern facilities. A *généraliste* (GP) can charge only 23 euros for a consultation and the rates for consultants are similarly regulated. Indeed, the official tariff includes a maximum rate that can be charged for attending a patient via Skype. 'People knock on our front door when they have a cold,' complains one doctor's wife.

MEDIAPART
LEFTIST FRENCH DIGITAL NEWS WEBSITE

Digital information service with a long list of scoops and inside stories on various *AFFAIRES* that has 100,000 paying subscribers. The editor is Edwy Plenel who left *LE MONDE* after several tumultuous years. The project is inspired by the idea that the subscription model makes the journal accountable to subscribers only. Predictably left wing, but at least it is a fresh breeze in a French news landscape otherwise dominated by crippled, state-subsidised dinosaurs.

MERKEL, ANGELA
FRUSTRATED PARTNER OF FRANCE

President FRANÇOIS HOLLANDE likes to pretend that he stands alongside Angela Merkel, the German chancellor, as one of the co-heads of the European project. This is hardly credible. Although Merkel receives him in Berlin and caters to Hollande's vanity she has never ceased to lecture the French for their failure to structurally reform their economy and Berlin is said to regard

Hollande as a political lightweight who does not keep his word. She is seen to grimace when he plants kisses on her cheeks during their frequent encounters. There's no doubt who is the stronger figure. When Arnaud Montebourg, the divisive economy minister in the first Hollande government, compared Merkel to Bismarck, he was promptly fired.

MINI-COOPER
YOU CAN BUY ONE, BUT...
It is not permissible to name a child Mini-Cooper in France, a couple in the Roussillon have been informed by the prefecture. Other banned names include Nutella and Manhattan.

MISÉRABILISME
DESPAIR
The Germans call this *Weltschmerz* (world sorrow). In English, it's a state of dwelling on the dark side. It translates exactly to miserabilism. In the fifteen years I have lived in France, I have yet to meet anyone other than politicians who expressed optimism for the economic future of the country. See *BOVARYSME*.

MITTERRAND, FRANÇOIS
PRESIDENT OF THE REPUBLIC, 1981-1995
Unscrupulous political opportunist, shameless liar, narcissist, seducer, adulterer, constructor of pharaonic monuments to himself. Georges Pompidou, president of France from 1969 to 1974, said: 'Never let Mitterrand impress you. No matter what he tells you, never believe a word he says.' Polls say that French people consider him the second-best president ever, after De Gaulle. All available evidence suggests he was the worst, imposing employment rules that have progressively destroyed the economy. Infinitely crafty, slippery and economically ignorant, he lived like

a Borgia. Beginning his political career as a Catholic rightist, he had a murky war, was a *fonctionnaire* (civil servant) in the administration of PÉTAIN, and joined the resistance in time for the allied victory.

After the war he reinvented himself as a socialist party politician whose instincts were statist, protectionist and *clientéliste*. By 1973 he was allied with the French Communist party and after winning the presidency eight years later installed four communists in his government. It was Mitterrand who proposed the 35-hour week, nationalised swathes of the economy, vastly expanded the welfare state, lowered the pension age, increased the embedding of unions within the social institutions, imposed the wealth tax and enlarged the government. His monuments include the hideous *Bibliothèque Nationale de France* (national library) in Paris. Only when his funeral was attended by his wife, his mistress and his illegitimate daughter after his death from prostate cancer did the compliant French media disclose that he had a second family.

MONARCHISME
ROYALISM

In absence of a monarch of their own, the Queen of England is widely admired by French people nostalgic for the *ancien régime*. Monarchists mount candidates for the European elections, run web sites proposing various solutions to the existential Republican crisis, but are basically irrelevant. In addition to those who are wistful for a Bourbon restoration there are also Bonapartists, but if anything even less visible, although I did meet one once at a barbecue. Given Republican control of all media, it is hard to see the emergence of a credible claimant to the French throne or imperium although it would always be open to the French to import a royal household. My own suggestion, that William and Kate be leased to the French as required, at least for the near future, finds surprising support amongst my constituents, especially as the French consider Kate *trés jolie* (cute).

MONDE, LE
NEWSPAPER WITH LITTLE NEWS

Prestigious, precious and pompous French newspaper, as self-regarding and viscerally leftist as the *Guardian,* but less imaginative and not as humorous. The printed edition will never deign to stoop to publishing anything so coarse as news. Indeed, it simply cannot. Due to the archaic rules of the print unions, *Le Monde's* content is more or less a day old before it gets to any newsstands outside Paris. To be a shareholder in *Le Monde* is an exercise in frustration. The staff get to vote on who should be editor, which is not a recipe for effective leadership. In summer 2015 the newspaper was looking for its sixth editor in five years. The most recent candidate, Jérôme Fenoglio, was rejected by the staff partly for proposing to accelerate the newspaper's move towards digital distribution. With a circulation that has dropped below 300,000, the paper has never sold well outside the Paris media-political bubble and survives on 16m euros a year of government subsidies, equivalent to almost 10 per cent of the cover price, per copy sold. This figure does not include tax breaks.

MOUVEMENT SOCIAL
EUPHEMISM FOR STRIKES

Polite name for strikes. Social movement is a name given to work stoppages to make them sound progressive and justified rather than merely greedy and annoying. There are few strikes ever reported on French radio and television outlets - instead there are social movements. France Inter will solemnly announce that train services, for example, will be suspended 'because of a social movement.'

MUR DES CONS
WALL OF SHAME

The *Mur des cons* affair exposed the corruption of politicised French prosecutors, revealing their hit list of targets. In 2013 the website *Atlantico* published a video taken surreptitiously at the headquarters of the magistrates' union in Paris revealing a mural labeled *Mur des cons* depicting figures on the right. They included former President NICOLAS SARKOZY, MANUEL VALLS, then the minister of the interior who later became President FRANÇOIS HOLLANDE's second prime minister, the criminologist Alain Bauer, the businessman Alain Minc and the banker/writer/left-wing apostate Jacques Attali. The suggestion that this constituted a target list for magistrates was implausibly denied and the journalist who exposed this scandal was censured by his union for breach of professional ethics, having photographed the wall without permission (!) from the union of magistrates. The head of the union, the austere leftist Françoise Martre, was eventually declared by the Paris prosecutors (members of her own union) to have committed no criminal act. The mural has nonetheless been painted over.

MUSULMANS, LES
MUSLIMS

A marginalised religious minority, suffering educational and employment deprivation and discrimination. It is extremely difficult to determine the precise economic status of Muslims in France because the state does not recognise them as a separate ethnic group so it collects no statistics revealing their education achievements, average income, rate of employment, housing status, household wealth or health. Indeed when the mayor of Béziers was accused of trying to collect such data in his city, he was investigated by the police. Of course on all of these metrics, empirical observation and independent data demonstrate that Muslims do not fare well. Casual racism directed at Muslims is common.

Even when Muslims know better than anyone else what they are talking about, nobody listens to them, as I learned when I tried to buy an infant seat from a local car dealer, only to encounter mass confusion among the sales staff. The only guy who seemed to know anything was a junior employee named Mohammed, who pointed out that the proposed solution could never work but was ignored. Muslims are subject to naked employment discrimination in France. Unemployment among Muslims across France is at least 40 per cent, higher among youth, while 60 per cent of prison inmates are thought to be Muslim.

'MY TAILOR IS RICH BUT MY ENGLISH IS POOR'
ENGLISH PHRASE KNOWN TO ALL FRENCH PEOPLE

Once upon a time every French student was taught this bizarre phrase. Its first recorded appearance is in the standard textbook *L'Anglais sans peine* (*English Without Pain*), by Alphonse Chérel, published in 1929. Although not taught in French schools for decades, the expression has ironically become firmly embedded in the French language. It was used in *Astérix chez les Bretons*, and even made a cameo in *The Exorcist* (William Friedkin, 1973) when the devil-possessed girl Regan announces from her bed that her tailor is rich, a reference that will have entirely escaped 99.9 per cent of the film's audience. It is still sometimes used by French pilots to test their radios, as an anglophone might say 'testing, 1,2,3'. It is of course almost impossible to use this phrase in any conversation - but not totally. At my first municipal council meeting, complimented on the cut of my suit, I was able to reply, and truthfully given the price of the suit, 'my tailor is rich', producing gales of laughter. British children were taught to recite an equally challenging phrase for everyday conversation, '*où est la plume de ma tante?*' It is not unknown for Britons in France seeking to purchase a writing instrument to ask shop assistants for a '*plume*' rather than a *stylo* (generic name for a biro or pen). I know this because I actually saw it happen at a French motorway service area when a British tourist gormlessly asked for one. The shop assistant was baffled since it has been some time since the French plucked a goose to write a letter.

N

NAPOLÉON BONAPARTE
AMBIVALENT NATIONAL FIGURE

The French are massively ambivalent about Napoléon (1769-1821). The number of roads named rue Napoléon Bonaparte in France is zero. Though, to be fair, he has two avenues. And there is an unassuming Bonaparte street in Paris, though the forename is absent. By contrast, André Breton, the surrealist poet, has more streets named after him. The communards proposed memorialising Bonaparte on a Monument to the Accursed but this came to nothing. WALTER BENJAMIN notes that the stations of the Paris Metro named after his victories made them 'gods of the underworld.' The Arc de Triomphe was conceived by Napoléon, and most of his body is interred in the most magnificent tomb in Paris at Les Invalides, although a urologist in New Jersey claims to have his penis.

Bonaparte presents French people with a problem. The most gigantic figure in all of French history, he was not really French but a Corsican of Italian extraction. His legacy is fundamental to France and he put in place much of the foundation of the modern French state. He defended the revolution but proclaimed himself Emperor. He was the most successful French general of all time, but his career ended in humiliation. He is irreconcilable as both a war lord and social reformer, a tyrant and a law-giver. His famous legal code (see CODE CIVIL) was progressive and reactionary at the same time, supposedly forbidding privileges based on birth, establishing freedom of religion, and imposing a meritocracy on government jobs, while bequeathing enormous power to the state and institutionalising discrimination against women. He brutally restored slavery in the Caribbean and massacred those trying to free themselves from its yoke. Andrew

Roberts in his 2015 biography, sympathetic to Bonaparte, is hardly sympathetic to the leader of the Haïti rebellion, Toussaint Louverture, noting that he was pretty brutal himself and also a slave-owner. This hardly excuses Bonaparte's remark: 'What could the death of one wretched Negro mean to me?'

NAPOLÉON II
FORGOTTEN SCION OF BONAPARTE
François Charles Joseph Napoléon, 1811-1832, son of Bonaparte, was arguably Emperor for a fortnight, but he died at 21.

NAPOLÉON III
THE LAST EMPEROR (1808-1873)
To visit the remains of Napoléon III, you must go to Farnborough, in Hampshire. The Imperial Crypt is a short walk away from the train station at St Michael's Abbey, where it is tended by Benedictine monks. A jolly, hospitable Abbot, Cuthbert Brogan, showed me around, ushering me into the chilly crypt that the Emperor shares with his wife Eugénie de Montijo and their son, Napoléon Eugene, the Prince Imperial. After the disastrous conclusion of the Franco-Prussian war, Napoléon III and his entourage were held in captivity in Germany for several months before he was released by Bismarck and made his way to England, where he was joined by Eugénie. They settled first at Chislehurst in Kent, where the Emperor died in 1873. He was buried at St Mary's Catholic church. When their son, Napoléon Eugene, who would have been Napoléon IV, died in 1879, Eugénie moved the bodies to the abbey she built in their memory. She installed herself in a nearby mansion, now a Catholic girls' school, and plotted against her enemies.

The Crypt is not especially grand. Napoléon is entombed in a sarcophagus donated by Queen Victoria, very similar to those of the British royal family at the Frogmore mausoleum at Windsor, with some added Catholic iconography. Neither is it a major tourist attraction, being open only once a week and attracting a mere handful of visitors. Queen Victoria, in her diaries, expressed great admiration for the Emperor. 'If we compare him with poor King Louis-Philippe, I should say that the latter was possessed of vast knowledge upon all and every subject, of immense experience in public affairs, and of great activity of mind; whereas the Emperor possesses greater judgment and much greater firmness of purpose, but no experience of public affairs, nor mental application; he is endowed, as was the late King, with much fertility of imagination. Another great difference is that the poor King was thoroughly French in character, possessing all the liveliness and talkativeness of that people, whereas the Emperor is as unlike a Frenchman as possible, being much more German than French in character.'

From time to time, French politicians have demanded that the Emperor's remains be returned to France but Father Brogan dismisses these suggestions with contempt. He recalls that when Queen Victoria was criticised by the French press in 1871 for entertaining Napoléon and his wife Eugénie to dinner, she described the French in her diary as 'incomprehensible and impertinent,' a sentiment with which he is plainly in accord. 'The French seem to think we are some kind of insurrectionist Bonapartist cult,' he told me. 'Frankly, I am more concerned with chickens, bees and bookbinding. We have to earn a living. The best we can do for the Emperor is to pray for his soul every day, which is the only thing that will do him any good.'

Napoléon III presided over the industrialisation of France and the ascendance of the bourgeoisie. Elected the first president of the second Republic in 1848, then denied a second term, in December 1851 he seized power in a coup (with considerable popular support). The next year he engineered a referendum in which an implausible 97 per cent voted to name him Emperor. Victor Hugo famously loathed him, and was forced into exile in the Channel Islands. The catastrophic military campaign and disaster of Napoléon III's Franco-Prussian war is pitifully rendered by Zola in his novel *Débâcle*. Yet it was the second empire that ushered France into the modern age. There are still Bonapartists in France but they are a tiny, indeed almost invisible minority. The best claimant to the Bonapartist legacy, Jean-Christophe Bonaparte, 28 in 2015, is the great-great-great-great-nephew of Napoléon Bonaparte, and lives in London, like so many of his compatriots. He works as an investment banker and although he attended the 200th anniversary commemorations of the Battle of Waterloo, has never pretended to the imperial throne, being comfortably installed in Sloane Square.

A bizarre sidebar to this story is that after she was widowed, Eugénie hired one James Mortimer, an Englishman who had lived in Paris and was a friend of her family, to pursue a literary feud against her enemy Henri Rochefort, journalist and communard, who had conducted a vicious campaign against her husband including the allegation that their son was fathered by another man. Mortimer subcontracted the job to Ambrose Bierce, the brilliant American journalist, who was at the time living in Leamington. This he did with great style, noting among other acidic insults that Rochefort was 'suffering from an unhealed wound. It is his mouth.' Bierce was subsequently 'commanded' to the presence of the princess to receive her thanks. 'My republican independence took alarm and I had the incivility to disobey; I still think it a sufficient distinction to be probably the only American journalist who was ever employed by an Empress in so congenial a pursuit as the pursuit of another journalist.'

NATURISME
THE PLEASURE OF NAKEDNESS

Toplessness is *de rigueur* on French beaches and bottomlessness fails to startle, although many younger women are reverting to bikinis as they examine the ravages of time and gravity on the naked bodies of their mother's less inhibited generation. France is a magnet for not just French nudists, but practitioners of nudity from everywhere in Europe and indeed most corners of the world. Naturist campsites are found throughout France but nothing compares to Europe's largest fully-nude city, Cap d'Agde, which attracts naturists and exhibitionists from all over the world. The village caters for all tastes and there are naked shops, hotels, restaurants, boulangeries and even a post office. Without irony, the central street of the naturist village is called the avenue de la Butte. At the distant end of its famous beach is the notoriously libertine *baie des cochons* (bay of pigs) described by Michel Houellebecq in *Les particules élémentaires* (Atomised, 1998). Although Cap d'Agde was conceived half a century ago as a wholesome family resort, a municipal policeman there described it to me as '*le plus grand bordel d'Europe*' (the biggest whorehouse in Europe). Many of the cars in the enormous car parks have British registration plates.

NEXTRADIOTV
PRIVATE MEDIA GROUP

Operator of BFM TV, a French version of Sky News, BFM Business, which is both a TV and a radio station, and RMC, the independent radio chain. NextRadioTV is the only real alternative to the public service radio and TV stations with their statist, leftist agenda. But NextRadioTV is itself compromised. Its TV operations have been massively privileged by a decision of the *Conseil supérieur audiovisuel* (the French broadcasting regulator) to award it the exclusive right to broadcast an over-the-air news channel, restricting its main competitor, iTELE, to subscription TV and the Internet. iTELE, owned by Vivendi, continues but with reduced staff and limited reach although the frequency award has subsequently been confused by continuing legal appeals. The NextRadioTV group is headed by Alain Weill, born 1961, a veteran broadcasting executive who is the company's founder, chairman of the board and chief executive officer. A graduate of the HAUTE ÉCOLE DE COMMERCE, Weill bought RMC as a failing business and turned it around by buying exclusive rights for the 2002 football World Cup for 500,000 euros, then refocusing the station on news, talk shows and sports. Although nobody can survive without patrons in high places in France, Weill has been shrewd and although he has not balked at taking advantage of the regulations, his stations do provide a centrist antidote to the leftist output of France Inter and the anodyne news broadcast by FRANCE TÉLÉVISIONS. BFM Business is especially sharp at exposing the contradictions that handicap French business and its journalists cover many subjects that France Inter does not recognise.

NI NI
NEITHER, NOR

Pronounced 'knee-knee'. Dozens of examples of this double negation have embedded themselves into French political and social discourse. *Ni Sarkozy, ni Le Pen* - (a plea to vote for the Socialist party, i.e., for neither NICOLAS SARKOZY nor Marine Le Pen); *Ni putes ni soumises* - neither whores nor doormats, a French feminist movement; *Ni ingérance, ni indifference* - President Valéry Giscard-d'Estaing's (VGE) 1977 description of French policy towards independence for Quebec, meaning that France will remain neutral but not indifferent to the debate over Quebecois independence.

NOIR, LE
THE BLACK ECONOMY

A rare healthy sector of French economy, the 'black' underground economy is huge but of course illegal. A third of French people admit to having undeclared income. It's estimated that 14 per cent of French people work off the books. It is likely the economy would collapse entirely without it. It is impossible to capture a full picture of what are inevitably millions of private arrangements by which goods and services are exchanged for cash (*liquide*). The *inspecteurs du travail* (labour inspectors) boast of their successes shutting down illicit corners of the economy, but it can be argued that without the black economy acting as a pressure valve for the otherwise suppressed practice of working, France might grind to a complete standstill. Even the government employs people on the black. The Ministry of Justice paid 40,000 temporary workers wihtout deducting taxes or adding social charges.

NORMAL, PAS
GRAVE ACCUSATION
The French and English versions of this word have different meanings. In French, to be not normal is to be wrong. It does not mean the same thing as normal in English where being not normal means being unusual. In French, an accusation of non-normality, *ce n'est pas normal* (that's not normal), can be reinforced by adding, *ça ne se fait pas* (it isn't done). To be not normal is a serious complaint, verging on an accusation of misconduct.

NOTAIRES
YET ANOTHER LAWYER WITH A MONOPOLY
Notaires are lawyers who deal with property and inheritance. For all the criticism, property conveyancing in France is usually reliable. There are very few cases like those common in Spain where people who buy houses can subsequently be dispossessed due to irregularities in the transfer. EMMANUEl MACRON, the economy minister, wants to open conveyancing to competition since many other ordinary lawyers say they can do it equally well and cheaper but the *notaire* profession has mounted a stiff defence. If the notaries are as smart and specialised and vital as

they claim, why would they not prosper in any case? Their protests sound feeble and defeatist.

O

OBÉSITÉ
FRENCH PEOPLE ARE NOT SO FAT
France is the 128th fattest country in global corpulence ranking and has the lowest obesity rate in Europe. Even if McDonald's serves one million meals a day, many French families seem still to sit down and eat lunch and dinner together, instead of having an all day meal like corpulent Britons or Americans.

OCCUPATION
COLLABORATORS
In 2014 I suggested to my mayor that we organise a colloquium (*une conférence*) to celebrate the 70th anniversary of the liberation of our village towards the end of World War Two. There are still a few villagers who remember the events of 1944 and I naïvely thought it might be a chance to allow them to share their recollections. I was ready to organise the event and expected a warm reception for the proposal. The mayor looked pained. 'Jonathan,' he said, 'it's really too sensitive' ('*ça reste trop tendu*'). In particular, he noted the numerous German people who now live in the village who might be offended. Such an event could re-open too many old wounds, he said. But there was more to his reticence than he acknowledged. It was not the Germans in the village who would find such an event uncomfortable. I know, because I asked them. It was the French.

For most of the war, our village was spared the worst. After almost 100 village men had perished in the Great War from 1914-1918, there wasn't much stomach for a fight. The German occupation in 1942 barely changed the rhythm of life. Dozens of Jews were deported from some of the nearby villages, but they were arrested by the French police, not the Germans. Nobody was deported from our own commune although some of the village men were prisoners of war in Germany where they worked as farm labourers. German soldiers were billeted in the village, some of them even housed in my *chai* (winery). They were hardly frontline troops and their relationship with the villagers was correct. They drank bad wine in the village cafés, for which they were cheerfully overcharged. There were sporadic episodes of resistance nearby, but few villagers were involved.

In the spring of 1944, as the invasion of Europe approached, everything changed. On May 12, British Halifax bombers based in Tunisia dropped containers of weapons and gold coins to the resistance group Bir Hakeim, who were based in a remote, abandoned chateau near the nearby village of Cabrières. The containers missed their target and fell close to my village. German soldiers manning an observation post in the church tower saw the drop and summoned reinforcements and a race began to recover the containers. Neither the resistance nor the Germans were to recover the prime prize. The container of gold was found by several villagers, who hid their loot in a well. After the war, they were able to buy land and businesses at knock-down prices. One family moved to Paris.

The Germans arrived soon after the airdrop. The *maquis* (resistance), well-concealed and knowing every nook and cranny in the countryside, killed nine German soldiers. The French officer, a 23-year-old named Lieutenant Jean Lucas, bravely led the assault, and was killed. A German column was sent up the *route nationale* from Béziers with orders to teach the village a lesson. But the local German commander in the village, a monocled Prussian officer who had spent the war happily cohabiting with a local girl, persuaded his superior to withdraw. Three weeks later, the Allies invaded Normandy and the atmosphere in the village became supercharged. The resistance was launching frequent attacks on the Germans nearby, but many of the resisters were denounced and massacred. By the summer, the liberation was imminent but there was one final horror to come in the triangle of three villages of which our commune is a part.

On the night of August 15, 1944, ten British soldiers of the Special Operations Executive parachuted into the hills with orders to make contact with the resistance. One of them, Lt Peter Fowler, a Royal Fusilier, aged 25, joined two French GENDARMES and began making his way to the resistance headquarters at Cabrières. On the way, on the road into the village of Fontès, they ran into a column of German troops. The three fled into the vineyards, chased by the occupiers. All were brought down in a fusillade. In a particularly disgusting episode which is still recalled with horror by villagers, the Germans then shot each of them in the head.

Days later, the first French army arrived in Montpellier, and in the Languedoc, the war was over. The remaining Germans withdrew to the north, leaving mayhem in their wake, most notably in the village of Oradour-sur-Glane in Limousin, where German troops massacred 642 people including women and children. Thirteen of the German soldiers were said to be *malgré-nous* (against-our-will) conscripts from Alsace, which had been annexed by Germany, others say they were willing French volunteers.

How to remember these events? The grandchildren of the German officer's girlfriend still live here. As do some of the families whose ancestors stole the gold. Outside Fontès, hidden in the vines, there are memorials to Peter Fowler and the two gendarmes who perished at his side. On the flank of an ancient volcano in our own village, there is a well-tended memorial to Lt. Lucas. Fowler's body was recovered and is buried in the cemetery at Mourèze where it is the only Commonwealth War Grave in the churchyard. Nearby is a memorial to the 105 members of the maquis who also died in the liberation struggle. Every year, British residents put poppies on Fowler's memorial and headstone.

In Britain, World War Two is remembered as the ultimate expression of national solidarity and there is little nuance to the memories. Here in our corner of France, it is all much more complicated. Memories are painful and often shameful. It was hard to be heroic. Most people were neither collaborators nor resistants, but simply struggled to keep their heads down and protect their families. Some collaborated. Others were opportunists and profited handsomely. Some were victims. It is difficult to imagine that had the Germans invaded Britain we would have behaved any differently. The events in our village were particular but not unique. They reflect the broader history of France during the occupation and even now, the memories unsettle.

OGM
FOOD OF THE DEVIL

Organismes génétiquement modifiés (genetically modified organisms) are outlawed in France due to the paranoia of ecologists who consider all such innovations to be an Anglo-Saxon plot and have intimidated the government into maintaining an outright prohibition in the absence of any scientific evidence of harm.

P

PACTE DE RESPONSABILITÉ ET DE SOLIDARITÉ

BROKEN PROMISE, FAILED REFORM

The notion that employment can be created simply because the government orders it is particularly French. Announced in 2013 by President FRANÇOIS HOLLANDE, this was a grand bargain by which private industry would create 500,000 jobs in return for a lowering of social charges. Naturally, the CGT union (still essentially controlled by the Communist party, although this is ritually denied) rejected the idea. Other elements of the plan were rejected by the Senate. Still further elements were declared out of order by the *CONSEIL CONSTITUTIONNEL* (constitutional council).

PAIN

STILL A SMALL GLORY

Twenty-five years ago I had the idea of opening a bagel shop in Paris which I intended to call *Fabrique nationale de bagels*. French friends told me this was an insane idea as nobody would ever persuade the French to consume anything so barbaric. This was bad advice as there are now bagel shops all over Paris (bagel with *foie gras* is a speciality) and even in the south I can buy quite good frozen bagels (and Philadelphia cream cheese to smear upon them). The best of these frozen bagels claim to have been baked in the Bronx.

The totemic French loaf, the *baguette* (literally, a stick), must by law be made from basic lean flour which has a low protein content. This is quite different from the strong flour used in British bakeries. The shape is designed to bake quickly, allowing the baker to sleep a little bit later before preparing for the morning rush. The nature of the prescribed flour is that a baguette has a half life of only a few hours. A day-old baguette can be cut into cubes and fried in olive oil to make *croûtons*, but otherwise is rock hard and good mainly for bird food.

Only a bakery constructing bread from its basic elements can describe itself as a *boulangerie*. Other shops that reheat frozen dough are not entitled to this status. The best *boulangeries* in France have diversified well beyond the traditional baguette and the standard accompanying loaves such as the *pain complet* (whole wheat) or *pain de campagne* (country loaf). Most towns boast artisan bakers offering dozens of loaves made with speciality flours. Bakers as a trade seem often to be more enterprising than other French merchants, opening longer and in some cases 7 days a week (although this has been cracked down upon by the employment inspectors). Some have boldly added wine and catering counters to their shops.

Even as bagels have begun to infiltrate France, the French retain a strongly positive balance of trade in bread. The best-known French baker, *Paul, maison de qualité fondée in 1889*, is active in Europe, Africa, the Middle East, the United States and Asia with more than 500 sales points and 100,000 employees. Founded near Lille in the north of France, the chain is ubiquitous but less prestigious in France than elsewhere. Because much of the bread and dough is prepared in commissaries, it is not strictly speaking a *boulangerie*. Paul tends to operate in railway stations and autoroute service areas in France, whereas it has installed itself in well-fitted shops in posh neighbourhoods in London and Singapore. It presents itself as a family business but is part of the gigantic Groupe Holder, which also owns the equally faux Ladurée. Real *boulangeries* face numerous challenges including cut-price supermarket bread (often terrible, sometimes not bad) and a diet-obsessed populace that consumes less starch than it used to. Still, a fine *boulangerie* in France will attract queues.

PANTHÉON
POSH ADRESS FOR DEAD PEOPLE

Most exclusive mausoleum in Paris, other than Napoléon's tomb at *Les Invalides* (whose overwhelming enormity is, one must suppose, designed to ensure that the tyrant remains entombed for eternity). A Republican temple, the Panthéon is housed in a deconsecrated church. How do you get in? Obviously it helps to be dead, but also to be male. Only one woman is interred there on her own merit, other than as a spouse, and that is Marie Curie, the Polish-born physicist who discovered radium and polonium. She was lucky to get in since it does say clearly on the inscription above the door: *Aux grands hommes la Patrie reconnaissante* (The homeland recognises its great men). For those unable to rest for eternity at the Panthéon, an acceptable and perhaps funkier alternative is the Père-Lachaise cemetery in eastern Paris whose residents include Edith Piaf, Jim Morrison and Oscar Wilde.

PARAÉTATISME, PARAÉTATIQUE
THE STATE BY ANY OTHER NAME

Paraétatisme (semi-government) describes the myriad of supposedly private enterprises that are not independent from the state at all. They are controlled by highly distorted share-ownership structures that give ministers de facto veto power over every important decision. These companies include Air France-KLM, France Télécom, PSA Peugeot Citroën, EDF, the world's largest electricity company, Areva, the nuclear power plant constructor, Engie (formerly GDF-Suez), the world's largest energy company, Thales, the engineering group, Aéroports de Paris, France Télévisions, La Poste, Radio France, Française des Jeux, the betting monopoly, SNCF, the state railway, and the ports of Bordeaux, Le Havre, Marseille and Rouen. The state's official share of GDP is admitted to be 54 per cent, but with the commanding heights of the economy under state ownership or operating under an effective state veto, there are really very few important parts of the economy that are not semi-governmental.

PARIS
VENICE WITHOUT THE CANALS

So pronounced FLAUBERT. Victor Hugo, author of *LES MISÉRABLES*, wrote:

> *Toujours Paris s'écrie et gronde.*
> *Nul ne sait, question profonde !*
> *Ce que perdrait le bruit du monde*
> *Le jour où Paris se tairait !*

> Always Paris cries and mutters.
> Who can tell, unfathomable question!
> What would be lost from the universal clamour
> On the day that Paris fell silent!

Paris is not yet silent but is no longer so central to the universal clamour, and is more *ville musée* (a city that is itself a museum) than indispensable global metropole, much as Parisians might imagine themselves at the centre of the universe. With 3 million inhabitants at the beginning of the 20th century, 2.1 million at the beginning of the 21st and 1.9 million forecast by 2024. Many apartments in Paris have been vacated by their owners and are now let short-term to tourists via Airbnb. There is still plenty of style in Paris, but perhaps less of substance.

Outside the touristic hotspots, the city is no longer dynamic. Much of the basic infrastructure is crumbling. There is a feeling of insecurity, especially in the northeast. It's hard not to notice the feral gangs at the GARE DU NORD. If the centre is overrun by gawping tourists during the day, by 9pm much of the city is deserted. On Sunday, with the shops closed to protect the workers from having to work (see TRAVAIL DOMINICAL), Chinese tourists take the Eurostar to go shopping in London.

Paris is a city sculpted by pharaonic urban renewal projects, rather than organic consolidation of older settlements. George Eugène ('Baron') Haussmann was the principal architect of modern Paris. Working for NAPOLÉON III in the time of high empire, it was his blueprint that has produced the city that everyone knows today. What was lost is barely recorded: Haussmann boasted that he was an *artiste démolisseur* (demolition artist) and set about his mission without sentiment, driving great new boulevards through ancient neighbourhoods, even razing his own boyhood home, pushing the poor to new slums in the suburbs.

ÉMILE ZOLA vividly describes Haussmann's destruction of Paris in *Au bonheur des dames,* (*The Ladies' Paradise*, 1883) with harrowing descriptions of the razing of the neighbourhoods and the societies and cultures within them, and how in the centre the great department stores rose from the dust of the destroyed settlements, introducing an entirely new way of life to the capital. The EMBOURGEOISEMENT left Paris a paradise for some. WALTER BENJAMIN in *Passagenwerk* (*The Arcades Project*, 1940), his masterful work on Paris, said the 'true goal of Haussmann's projects was to secure the city against civil war. He wanted to make the erection of barricades in Paris impossible for all time' by creating straight avenues that could be cleared by cannons in case of a rebellion. Pierre L'Enfant used similar military logic laying out Washington, D.C.

Although very energetic, Haussmann cannot claim credit for all of modern Paris. After the Commune there was another great urban renewal scheme entered on Montmartre, headquarters of the Communards, whose *quartier* (neighbourhood) was razed to build the hideous basilica of Sacré Coeur. Then, between 1971 and 1978 there was the extraordinary vandalism of the glorious pavilions of Les Halles in central Paris and the replacement of this priceless market district with a soulless plaza and an egomaniacal museum by Richard Rogers and Renzo Piano, named after Georges Pompidou, the President of the Republic who inspired this destruction.

Grand Paris (the Metropolis of Greater Paris) is a big idea that's come to nothing much, so far. A scheme for rebuilding Paris including the first new skyscrapers in the city since the hideous Tour Montparnasse was erected in 1975, the initiative was launched by former president Nicolas Sarkozy in 2007. Much discussed, hugely criticised by politicians, architects and ecologists, proposals for improved suburban transport networks have become a renewed talking point as thoughts turn to another scheme to integrate the *ghettos*. Compared to London, Paris remains a resolutely low-rise capital, and many prefer to keep it that way. Transportation in the city is a catastrophe with the ring road (*périphérique*) completely congested, the interior boulevards in a perpetual state of chaos and the metro and suburban rail links in a state of decay. A shocking 100 per cent of French women surveyed report having been sexually harassed on the metro. The Paris city council has recently approved a scheme for *La Tour Triangle*, a 180-metre glass pyramid already being called the *Toblerone*, for its resemblance to the Swiss chocolate bar, and Renzo Piano's scheme for a 160m *Palais de Justice* is also supposedly going ahead. But these are both on the city perimeter. The bid by Paris for the 2024 Olympics, if successful, may stimulate progress on the Grand Paris project since the city is in no condition to welcome the games in its present state, which has barely evolved since the 19th century.

It sounds philistine to doubt the grandeur of Paris but it takes more than grandeur to be a world city. The cityscape looks in dire need of maintenance and investment. Away from the posh *arrondissements* (districts) Paris gets grim quickly. Walk up the Canal St Martin to *La Villette*, the modernist science city, to see the stark contrast between promise and performance. The banks of the canal are home to a sordid camp of homeless migrants. The space bears no comparison at all to the canals of

Amsterdam, and the sympathetic development that makes them captivating. Eventually, one arrives at the brutalist installations at *La Villette*, approached over an endless concrete plaza, and Paris doesn't feel quite so chic after all.

PARLEMENTAIRES
PRIVILEGED, OFTEN CORRUPT POLITICAL CLASS

France's too-frequently grasping, greedy, lavishly compensated parliamentarians comprise 577 National Assembly deputies and 348 Senators. They inhabit a world entirely divorced from the economic realities of modern France. An acquaintance of mine, let me call him Jean-Marc, was a deputy in the National Assembly. He was also the mayor of his hometown and the president of the local government *agglomération* council. So he had three *mandats*, that is to say three jobs, three salaries, three sets of tax-free allowances and three pensions. Before embarking on his political career he was an officer in an intelligence branch of the national police and took home 3,300 euros per month. His terminal emoluments, before he carelessly lost two elections, including various allowances and indemnities (tax-free payments) were, he calculates, just short of 30,000 euros per month. The system of mandates has been reformed, so while double-dipping will continue, triple-dipping has been disallowed - this, after one senator was revealed to be making 360,000 euros a year.

To be elected a deputy in the National Assembly of France is to inhabit a different planet. It is not just the gilded surroundings, but the constant *enveloppes* (packets of cash). One socialist member told me he was a little shocked at first at the range of tax-free allowances being thrust in his direction, but he seems to have overcome his initial surprise.

Everyone else working in the parliament is also generously paid - an average of around 8,000 euros per month for each of the 1,212 fortunate servants on the payroll. Being a Senator is another golden privilege with a monthly salary, a hefty series of tax-free indemnities, as many free tickets on Air France as you can use, free train travel, etc., etc., etc., and of course no need to give up your day job since there is almost nothing to do, the place being stuffed with individuals who might once have been important. All around the Senate is golden. The gardeners who look after the Senators' gardens at the Palais de Luxembourg earn 7,000 euros a month.

The French hold their parliamentarians in contempt. They say, *On y parle, on y ment* (as they speak, they lie). But they still vote for them.

PARTI SOCIALISTE
CLIENTELIST AND STATIST PARTY

As an elected official in France, I meet a lot of politicians. Before the recent departmental elections, the socialist candidate dropped by for a private meeting with members of our council. I asked him a few questions, admittedly provocative, to test whether he had any clue at all. What about the employment code, doesn't this make it hard to employ people? Oh no, he said, that couldn't be touched. How about the ghastly killing of a schoolgirl by a classmate in the city where he is mayor? Had he learned anything about leadership from the experience of being mayor during such a terrible time? Apparently not. Not really his business, he said, it was a matter for the police and the school. Then, evidently bored with my attempts to discover how he approached leadership, he cut to the chase, pulled out his notebook, addressed himself directly to the mayor, and came to the point of the meeting: what did we want? What were our commune's priorities, and what subsidies did we seek? It was a straightforward bargain on offer: our votes, for his cash. He was subsequently elected and at the first meeting of the new council, voted to raise his own salary by 8 per cent - an intention he neglected to mention in our interview.

While genuflecting before the saints of French socialism like Jean Jaurès, with their agenda for social reform, the modern Socialist party is led by a class of elite, bourgeois career politicians who know nothing of the working class and whose concern for social justice is purely theoretical. At the top it is an elite composed of people who have attended the elite *grandes écoles*. Lower down the pecking order, they are machine politicians drawn from the unions, the civil service and local politics. The modern socialist party pays lip-service to socialism but is less a socialist party than a party of *CLIENTÉLISME*, allied with the civil service, the teachers, the unions and *PARAÉTATIQUE* (semi-governmental) semi-privatised monopolies, devoted to power for its own sake and the privileges that come with it. Real socialists in France hate the Socialist party, although their reaction is to become even more irrationally left-wing.

PASTEUR, LOUIS (1882-1895)
GREAT SCIENTIST, ETHICALLY DUBIOUS

Invented pasteurisation, developed vaccinations for anthrax, cholera, TB, smallpox and rabies. A graduate of the *ÉCOLE NORMALE SUPÉRIEURE*. Has been accused of arrogance, dogmatism, unethical experimentation, secretiveness, claiming credit for the discoveries of others and even of practising deception. His notebooks were only made available to researchers in 1971, provoking further controversies. But his achievements are beyond dispute and millions if not hundreds of millions owe their lives to his work. France's Sanofi-Pasteur, originally founded by a student of Pasteur, now a division of the Sanofi-Aventis group, is today the largest vaccine company in the world. There are 2,020 streets named Rue Pasteur in France, more than any other Frenchman.

PASTIS
FRENCH CAFÉ BREAKFAST

What French peasants often drink at the café in the morning to fortify themselves for the labours ahead. Pastis, an alcoholic drink flavoured with aniseed, is a basic ingredient in the great French peasant breakfast (Pastis, cigarette, coffee). Fernandel (1903-1971), the great French comic actor, said: *Le pastis c'est comme les seins, un c'est pas assez et trois, c'est trop.* (Pastis is like a woman's breasts. One isn't enough, three is too many.)

PAYSAN
A PEASANT

To call somewhat a peasant in England is somewhat akin to calling them a bumpkin. In France, to be a *paysan* is an honourable calling, and *paysans* are seen as an authentic expression of the soul of rural France, the salt of the earth. In ancient French, a *païsan* could also mean a villain - and this remains sometimes true. Peasants are not necessarily poor, many have accumulated substantial land holdings. And they are not always as charming as those I often encounter on my perambulations through the countryside, often ready to hand me a basket of apricots from their orchard or a bunch of grapes from their vines.

LE PENS, LES
FRENCH NATIONALIST POLITICAL DYNASTY

Jean-Marie - Founder of the *Front National* (National Front) and its leader for almost 40 years, made it to the second round of the 2002 presidential election, losing to Jacques Chirac. Channeling a long history of French fascism, he sounds increasingly demented. Suspended from the party for his outrageous and barely concealed anti-semitism. Still a member of the European Parliament, has health problems (he was 83 in 2011 when he gave up leading the party), is a fading figurehead of the party's unreconstructed right-wing - more nationalistic, more to the right economically, a champion of traditional moral values and advocate of *les Français de souche* (French people grown on the soil of France). Provocative statements on the Holocaust and unconcealed nostalgia for the collaborationist Vichy regime warranted the depiction of the Front as a party of the extreme right, although since he relinquished the leadership to his daughter Marine Le Pen the party has moved to the centre on social policy and to the left on economics. He has subsequently disowned his daughter and remains embraced in a bitter feud with her.

Marion Maréchal Le Pen - Elected youngest-ever deputy to the National Assembly at 22, and still just 25. Fearless in the Assembly, provoking prime minister Manuel Valls to quivering rage and afterwards urging her supporters to give Valls a heart attack. Granddaughter of Jean-Marie Le Pen, much closer to him politically than her aunt, Marine Le Pen, although she has stayed quiet about the Holocaust. Seen as an eventual leader of the party.

Marine Le Pen - *papa* problems, *maman* problems, and now the problem of keeping her politically rightist base on-side while denouncing her father's anti-semitic provocations, softening the rhetoric generally, and moving her party further to the economic left. Born in 1968 and aged 46 in 2015. Her mother once posed for the French edition of *Playboy,* dressed as a chambermaid. This was supposedly to make money after Jean-Marie failed to give her enough to keep the house. He supposedly told her that if she wanted more, she should go out and *faire des ménages* (work as a cleaning lady). So it's fair to suppose that Marine's family was always pretty dysfunctional. After inheriting the leadership of the party from her father, she has surrounded herself with advisors who are less obviously gorillas than the blokes who still hang out around her dad.

She is friends with gay people, avoids overtly racist rhetoric as she proclaims nationalism and demands a return of the death penalty. If she can be said to have an economic policy it is protectionist, hostile to labour-market reform, anti-European and in policy detail hard to tell apart from that of Jean-Luc Mélenchon, the ultra-leftist leader. 'Marine has stolen our economic policy,' wails one advisor to the extreme left. But she has foes on the right, too. There are those who do not approve of her close political relationship with advisor Florian Philippot, a graduate of both ENA and the HAUTE ÉCOLE DE COMMERCE in Paris, who was outed as gay by *Closer* magazine in 2014. It was once considered impossible that Marine could ever survive the second round of a presidential election but there are new calculations that suggest she has handsomely profited by the rise of Islamic extremism, where her nationalist, integrationist ideas find resonance with threatened, disaffected voters.

PÉRIPHÉRIQUE
TOXIC ORBITAL MOTORWAY

The *Boulevard Périphérique* is the rough Parisian equivalent of the M25 or the Washington Beltway. The busiest and most congested road in Europe, in a perpetual miasma of carbon monoxide fumes and photochemical oxidants, with no hard shoulder, it marks the division between Paris and the suburbs. It is almost impossible to drive from the north to the south of Paris without passing the *périph'*. It is claimed that when travelling at the legal speed limit of 70 km/h (45mph) it takes 30 minutes to circumnavigate the city. Perhaps at 3 a.m. My own experience is that it can take 30 minutes to travel 2 km and the crumbling road is made more terrifying by motorcyclists weaving suicidally through the crawling traffic. Plans to build a new outer ring-road have stalled.

PERPIGNAN
CROSSROADS OF THE WORLD

Salvador Dali said Perpignan railway station in the department of Pyrénées-Orientales in the region of Languedoc-Roussillon, on the Spanish border, was the centre of the universe but if this was ever true, is no longer the case. Although the exterior facade remains glorious, all interior character features have been eliminated by SNCF. Tucked away in the bottom left-hand corner of the *HEXAGONE*, Perpignan has been neglected at the expense of Montpellier.

PÉTAIN, MARCHAL PHILLIPE
NOTORIOUS COLLABORATOR

Hundreds of thousands of French men and women revered him during World War Two, before abruptly switching allegiance to de Gaulle when the Nazis started losing. Pétain (1856-1951), austere, unsmiling despot, spawned an ideology known as *Pétainisme* and also as *Vichysme,* after Vichy, the capital of the French collaborationist government. Subsequently sentenced to death for treason, although he was never executed. Died in exile on the Île d'Yeu, an island off the French Atlantic coast. There may be a certain amount of nostalgia these days for *travail, famille, patrie* (work, family, country), the slogan that replaced *liberté, égalité, fraternité* during the dark days of Pétain's dictatorship. Or maybe not so dark days in the minds of many French people with an odd *nostalgie* for the imagined discipline and order of *Pétainisme.* 'If we'd been overrun by the Germans we'd be better run,' said Emmanuel Petit, the French footballer. 'I have great difficulty with the French, I have never seen such arrogant, smug, lying and hypocritical people,' he declared, before thinking better of it and withdrawing the remark.

LE PETIT JOURNAL
JOLLY TV SHOW

French equivalent of Jon Stewart's Daily Show. It is presented by Yann Barthès, can be watched on the Canal+ television channel and online. Gentle mocking of the Parisian media establishment (but not too mocking), often very funny, ratings success gives them license to be a little subversive (but never really questioning the fundamental precepts of French statism; they feed from the same trough of subsidies after all).

PHILOSOPHIE
TORTURE FOR FRENCH STUDENTS

Compulsory subject on the *bac*. Students must study philosophy for up to eight hours per week and are then subjected to a four-hour examination on such questions as whether truth is preferable to peace and whether it is possible to be right in spite of the facts. Very little of this is likely to prepare French students for life in the 21st century. Deep down, much of what has passed in the Anglo-Saxon academy as profound French thought - EXISTENTIALISM, structuralism - is pretty obscure and self-regarding, even as it seduces intellectuals elsewhere. The French would be well-advised to substitute economics for philosophy and to include Adam Smith in the curriculum, since their enlightenment seems to have skipped over the fundamentals of wealth creation.

PIGEON
A DINNER - OR A VICTIM

(1) Bird often cooked with garlic and red wine. (2) In general, victims. *Les pigeons* is the name adapted by an ad hoc movement of small business people to protest against France's strangling regulations and social charges. *Génération pigeon* is the name given by the magazine *Le point* to young people in France who have

been betrayed by a social model that protects the already employed at the expense of young people.

PIKETTY, THOMAS
FRENCH ECONOMIST, ENEMY OF THE RICH

Celebrated but widely unread French economist whose enormous tome on inequality, *Le capital au XXIe siècle* (*Capital in the 21st Century*, 2013), demanding higher taxes on rich people, drew much comment and admiration from the likes of the Princeton professor and *New York Times* columnist Paul Krugman ('serious, discourse-changing scholarship.') Amazon said its tracking of electronic readers showed most buyers gave up reading its dense argument after just a few pages. Piketty is the Marcel Proust of economics. Admitting that I am reviewing a book I have not read, if I understand Piketty's reported arguments correctly, the solution to inequality is for more progressive taxation, to redistribute from the rich to the poor. It is true the rich are richer than ever, but will making them poorer make the poor richer? Has this ever worked? In a country like France, won't it just feed the voracious civil servants, with very little trickling down, and won't that which does drip-feed itself to the lumpenproletariat perversely create an ever more dependent and infantilised population, who will vote forever for the munificence to continue? That's assuming the rich people stay put. Indeed, this is exactly what has been tried in France with entirely predictable results. Wouldn't an easier solution be to raise the minimum wage and make employers pay their labour better? Conservatives hate this idea, of course, claiming it will bring higher unemployment. But instead of paying more taxes, why can't we just pay a dollar, pound or euro more for a hamburger, with the money going to the person who makes the hamburger? Let the people who work at McDonald's be able to afford to eat there, to channel Henry Ford, who paid his workers $5 a day, so they could afford to buy a car. Piketty is more convincing when he argues for the demolition of anti-competitive structural obstacles. He seems a bit precious.

PISTON
PRIVILEGE, INFLUENCE, CONNECTIONS

Literally pull/push, meaning influence. Through family connections or shadier masonic networks, it is possible in France to gain access to privileged positions. In principle, jobs in the *gendarmerie*, for example, are awarded strictly on the basis of a competitive exam (*concours*). But everyone knows that the children of GENDARMES become *gendarmes*. *Piston* helps children of the privileged gain admission to elite schools. And piston is the best passport to jobs in local government. *Piston* gives the lie to French claims to have established a meritocratic society.

PLANQUES DE LA RÉPUBLIQUE
A SINECURE THAT PAYS WELL

Also known as a *fromage* (cheese) *de la République* or *un job en or* (a golden job). A *belle planque*, not too stressful, is one of the blessed jobs of the Republic that do not require much in the way of heavy lifting, or often any actual work at all, other than a ceremonial presence at the occasional meeting. (While there are as many as 1000 of these plum jobs, arguably, the entire French economy - largely comprised of the state and semi-governmental corporations - is itself best characterised as an overripe *fromage*.)

The French have not gone down the road of quangos (quasi public organisations, such as the BBC) quite like the British and so the *planques* remain for the most part jobs directly attached to some function of the state. There are numerous obscure inspectorates, high-counsels and other jobs sometimes involving the wearing of a uniform and usually coming with a LÉGION D'HONNEUR. The average pay is 110,000 euros per year but the best jobs are even more lavishly compensated. The regulator of radio and TV channels is paid 10,000 euros a month. She is Christine Kelly, author of a hagiography of former prime minister Francis Fillon before she was appointed to a six-year term at the CSA. The troughs are numerous: controller-general, first class: 8,000 euros a month; controller-general, economics and finance, 8,000 euros per month; inspector of social affairs, 6,500 euros per month; inspector of the academy of Paris, believed to be an especially untaxing position, 3,800 euros per month. Some of them come with other privileges, like chauffeurs, sumptuous Parisian apartments, secretaries, although the details are kept very hushed-up.

POLICE MUNICIPALE
LOCAL POLICE

We have three of these in the village and they are very effective. They are unarmed and run errands for the *mairie*, keep an eye on parking and tell-off dog owners who let their animals foul the sidewalk. The *police municipale* is the third and smallest police service in France comprising around 20,000 officers in 4,000 communes, reporting to the local mayor but also required to co-operate with *la police nationale* and *gendarmes*. Increasingly armed with immobilising weapons such as Tasers and sometimes pistols, they are supplemented by ASVPs, *agents de surveillance de la voie publique* (equivalent to British community support officers).

POLICE NATIONALE
NATIONAL POLICE

Not to be confused with *gendarmes*. Pathetic to useless in confronting blatant lawlessness by trade unionists, ignoring road blocks on approaches to the Channel Tunnel, refusing to arrest unionists who invade railway tracks and frontiers inconveniencing thousands, refusing to intervene when unionists take bosses hostage, yet assiduous in issuing tickets to motorists who fail to update the address on their driving license. A dedicated squad of police, however, is assigned to arresting Uber drivers for the crime of competition - France's greatest taboo.

A force created under Vichy, the *police nationale* work for the Ministry of the Interior. Its 145,000 officers are responsible for large towns and cities including Paris. In major crime investigations, the French police often seem more Clouseau than Maigret. Paris and the Riviera are known for spectacular criminal escapades that leave the *flics* (cops) flat-footed. The notorious *Compagnies républicaines de sécurité* (CRS) riot police are an elite squad. They are the heavy-police mob trained to repel the rebels, should they ever lay siege to the Elysée palace. They have a reputation for toughness and were recently filmed in action against refugees, in Calais, tossing them over the parapet of a bridge. The top of the *police nationale* is very keen to talk about its technological future. The interior ministry has been envious of the British closed-circuit TV panopticon and there have been recent heavy investments in surveillance.

POISSON D'AVRIL
APRIL FOOL

An April fool's day joke is a *poisson d'avril* (literally, an April fish). On April 1, 2015, the local *Midi libre* newspaper published a story reporting that the British had seized control of my village, that the monarchy was to be restored, that residents were henceforth to drive on the left and cricket would be played at the village *boulodrome* (*pétanque* pitch). The article was accompanied by a photograph showing a Union flag flying insolently from the *échauguette* (watchtower) atop the old village ramparts. I cannot say who might have been responsible for this.

POLITIQUEMENT CORRECT
INEFFECTIVE FOIL TO FRENCH RUDENESS

The French have blessedly avoided the worst excesses of political correctness but it is starting to catch on. Since the French can be especially good at causing offence, indeed have practically perfected it, the new rectitude is not always welcomed. Political correctness with its horror of causing embarrassment is 100 per cent an Anglo-Saxon import but is nonetheless infesting campuses, businesses, and the administration. Lists for local elections must now be equally balanced between women and men, even if French women are still expected to make the coffee. The city of Paris has a team working full-time to rename streets that carry racist or colonial overtones, or that honour individuals whose sentiments at the time are no longer deemed worthy of memorialisation on the local plan. It's a war against bad memories. I have yet to spot a French trigger warning but doubtless this will come and the *Académie française* will have to think up a French phrase for it. *La marseillaise*, the national anthem, is definitely not compatible with political correctness.

PLOMBIER POLONAIS
DANGEROUS POLISH PLUMBERS

In 2005 the Polish plumber became the symbol of French discontent with the single market and special measures were adapted to keep Polish and other new EU citizens from working in France, where they might compete with the locals. Given the number of toilets that remain to be modernised, the French needed the Poles more than the Poles needed the French, and so they went to England instead, greatly improving the standard of British sanitation and leaving France looking for their missing toilet seats. See *toilettes*.

POMPIERS
FIRE AND RESCUE SERVICE THAT WORKS

The *Sapeurs/pompiers* are both firefighters and paramedics. In a country characterised by dysfunctional official institutions, the French have somehow got this one right. There are 250,000 *pompiers* and 80 per cent are volunteers. It was the *pompiers* who led the extraordinary and difficult effort to recover the remains of the crashed Germanwings/Lufthansa flight in March 2015. It is the *pompiers* who battle every summer with terrible fires in the dry southern scrubland called the *garrigue*. *Pompiers* are sent by the government to civil emergencies all over the world, and it is the *pompiers* who come if your neighbour falls off a ladder. And they never strike.

PRÉFECTURES
CATHEDRALS OF THE STATE

The State's physical presence in provincial France is the inevitably grand *préfecture,* which is equivalent to a federal building in America. The division of France into regions governed by prefectures was the idea of NAPOLÉON BONAPARTE and the modern French state still uses the *préfectures* to enforce its will. There are *préfectures* in each of the 101 French departments located in the principal city of the department, and usually one or more *sous-préfectures* in subsidiary cities. The *préfecture* is headed by a senior FONCTIONNAIRE (official) called a *préfet* (prefect), and is technically an outpost of the ministry of the interior. The *préfet*, who wears a splendid uniform on high days, is the ultimate law enforcement authority and bishop of the state. The *préfectures* are often sinister, operating largely unscrutinised by local media and rarely user-friendly for those seeking to transact business with them. It is assumed they hold a dossier on just about everybody. They are often installed in magnificent heritage buildings whose inefficiency is almost legendary: members of the public wait for hours to have their papers stamped and car registrations approved by austere, unsmiling functionaries. If one were looking to entirely abolish a layer of government in France to save money the *préfectures* would be a good place to start.

PRÉPAS
ACADEMIC CRAMMERS
French swots who want to gain admission to the elite colleges must pass still more rigorous examinations even after getting top scores in the bAC. The *Classes préparatoires aux grandes écoles* separate the wheat from the chaff, or perhaps not, since those who make it through are not proven especially good at thinking, only at passing exams. The ruthlessness of the process is startling. Typically 40 places are allocated for every 1,500 applications.

PROCÈS VERBAL
SUMMONS
Under French law a PV (which is not, in fact, verbal, but always written) can be issued for a traffic infraction, a parking violation, failure to bring in your wheelie bins at night, and numerous additional reasons. To receive a PV is to be *verbalisé*. If you know the mayor, a PV for a parking violation is readily suppressed.

PRODUCTIVITÉ
FRENCH MIRAGE
Homer Simpson famously said 'you can come up with statistics to prove anything.' Even if he is not an economic authority, it is clear that productivity measurement tells very little about the overall health of an economy, especially in France. The French often claim to be the most productive economy in Europe (although according to Eurostat they are fourth) but it is hard to reconcile personal observation and real-world competitiveness

with the French data. Productivity measurement is in any case highly misleading but the official French numbers are, literally, incredible.

I will ask this: who is measuring productivity in a state-centred economy but the very bureaucrats whose productivity is to be measured? The distortion of a state-heavy economy is itself enough to produce the mirage of a productive economy. But do we always benefit from what they produce: endless regulations, constantly multiplying layers of administration, bottomless pits of entitlements and unlimited interference in the private sector? So many French economic claims are dodgy but the boast that the French are productive is an example of a self-deception repeated so often that many people have come to believe it, including some British politicians who ought to know better.

Here is the sniff test: If the French are so magnificently productive, why are they exporting capital and delocalising industrial production? Why are foreign investors putting their money elsewhere? Why have more jobs been created in Yorkshire than in France in the past five years? Who is rushing to exploit this alleged productivity? Why are 66 per cent of Germans aged 55-64 in work, compared to only 47 per cent of the French? If the French are so productive, why have they managed to produce only 0.3 per cent per cent growth in GDP over the past seven years? Why has inward investment in France fallen 77 per cent to the lowest level in 27 years, according to the United Nations ($5.7 billion in 2013, vs. $53 billion in the supposedly less productive UK)?

Perhaps the long lines at the cash registers in French super-markets (because they cannot afford to hire more workers), produce more productivity per cashier employed, but the statistics do not measure the time wasted by frustrated customers waiting to pay.

PRODUIT INTÉRIEUR BRUT
GROSSLY MANIPULATED DOMESTIC PRODUCT

The French love to boast that they have a higher gross domestic product than Britain but this is a claim that should be taken *avec des pincettes* (literally with tweezers, or as we would say, with a grain of salt). The French belief in this obviously ridiculous metric evidences the poor quality of much of the Gallic economic discourse. The two economies are very similar in size and therefore which one is the biggest can be largely a matter of the exchange rate chosen to compare them. But the real flaw is that in France, 54 per cent of GDP is represented by state expenditure and of that, 50 per cent is represented by taxes and social charges. The state can literally employ workers to dig ditches and fill them in again (and does, by all accounts), and this counts as GDP. In the UK, government spending represents just over 40 per cent of GDP. Hence, the claim that France has a higher GDP than the UK, even discounting exchange rates, relies on France collecting higher taxes and social charges, which it then cheerfully counts as GDP. The inflated GDP figure plays into another set of misleading claims relating to *PRODUCTIVITÉ* (productivity).

PROFESSIONS PROTÉGÉES
PROTECTED SKILLS

Lawyers, hairdressers, dentists, driving schools, massage therapists, pharmacists, pedicurists, insurance agents, ambulance drivers, taxi drivers and legal clerks are among the protected professions that the French government has failed to significantly reform since proposals were first mooted in 2008. The finance ministry reckons that French consumers pay at least 20 per cent too much for their services. France has ignored EU directives demanding that services be opened to competition. You cannot buy an aspirin in a supermarket in France as this would be unfair competition to the pharmacists.

PROFS
SCHOOLTEACHERS WHO CAN NEVER BE FIRED

They strike frequently. French teachers, from the *maternelle* reception classes through secondary *Lycée*, are called *profs* and they all go through rigorous and highly standardised training. Once in post, a *prof* enjoys the status of a *titulaire*, which means the job belongs to them forever. It is, essentially, impossible to be fired - certainly not for incompetence, although sexually assaulting a pupil is frowned upon. In principle, all *profs* are equal but the quality is of course mixed and the restrictive entry regime into the profession makes it complicated for foreigners, even from the EU, to work as teachers in France. There is a better representation of British teachers in the post-lycée technical colleges.

PROSTITUTION
CLOSING THE MAISONS CLOSES

Le Chabanais, le One-Two-Two, le Sphinx, and la Fleur Blanche in Paris were in their day the most reputed *maisons closes* (brothels) in the world, attracting clients including Edward VII, Henri Toulouse-Lautrec, Humphrey Bogart and Mae West. During the war, they were reserved for the use of the occupying Germans and selected collaborators. The glory days of prostitution in France have passed and it has become a more sordid affair. Working girls now park up by the side of the road outside many towns and cities, many are immigrants and some are trafficked. Najat Vallaud-Belkacem, the minister of national education, has attempted to ban prostitution in France but the project has descended into chaos. The prostitutes have protested that the repression of their profession will only make their life more difficult and dangerous and hundreds have taken to the streets to protest. The government's fantasy that it can end prostitution by passing a law against it is a classic example of the French worship of principle.

POSTES, TÉLÉGRAPHES ET TÉLÉPHONES (PTT)
A STUDY IN IDLENESS

The PTT hasn't existed in years since the telephone network was (sort of) privatised and *La poste* (postal service) became a *PARAÉTATIQUE* (semi-governmental) ward of the state. But PTT is still used in everyday conversations to describe the untaxing jobs performed by civil servants - *un petit travail tranquille* (a little quiet work). *La Poste* is now also cruelly known as *La Pause*, indicating delay.

PRUD'HOMMES
WHY IT IS SO HARD TO SACK THE USELESS

An employment tribunal in France is in theory a council of wise men (and increasingly, women), elected by the unions and the bosses. They adjudicate in disputes between employers and employed. These forums are not generally seen as likely to take an employer's side against that of a litigious employee, given the worker-friendly nature of the *Code du Travail*. It takes 25 months on average for the *prud'hommes* to resolve contested redundancies. Because of the likely intervention of the *prud'hommes*, it is difficult and costly to fire an employee in France. A small reform capping damages for unfair dismissal has been put into place but does not change the dynamic of this insane system.

36 QUAI DES ORFÈVRES
COMPROMISED SCOTLAND YARD EQUIVALENT
Equivalent of Scotland Yard; headquarters of the famous *Police Judiciaire* (PJ), the elite squad of Paris detectives charged with investigating the most serious criminal affairs. It is a curiosity that the real-life corruption at the headquarters of the PJ in Paris is even more profound than even the gritty TV series *Engrenages* has dared to suggest. In *Engrenages,* one of the principal detectives is taking cocaine. In real life in 2014, several *PJ* investigators were arrested accused of operating a drug ring from the evidence room, retailing 50kg of seized cocaine to their criminal accomplices. Sexual intimidation? In *Engrenages*, Captain Laura Berthaud orders her detectives to strip-search a teenage male suspect, while she watches, to humiliate him into talking: in reality, two detectives from the anti-gang squad have been charged with raping an Australian tourist, on the premises, in never-explained circumstances. In the show, Captain Berthaud's boss is a publicity-hungry, grandstanding political cop who will stop at nothing to get on TV. In real life, Bernard Petit, the chief detective, has been arrested and charged with obstruction of justice.

QUEBEC
INFERIOR FRENCH
The easiest North American bolt-hole for French exiles is Quebec. An estimated 10,000 French citizens are establishing residence in Quebec every year. Montreal has distinctively French neighbourhoods (i.e. not French-Canadian neighbourhoods but quartiers inhabited by French people from France).

But the new arrivals are not always popular. Quebecois are not known for being retiring personalities and neither are the French. Locals accuse the snooty French who arrive in Montreal of arrogance and the French reckon the local dialect to be inferior.

R

RADIO FRANCE
PUBLIC SERVICE RADIO, OFTEN ON STRIKE

La maison de la radio, (the house of radio) is the headquarters of French public radio. Perennially overspent, on strike, politically-compromised nest of vipers, housed in great splendour on the right bank of the Seine, responsible for seven national radio networks including the hugely influential FRANCE INTER plus the France Info all-news station, the France Bleu network of 44 local radio stations, and separate stations specialising in culture, classical music and modern music. A recent documentary (*La maison de la radio*, Nicolas Philibert, *2013*) was striking for its exposé of the Parisian elite at work. Parisian *bobo* and right-thinking (more accurately, left-thinking), Radio France preaches to a dwindling constituency of true believers, given the vigorous competition mounted by BFM Business which inhabits something resembling the real world. See NextRadioTV.

#RADIOLONDRES
SUBVERSIVE FRENCH TWITTER CHANNEL

Nothing to do with London. Or radio. Just the ironic name for an occasional hashtag containing off-message news about French elections including exit polls suppressed by French broadcasters. Named after BBC broadcasts from London during World War Two with coded 'personal messages' to the resistance.

RAFALE
FIGHTER JET OF CHOICE FOR DESPOTS

Impressive aircraft manufactured by Dassault Aviation, second largest French aviation enterprise. When you absolutely, positively want to bomb your enemies in the chiquest way possible, you would definitely want to consider the Rafale, which has defied American and British sceptics to become one of the best combat aircraft in the world. Used by the French air force and navy, and sold in dubious circumstances to Egypt, Qatar and Abu Dhabi. The Rafale is a lethal machine but whether these exotic and enormously expensive aircraft are of much relevance in a world of asymmetric warfare is another question. See ARMES.

RAINBOW WARRIOR
GREENPEACE ATTACKED POUR LA FRANCE

This gaily painted ship was bombed in Auckland Harbour, New Zealand, by French secret agents in 1985, killing a Greenpeace photographer. The operation was authorised by FRANÇOIS MITTERRAND, the socialist president, to stop Greenpeace from disrupting French nuclear tests in the Pacific. The French ridiculously tried to blame the British. Two French secret service officers were swiftly arrested, convicted of manslaughter and sentenced to 10 years imprisonment. This, by agreement with the French government, was to be served in military detention on a French island in the Pacific. France predictably reneged on the deal and released the agents after two years. Both were subsequently promoted. A curious sidelight to this incident is that Gérard Royal, one of the French agents involved in the affair (but never arrested) is the brother of SÉGOLÈNE ROYAL.

À LA RECHERCHE DU TEMPS PERDU
MAYBE NOT THE GREATEST BUT AT LEAST THE LONGEST NOVEL EVER

'The man ate a tea biscuit, the taste evoked memories, he wrote a book,' summarised A.J. Liebling, the *New Yorker* journalist, of the iconic novel by Marcel Proust (1871-1922). 'In the light of what Proust wrote with so mild a stimulus, it is the world's loss that he did not have a heartier appetite.' *In Search of Lost Time* by Marcel Proust is the quintessential expression of French yearning for an often imagined past. The novel is claimed to be the greatest ever written in French but few of those making the claim are likely to have read all five volumes of it (it was originally published in seven). WALTER BENJAMIN began but never finished a translation into German. 'I am reading Proust for the first time. Very poor stuff. I think he was mentally defective,' said Evelyn Waugh, the English novelist. The longest novel ever, according to the *Guinness Book of World Records*. Said to be funnier in French than translation, a little Proust goes a long way. I have not progressed beyond halfway through volume one, with the French and English texts side by side.

The iconic madeleine cake which triggers Proust's masterpiece is all most people remember about this great work. Indeed, I could never buy a madeleine without thinking of Proust, so I stopped buying them and in any case they are incompatible with my *régime* (diet). In 1922, Proust met James Joyce at a dinner at the Majestic Hotel in Paris, organised by Violet and Sidney Schiff. The other guests included Igor Stravinsky, Serge Diaghilev, some pretty ballerinas and Clive Bell. This historic literary encounter reconstructed by Richard Davenport-Hines (*A Night at the Majestic*, 2006) might be better remembered had it not rapidly descended into banality. Proust arrived late and promptly informed Joyce that he had never read his books and Joyce, already drunk, told Proust he'd never read his.

Novelist Joanna Kavenna identifies the central problem: Proust is 'one of the most revered and least-read of all the so-called modern greats.' He nevertheless remains an inspiring figure to generations of authors. He was a sickly chap who really never worked in anything resembling employment, but he did have a 'job' at the Bibliothèque Nationale (national library) and spent years collecting sick pay. An asthmatic, who gasped for days on end, he couldn't report for duty, he said, because the paper dust in the library made him sneeze. So he stayed in bed, dosing himself with various strong medicines including opium, morphine, Stramonium cigarettes and Epinephrine, writing and writing and writing, sometimes palely venturing forth at night, before dying at the not-so-ripe age of 51.

RÉFORMES
POLITICAL SOUFFLÉS

Reforms are periodically announced by the government. They are introduced amidst great fanfare, watered down in the National Assembly under pressure from the unions and protected professions, subsequently adopted as law and then loudly proclaimed to the world as evidence that France is open for business. Nobody but the government itself believes these to be more than window-dressing. Chancellor Angela Merkel wants the European Union to have the power to impose 'programme' reforms to coerce recalcitrant countries, like France and Greece, to get serious. *The Times* in July 2015 quoted a 'senior German conservative' saying that in countries like France and Italy, the only instrument to force reforms is the programme approach. He was scathing of so-called reforms in France that 'need reform but have no programme.'

RENSEIGNEMENT, LOI SUR LE
THE FRENCH VERSION OF THE PATRIOT ACT

Intrusive law passed in May 2015 following the *Charlie Hebdo* massacre greatly extending the authority of French intelligence services to intercept all forms of communication. Ironically, the law passed even as WikiLeaks was revealing that the French themselves were being surveilled by the Americans. See *espions*.

RENTRÉE, LA
AFTER THE SUMMER BREAK, THE GREAT RETURN

Nothing much happens in France during August (and little more in July). The *rentrée* (the return) marks the resumption of school (*la rentrée scolaire*), of political activities (*la rentrée politique*) and the publication of new books (*la rentrée littéraire*). *La rentrée* is presaged by gigantic traffic jams that paralyse French AUTOROUTES as vacationing French people return to their homes from their *résidences secondaires* (holiday homes).

RÉPUBLICAINS, LES
CONSERVATIVES, PART OF THE LEFT CONSENSUS

New name for the UMP, *Union pour un mouvement populaire*, which is the French equivalent of British Conservatives and American Republicans, but that analogy is really in appearance only. The new name is intended to put distance between the party and funding scandals that enveloped the UMP during the presidency of NicoLas SarKozy. The right is a party without an apparent project, only politicians. This flaw notwithstanding, it has been by default the main conservative/centrist political party in France, emerging from the candidacy of JacQues CHiRAC for president of the Republic. It has ever since been a party that reflects the personality of whoever its candidate at the time might be, rather than any founding ideology. Sarkozy seems to be its de facto leader in his effort to regain the presidency, but he is promising things he failed to deliver last time and French hearts have not grown any fonder in his absence from power. Indeed the problem is that the more people see of him, the less they like or trust him. The reason for existence of the UMP seems to be, or have been, that it is not the Socialist party, and that it has at least a notional respect for the efforts of businesses. In practice the UMP has played the same *clientéliste* politics as the Socialists and has no intention of reforming

France's sclerotic economy and its system of jobs for the boys (and, increasingly, girls).

RÉPUBLIQUES 1, 2, 3 ET 4
FAILURES

To wreck one republic might be considered a misfortune, to wreck four suggests supreme carelesness. The first Republic was a brief affair founded in 1792 and lasted until Napoléon Bonaparte's seizure of power in 1802, though technically it limped on for two more years until Bonaparte declared himself Emperor. After 10 years his career ended in military defeat at Waterloo and exile to St Helena. The Bourbon dynasty then returned for 34 years, making various futile attempts to wean the French onto the idea of a constitutional monarchy, before being violently replaced by the second Republic in 1848.

The second Republic lasted but four years. The Second Empire, Napoléon III's, took over from 1852-70, ending again in military catastrophe, before any semblance of Republicanism reappeared with the third Republic, which lasted 70 years, until the Second World War. Then it was Vichy for four years, then a provisional government, and finally in 1947 the fourth Republic, but again with little durability, collapsing in 1958 when General Charles de Gaulle led France out of the constitutional wilderness, for a while at least, as the president of the fifth Republic. Republicanism has utopian origins so it helps to be an optimist about these things.

RÉPUBLIQUE, 5ÈME
SUPERANNUATED FRENCH FETISH

In 1958 the French replaced the disputatious parliamentary character of previous republics with a fifth edition that came equiped with a strong executive power, which it was imagined would lead them to success. (Flaubert said the French had to be led by the sword.) Born during the 30 glorious years of economic prosperity, Johnny Hallyday provided the background music and Brigitte Bardot the glamour. With General DE GAULLE at its head, France seemed to be standing tall in the world once again.

Half a century later, the Fifth Republic has become pretty degenerate. It is not delivering much liberty, equality, fraternity, *laïcité,* jobs or much else to ordinary Frenchmen, but the mainstream politicians are doing very well out of it and have little incentive to change.

The problem is that nobody has so far proposed a credible-sounding alternative. The fifth Republic was specifically architected by de Gaulle to bring stability to government and in some ways it has worked too well since stability has become sclerosis and today's French government looks to be completely immobilised, albeit on full pay and rations.

RÉPUBLIQUE, 6ÈME
NOT IF BUT WHEN

Coming… coming… It seems likely that a sixth attempt at constitutional renewal will arrive at some point, given the limited durability of previous efforts but there is no defined project currently before the French people and MONARCHISME seems unlikely to mount a significant comeback. Jean-Luc Mélenchon, a leader of the extreme left, and Marine LE PEN, leader of the nationalist Front National, both speak of repatriating powers to France from Europe and protecting French industry. NICOLAS SARKOZY pays lipservice to changing the constitution to limit the size of the state. With so many snouts in the trough, there is little organic desire for change.

What nobody seems to be suggesting is *une nouvelle république* in which it is permitted to talk of liberated ambitions, one that is future-pointing and confident, not reactionary and protectionist. It was once believed that Sarkozy thought this, but it was evident during his presidency that these were just words: he proved to be more and he was going to disappoint those who saw him as a Margaret Thatcher.

RÉVOLUTION FRANÇAISE
THE FOUNDING EVENT OF REPUBLICANISM

Zhou Enlai, the Chinese communist leader, asked what he thought of the French revolution, supposedly replied, 'It's too soon to tell.' In fact, he didn't really say this, having misunderstood the question. But it's a quote too good to waste. The French like to talk about their revolution as if it were a singular act of secular enlightenment, but from the storming of the BASTILLE in 1789 (an event subject to considerable Republican exaggeration thereafter) it was much more messy than that and a good case can be made that the revolution and its aftermath have been disasters, trapping the French in a mythology they are unable to puncture.

Joseph de Maistre, a Savoyard lawyer and philosopher (1753-1821), wrote of the revolution's 'satanic character' in which priests were hunted, butchered, humiliated and robbed. 'Those who escaped guillotines, stakes, knives, firing squads, drowning and deportation are now begging instead of helping the poor, as before. Altars are vandalised, prostitutes stand naked on the altars watched by terrified cherubs.' Edmund Burke drew from the revolution the lesson that it had transferred power from aristocrats to an 'enlightened' elite who were more heartless, tyrannical and incompetent than the aristocrats they replaced. Violence was not only a symptom of the revolution but the fuel of it. A comparison with the terror of the Islamic State in Syria is unavoidable.

Perhaps one might not expect British historians to be sympathetic, but it is easy to be revolted by this supposedly glorious chapter in French history. Thomas Carlyle describes the 'hideous' cry emitted by Robespierre when the axe severed his head. Simon Schama, historian of the French and hardly a fan of the republic, author of *Citizens: A Chronicle of the French Revolution* (1989), contests the entire basis of the revolution and the argument that without it, we would not have the liberty, equality and democracy we know today. He says there is a fundamental difference between the American revolution and the revolution in France, both in the violence that propelled the revolutionary French project, and the failure of any French constitutional solution to endure. The late Tony Judt, the brilliant British historian of France, wrote that whoever controls the understanding of the French revolution controls France. Despite massive scholarship discrediting the Marxist historiography portraying the revolution as class struggle, this remains the prevailing doctrine in France, with disastrous consequences as republicanism has become statist authoritarianism.

When I came to France I used to joke that I was a republican in England and a monarchist in France, which produced gales of laughter at the village café, but it is hard to think of any events in monarchical Britain in modern times that come close to the horrors of the French Revolution, or to imagine that Britons today are any less free than their French cousins. Indeed, it is impossible to argue that citizens in any of Europe's constitutional monarchies are less free than those in republican France. Are the Dutch, the Norwegians, the Swedes, the Belgians or the British less equal, free or fraternal than their French cousins? Can anyone argue with a straight face that they are not? The quasi-religious worship of revolutionary republicanism in modern France is among the most powerful of French perversions.

ROYAL, SÉGOLÈNE
MADAME DE POMPADOUR

The woman who would have been president. Failed presidential candidate, losing to NICOLAS SARKOZY in the second round of the

2007 presidential election. Graduate of the ÉCOLE NATIONALE d'ADMINISTRATION (of course). Despite her baby-daddy's serial infidelity, she remains close to him and is seen in France as being effectively the vice-president and bolder French journalists suggest they are not just politically intimate. A member of MANUEL VALLS's government as environment minister, she urged the French to stop eating Italian-made Nutella because it is made from palm oil, before executing a swift U-turn when the Italian government protested. Halted work on the Sivens dam in the Tarn, to avoid upsetting ZADISTES, the militant ecologists.

RMI
WELFARE

The poorest you will be allowed to get, if you qualify, is still pretty poor. Another obsolete set of initials that still lives on, meaning *revenu minimum d'insertion,* in effect a minimum-income platform. It is now officially called the RSA (*revenu de SOLIDARITÉ active*) and offers a means-tested minimum-subsistence benefit of up to 600 euros per month. As in Britain, in addition to the RMI, claimants can get free housing and many other allowances, especially if they have children. My friend Céline, who works in the administration of this programme, says many of her clients have an effective income exceeding her own, without doing anything at all.

RUGBY
POPULAR PASSION

Another sport copied from the English, practically a religion in the south. The French word for a rugby player is *rugbyman.* A female player is accordingly a *rugbywoman.* The Top 14 has become the richest league in the world for players and even French towns with minor league teams now boast their complements of imported players drawn by the professionalism of the sport. The history of French rugby is murky, with well-founded allegations of massive amphetamine use before international games including the classic encounter with New Zealand in 1986. During the war, Marshall PÉTAIN suppressed rugby league in France because of suspicions it was too close to the unions and dominated by communists. Rugby union was encouraged, however, and remains the dominant code.

Jonny Wilkinson CBE, the England international who played for Toulon from 2009-2014, is regarded by many French people as the greatest living Englishman, a true role model, epitome of sportsmanship, admired for his on-field performance (141 caps, 1,884 points) and his wonderful French. 'I fall more and more in love with the French language as the days go by. It becomes more and more natural being able to move around the tenses from past to future into conditional without being able to consider it,' he says. After retiring as an active player, Wilkinson remained in Toulon as an ambassador for the club, coaching, recruiting new players and inspiring the team.

RYANAIR
HATED IRISH AIRLINE

Despised by French pilots and the air traffic controllers' union. Hugely influential Irish low-cost operator with an immense fleet of Boeing 737 aircraft; 300 in service, many more on order and being delivered. Ryanair flies to every corner of France and despite misadventures with the French employment inspectors, plays an influential role in the tourist and broader social economy of the regions it serves. Michael O'Leary, the boss of Ryanair, used to revel in his bad-boy image. The Mr Nasty culture is starting to change, but there are still those who would rather crash than fly on Ryanair. EasyJet, Ryanair's British competitor, has meanwhile become the second-largest domestic airline in France even though its French-based crews have already gone on strike.

S

SAFER
GUARDIAN OF A FALSE MARKET FOR FARMLAND

Often accused of corruption, the *Société d'aménagement foncier et d'établissement rural* is the arm of the state controlling sales of agricultural land. Safer exercises a right of pre-emption on sales of agricultural land to those who do not have official status as an existing farmer. The supposedly noble intention of Safer when it was established in 1960 was to protect the French rural way of life by ensuring that when farmland came on the market, it was available first of all to the existing farmers and their children in the same area. Safer's right of pre-emption has created a false market - like so many in France - in rural land that has allowed peasants and their families to steadily increase their land holdings, but has made it a tribulation for outsiders to invest in agricultural holdings. Safer is justified as integral to the preservation of rural culture but it is also structured to produce conditions ripe for suspicion. The words *scandale* and *Safer* produce links to numerous *affaires* when Googled.

SA GRACIEUSE MAJESTÉ
WHAT THE FRENCH CALL THE QUEEN

Although the Queen is in English merely Her Majesty, the French lay it on even thicker by making her gracious and sometimes *très gracieuse*. The Queen is hugely popular in France where she is admired for her dignified longevity, stoicism and wardrobe (especially hats). It is also widely known and appreciated that she is francophone, speaking French with an accent that is *terriblement British*. The enduring fascination of the French with the Queen and British royal family, doped by the death of Diana, Princess of Wales, in Paris, is yet another contradiction in a proud republic that drove their own royal family from the throne in 1792 and decapitated their last queen, Marie-Antoinette a year later, her executioner brandishing her severed head and crying, '*Vive la République.*'

SANTÉ
INSOLVENT HEALTH CARE SYSTEM

The French claim to have the best health care in the world is pretty dubious, like so many claims of French exceptionalism. It costs just 23 euros to visit a general practitioner but first there has to be a general practitioner to visit. There are health care deserts in much of rural France, with a shortage of generalists and specialists. The ministry of health reported in 2014 that 2 million French people live in these deprived areas. Delivery of actual services on the ground can be pretty hit or miss. The ultimate outcome of healthcare is in any case measured in data that is hard to fake, that is to say life expectancy, where there's not much in it between France and other first-world countries. This data shows France at 81.5 years, in 17th place globally, while the United States, which spends more than anyone, is at 79.8 years in 36th place. So life expectancy isn't dramatically improved, it seems, even with statistically impressive health services. If you need medical intervention, the quality of health provision depends on when and where you are ill.

If you are lucky, the healthcare can be excellent. My carpenter severely injured himself skiing and was airlifted off the mountain in a helicopter, flown to a specialised unit, saved from what would under other circumstances have been death or permanent disablement, and eventually discharged after care that can only be described as proficient, paid for by his social charges. If you are poorly, the Sécu will pay for you to take a cure at one of France's elaborate spas. But visit the general hospital in Béziers with its broken elevators, grim unpainted corridors and harassed and demoralised staff, and it is another story. Health services are not always very innovative in France, especially at the primary care level, where there are numerous obstacles inhibiting greater efficiency. The quality of French medical training is high but the sector screams for investment and innovation: with a deficit in the national insurance fund of 12 billion euros in 2014, it is hard to know where this will come from.

SARKOZY, NICOLAS
FAILED PRESIDENT

Political pygmy, literally and figuratively. At 1.65m, even shorter than the non-statuesque FRANçOIS HOLLANDE. Married to the *chanteuse* Carla Bruni, who towers above him, even in his elevator heels. President of the Republic 2007-2012. Entered office with a swagger and left it defeated having changed little. Keen to return. Known on francophone Twitter channels as #rolex - reference to his taste for bling. The story is odd. Sarkozy seemed to start out as a rare French politician with balls, a relative outsider as he did not attend ÉCOLE NATIONALE d'ADMINISTRATION, the only to lose them entirely once cocooned in the Arabian splendour of the ELYSÉE presidential palace. As mayor of Neuilly, the tony Paris suburb, Sarkozy made his reputation as a gutsy politician, walking into a school where a gunman was holding children hostage, persuading the gunman to release the children and finally to surrender.

He failed to seriously reform the economy or the tax system, became distracted by law and order, taking a tough line and dividing public opinion. Perhaps too much was expected, although he must be responsible for this since he promised so much. It is true that Sarko was attacked from the first five minutes of his mandate by the media. When he chose to celebrate his victory with a dinner at Fouquet's, a classy restaurant in Paris, he was pilloried for this supposedly vulgar display. Are you not allowed to go to dinner if you have just been elected president? Are nice restaurants immoral? Apparently so, in the eyes of the French media, even if they patronise the same establishments. A smarter operator might have looked to live a humble life, to speak softly and persuade but this was never going to appeal to Sarkozy.

Sarkozy as President should have been able to wipe the floor with Hollande during the televised debates at the last election, but instead he came across as smug and arrogant. Despite all of this, he almost won. His attempted political comeback since his defeat has once again seen Sarkozy talk about fundamental reform.

SARTRE, JEAN-PAUL
DEAD END

A bit of a shit, actually. A *normalien* (i.e. graduate of ÉCOLE NORMALE), grand patron of existentialism, structuralism, communism. When the surrealist poet ANDRÉ BRETON, one of the exiles in America during the Second World War, returned to Paris, Sartre insulted him. Sartre feuded with ALBERT CAMUS, sucked up to Mao and Guevara, enjoyed a famously promiscuous left-bank lifestyle, and finally has been largely forgotten, along with his *EXISTENTIALISME*. You can still buy overpriced coffee at the Deux Magots café favoured by Sartre and his wife Simone de Beauvoir but outside a corner of the academy that doesn't matter, nobody talks much about existentialism these days, except to parody it. Breton's surrealism and Camus' humanism are meanwhile more compelling than ever.

SCIENCES PO
OXBRIDGE PRETENDER

Seven campuses in France, the most elite being *l'Institut d'études politiques de Paris* (institute of political studies), classed as a *grand établissement* (major institution) by the ministry of education.

Sciences Po does not prepare students for any particular career but offers a multi-disciplinary course including law, economics, history, political science, geography and sociology, somewhat similar to a British PPE (politics, philosophy and economics). At Sciences Po, a Marxist faculty graduates students who sign up as fast as they can for corporate jobs in London, where the alumni are a powerful group. Sciences Po graduates often share that particular arrogance characteristic of Oxbridge graduates, and waste little time telling everyone that they have *'fait sciences po.'*

SÉCU
INSOLVENT SOCIAL SECURITY SYSTEM
The basis of the French social model, a monstrous, un-reformable racket. The Sécu broadly refers to the four branches of French social security: medical care, pensions, health and safety at work and family benefits. Employees of the state receive pensions based on their final salaries at retirement; private-sector employees are pensioned at the average of their salary during 25 years of employment. There are also dozens of special regimes for such privileged groups as railway workers, miners, lawyers, parliamentarians, gas and electricity workers and Paris Metro workers. All aspects of the system are in deficit, estimated at 13 billion euros in 2014.

SERVICES
BLACK HOLE
France is a country where 'the customer is always wrong,' according to Maureen Dowd, a columnist for the *New York Times*. Where services are not banned altogether like dental hygiene and private hire cars, they do not exist because wage overheads make them impossible to provide. Although 10 per cent of the population is unemployed, it is too expensive to hire workers to perform services that are commonplace elsewhere.

In Britain, there is pretty much nowhere you can't get at least one supermarket to deliver to your door, and sometimes there are three or four. In France, this is a very limited service. If you go to a supermarket, expect a long wait at the undermanned checkouts. It is possible to order your groceries by Internet but you usually have to go to the store to pick them up. If your computer needs fixing, expect to wait. If you want your car washed, a machine will do it, or you can do it yourself, but don't expect anyone to do it for you.

SEXE
SEX, OR TOTAL CONFUSION

French attitudes towards sexuality span the range from extreme prudishness to *libertinage* all of it confused by a thick fog of hypocrisy. Chantal Thomass, the celebrated female-underwear designer, once told a friend of mine that in France, 'everybody does their own thing in their own corner'. 'No-one is faithful in France,' she states. 'And age is no barrier to being sexy, even 65-year-old women insist on matching underwear.' With testimonials like this, you could be mistaken for believing that the French are more promiscuous than other Europeans. I suppose it depends on your postcode. There is a size of woman's handbag called a *baise en ville* (literally: fuck in town) supposedly capacious enough for the change of underwear necessary after an illicit *affaire* between the hours of 5pm-7pm (the famous *cinq-à-sept*). I am not convinced any of this is true or that any of the at best empirical evidence can be believed for a second. My guess is that sexuality is sometimes more open in France but that this behaviour is not greatly different to that elsewhere.

SNCF
SQUALOR ON WHEELS

The terrestrial analogue of AIR FRANCE. The nationalised railway

(SNCF) is an employee-benefits scheme with a not especially impressive railway attached. The French railways are attractive to those who are not required to use them. Whenever I hear an Englishman wax lyrical about the quality of the train network in France, I can be sure he has never put a foot on any train other than a high-speed *train à grande vitesse* (TGV). To ride the stopping service from Montpellier to Béziers in the summer with no air conditioning is to be nostalgic for Southwest Trains in England. *Société nationale des chemins de fer* has a debt of 40 billion euros - a figure only marginally smaller than Egypt's national debt - which is predicted to double in coming years since the necessary drastic reforms to its network and its bloated bureaucracy and wildly generous pension scheme are not occurring at all. Train drivers retire at 50. If the TGV is a symbol of French technical accomplishment, then the rest of the trains in France are dilapidated, often dangerously so, with the most approximate of schedules. There remain ghosts of a glorious past. *Le Train Bleu*, the spectacular restaurant at the Gare de Lyon, is one of the most magnificent dining rooms in Paris. Their *steak tartare* is epic. But descend to the platforms and even if the *cheminots* (railway workers) are consenting to work that day, the trains are likely to be late and dirty. The Gare du Nord is squalid.

SOLIDARITÉ
HYPOCRITICAL MANTRA

The proclamation of solidarity is the substitution of sentiment for activity. Politicians insist on solidarity with the unemployed, while doing nothing about unemployment. They express *solidarité* with refugees, while doing everything they can to move them out of France. When there is an earthquake in Nepal or a tsunami in the Pacific, political expressions of *solidarité* are as ritualistic as they are meaningless. It is perhaps the most overused and hypocritical word in the French political dictionary. President FRANÇOIS HOLLANDE cannot make a speech without insisting on *solidarité*, but everyone else uses the word, too: there is a national federation of solidarity amongst women, one for farm workers, another for students, a federation for socialist solidarity and even an Internet site in which the Carrefour supermarket chain expresses its commitment to solidarity. In the context of taxation, *solidarité* is a simile for confiscation. There is the IMPÔT DE SOLIDARITÉ SUR LA FORTUNE (ISF), the notorious wealth tax, introduced by former president FRANÇOIS MITTERRAND. All employers in France must pay a payroll tax called the *contribution solidarité autonomie* (CSA) to support aged and handicapped people. A French pay slip now runs to two pages, to leave room to enumerate all the deductions. Then there is President Hollande's absurd PACTE DE RESPONSIBILITÉ ET DE SOLIDARITY. Every French town has a *maison de solidarité* that serves as a gateway for claiming benefits. Ultimately, solidarity boils down to a way for politicians to make themselves seem sympathetic, for unions to pretend they act in the interest of anyone other than themselves, and for justifying the imposition of new taxes. See *langue de bois*.

START-UPS
NOT A THING IN FRANCE

There is not really a French word for a start-up, hence it is borrowed from English; neither does the word ENTREPRENEUR have the same meaning in French as in English. Start-ups are frequently sued by those who feel threatened. 1001Pharmacies, a Montpellier-based start-up that wants to disrupt the protected drug-store market, raised 8 million euros in 2015 and has ambitious ideas to roll out their online service across Europe, although for the moment they are still banned from offering prescription drugs in France. 'It's the kind of thing that breaks your heart, when regulation gets in the way of innovation,' wrote *Rude Baguette*, the French start-up blog, after the French courts banned the company from delivering prescription drugs in a case brought by the *Conseil National de l'Ordre des Pharmacies* (one of numerous drug-store trade groups). Other recent start-up deals have been for between 1.5 million euros and 31 million euros - decimal points away from the venture capital investments being made elsewhere.

Ubisoft, the number three computer game company globally, is the only French gaming software company with any kind of global recognition but it has been doing everything it can to delocalise and has grown the most largely outside France. Its biggest studio is in Montreal and it expects to employ 3,500 staff in its rapidly expanding business cluster based around Montreal and Quebec City.

Esker, a business process software developer and Vupen, a Montpellier-based Internet security company, are accoladed in the French business press as examples of cutting-edge companies but are in truth small potatoes. It's taken Esker 30 years to get to 40 million euros in sales. Parrot, a Paris start-up that designs multi-rotor drones, is highly regarded for its technical innovation but has already been overtaken globally. Its modest 243 million euros in revenue in 2014 does not inspire confidence that it can maintain its market place. The French have a minister for digital innovation, Canadian-born Axelle Lemaire, who is also a deputy in the national assembly, representing French citizens in 10 countries in northern Europe, including the UK. Her influence is minimal. *Rude Baguette* says she has failed to fight for entrepreneurs and failed to object to the recent Loi sur le renseignement, the French law permitting virtually unlimited electronic surveillance by the government. She is, in any case, reported to be barely on speaking terms with her boss Emmanuel Macron, the minister of the economy. He is planning new legislation encouraging digital start-ups: what about less legislation, *eh*?

SUICIDE
ENDURING ARTISTIC THEME

Individual suicide is a constant theme in French literary and filmic discourse. National suicide has become a feature in France's management of its economy. Flaubert's Emma Bovary's terrible suicide sets the literary standard but the theme is readily seized by contemporary essayists with the gloomy polemic by Éric Zemmour, *Suicide Français,* at the top of bestseller lists in 2014. Michel Houellebecq's *Soumission* (*Submission,* 2015) also describes the auto-destruction of the Republic. *Le Petit Prince* (1943), the children's classic authored by Antoine de St Exupéry, can be read as a suicide note and indeed its appearance was swiftly followed by the death of St Exupéry, who despite being too old to be a combat pilot, and hardly current in his flying hours, was tortured by his failure to engage in combat. As the war drew to a close, his masterpiece finished, he returned to Europe and joined the Free French, taking out a tricky high-performance aircraft and recklessly, some say suicidally, flying into a hostile environment, where he was killed. The theme of national suicide is central to Marcel Carné's film *Hôtel du nord* (1938) where a young couple's suicide pact was a metaphor for France's own decision to live or die faced with the approaching forces of Nazism.

SUISSE, LA
WHERE FRENCH PEOPLE HIDE THEIR MONEY

In 2013, embarrassing President François Hollande, Jérôme Cahuzac, the French budget minister responsible for leading a crackdown on tax evasion, resigned after it was disclosed he held a secret bank account in Switzerland. In 2015, Arlette Ricci, heir to the Nina Ricci perfume dynasty, was sentenced to three years in prison (2 years suspended) and fined 1 million euros for hiding 18 million euros in Swiss accounts. Fifty other French taxpayers are being targeted in the ongoing investigation. HSBC was in 2015 accused of hiding 5 billion euros for nearly 9,000 French customers. Jean-Marie Le Pen, leader of the National Front, has been accused by the *Mediapart* online news service of hiding 2.2m euros in Switzerland but has denounced his accusers as politically motivated.

SYNDICATS
COMPULSORY TRADE UNIONS

Although French people do not especially love unions, anyone working for the government or a large enterprise is represented by a union whether they like it or not. Unions play a key role in negotiating employment reforms, despite representing only 8 per cent of private-sector employees. The largest is the *Confédération française démocratique du travail* (CFDT) and the most influential is the *Confédération générale du travail (CGT),* historically dominated by communists. Strikes do not require a membership vote, work stoppages are constant and the public be damned. Labour actions in France are not confined to the withdrawal of labour and picketing, but can comprise widespread social disruption. Electricity workers used to turn off the power to the entire country when they went on strike, though this practice has now been abandoned.

France lost more than a million days to strikes in 2013, 10 times as many as Germany. Strikes, which are described as '*mouvements sociale*', enjoy wide de facto immunity to the criminal law. Police will usually stand aside when workers block highways, set fires, occupy factories and hold their bosses hostage. Unions enjoy numerous privileges under French law. They have a statutory role as co-custodians of the enormous social security system and in companies with 50 or more employees, they have a right to statutory representation on a works council, and to be consulted on everything from company strategy to the arrangement of office furniture.

SUBVENTIONS
SUBSIDIES WITH STRINGS ATTACHED

France's many strata of local government are less autonomous than they pretend to be and are highly focused on extracting *subventions* (subsidies or grants) from superior layers of regional government. These are in turn focused on winning their own *subventions* from the state itself. Naturally, political support is expected up and down the line, and this is a pillar of the French system of *CLIENTÉLISME* (clientelism). It is by dangling the carrot of *subventions* that central government gets local governments to follow priorities established elsewhere, but the *subventions* on offer can be so attractive, a municipality would be mad not to grab at them. Who would not want someone else to pay to replace the sewers? Seemingly every town in France seemed simultaneously to install *ralentisseurs* (traffic calming). This is no bad thing, but the top-down nature of the decision-making means there is always a price. Subventions and the related *dotations* (transfer payments to collectivities from the state) are nevertheless decreasing as the state has forced austerity onto the collectivities while maintaining intact the core activities of the state itself, where there is needless to say no evidence of austerity. What might replace a reduced level of *subventions* in the future? There are structural problems that make it hard for local government to partner with the private sector to deliver developments and planning gains. In any case French local administrations have little experience of, and are not comfortable working with, private-sector partners.

SYSTÈME D
HOW THINGS GET DONE IN FRANCE

D stands for *débrouillardise* meaning making do, or resourcefulness. Applies to any quick-witted, improvised work-around to a problem, it can apply also to getting things done in the black economy. Also applied to the art of improvisation in a kitchen, popularised by chef Anthony Bourdain's book, *The Nasty Bits*, 2006.

T

TABAC
MORE SMOKERS

Cigarettes have never been more sublime than in the hands of a French person. Jean-Paul Belmondo with his dangling Gauloise in *À bout de souffle* (Breathless, Jean-Luc Godard, 1960) is an essential image of French cinema. Nobody who knows the French doubts the necessity for the government's vigorous campaign against smoking. The health minister, Marisol Touraine, said in 2014 that smoking deaths in France were the equivalent of an airliner crashing every day with 200 people on board. By 2016 it will be illegal to smoke in a car if there are children present and cigarette packets will have to carry even more prominent health warnings. Smoking has been forbidden in all public places including cafés since 2008 and in 2013, the government announced that it would extend the ban to electronic cigarettes to discourage mimicking behaviour. Since the 1960s, the proportion of smokers in France has fallen from 57 per cent to 32 per cent, but sales of cigarettes have shockingly increased 7 per cent since 2014 so smokers are puffing more or more people are smoking. A fifth of French women still smoke while pregnant. *Peut mieux faire* (must try harder).

The *buralistes* who have the right to sell tobacco in France are, like many of their compatriots, angry. They recently dumped four tons of carrots outside the headquarters of the Socialist party in Paris, to protest the planned introduction of plain cigarette packets. The carrot was chosen because it looks vaguely like the sign outside all shops in France that sell cigarettes. Before that they were angry that French people were buying their smokes in Spain. Indeed, they are usually angry.

TAYLOR JR, MAURICE
AMERICAN BUSINESSMAN, ENEMY OF THE STATE

Here is a cameo of how France sends the wrong message to foreign investors. Arnaud Montebourg was the minister for economic development in the first FRANÇOIS HOLLANDE government, before walking out of the government in a huff. He was trying to sell a strike-ridden, failing tyre factory in northern France to Titan Tire, an American company that has developed a reputation for hard-nosed turnarounds of bust businesses. After visiting the factory in Amiens and listening to Montebourg's pitch, Maurice 'The Grizz' Taylor Jr, Titan's no-bullshit chief executive, put it to the minister quite simply: 'How stupid do you think we are? Titan is the one with the money and the talent to produce tyres. What does the crazy union have? It has the French government. The work force gets paid high wages but works only three hours. They have one hour for their breaks and lunch, talk for three and work for three. I told this to the French unions to their faces and they told me, 'That's the French way!'

Montebourg's response was not measured. He might have said: 'Come to dinner, let's try and work it out.' Instead, he publicly called Taylor 'extreme' and 'insulting,' accusing him of 'perfect ignorance' about France and its strengths. 'Incendiary!' 'Insulting!' and 'Scathing!' were among the comments elsewhere, while the head of the communist CGT union at the plant said Mr. Taylor belonged in a 'psychiatric ward'. Very few voices were raised to say: perhaps Taylor has a point. (An honourable exception was the online journal, *ATlANTICO*.) How can you take a government seriously that has employed a minister with a temperament like Montebourg's? The factory has now closed after workers took managers hostage, an act for which nobody was punished or even charged. Another example of how the French police are utterly feeble dealing with unionists.

Montebourg was last heard of joining the board of the French 'eco' furniture store Habitat (long separated from its British roots). I recommend going short on this particular enterprise.

TAXIS
POLICE-PROTECTED MAFIA (LIKE ANY OTHER ORGANISED JOB)

While the French police fail to keep the Channel Tunnel open, they are doing everything they can to keep Uber closed. It's not surprising that the idea for Uber, which uses a smartphone app to summon private hire cars, was born in Paris, when Travis Kalanick, one of the founders of the company, tried and failed to hail a taxi. The number of cabs in Paris was capped at 14,000 in 1937 and is now only 15,900. London has 8 taxis for every thousand inhabitants, New York 6 and Paris 3. Uber has had a rough ride in France. When it opened an office in Paris, it was raided by the police. The minister of the interior, Bernard Cazeneuve, ordered the arrest of the CEO of Uber France and the general manager of Uber Europe. More than 400 police officers were sent to fight against Uber on the streets, pulling over cars with passengers in the back seat. And although Uber cars are still technically permitted, they must return to their base after every trip. So as it now stands, an Uber driver who takes a passenger from Paris to De Gaulle airport must return to Paris, 34km away, before he is allowed to return to the airport to pick up another passenger. This while Paris has some of the most contaminated air in Europe. UberPOP, an even lower cost version of the service, has been banned altogether.

When Phil, an Englishman in a nearby village who has lived in France a long time, finally persuaded his mayor to give him a permit to operate a *voiture de tourisme avec chauffeur* (VTC) - a sort-of taxi but limited to offering guided tours to tourists - he was promptly visited by the long-established taxi operator in the next village. 'Take one of my customers and you may find your car on fire,' he threatened. Phil, not to be intimidated, replied:

'That's not fair. You have nine taxis and I have one. It's going to cost me a lot more in petrol to burn your cars than it will cost you to burn mine.' He has heard no more. The French government, which instinctively sides with producers against consumers, hasn't the guts to stand up to the taxi mafia whose fight against Uber has been violent and nasty. Caught in a protest in Paris, the American singer Courtney Love tweeted: 'They've ambushed our car and are holding our driver hostage. They're beating the cars with metal bats. This is France?? I'm safer in Baghdad.' She added: 'François Hollande where are the fucking police???' In Marseille, taxi drivers have used the Uber app to summon private hire cars, which they then vandalise, beating up their drivers. When they are not physically attacking their competitors, taxi drivers punish everyone else with frequent *operations* ESCARGOT, blocking motorways during rush hours.

TELEVISIONS
DOMINATED BY CSI AND MASTERCHEF

France has long abandoned its eccentric SECAM television system (a product of French technical exceptionalism) and all broadcasting is now *numérique* (digital). Viewers can receive dozens of digital TV channels via satellite, over the air, or over broadband. But most of the TV in France is pretty dire, which probably makes it similar to, rather than different from, TV anywhere else. American imports are often the highlights of French schedules, especially on TF1, the principal commercial channel. *Les experts (CSI)* is wildly popular in France. Formats like *Masterchef* are imported from the United Kingdom. There are news, sports and music channels, an arts channel and some pretty marginal channels that have tiny viewing figures. A *redevance audiovisuelle* (television licence) of 136 euros is charged on every French household as an add-on to the *taxe d'habitation* (home-occupancy tax). The proceeds

finance *France Télévisions,* the public service television conglomerate whose president is appointed by the president of
the Republic. *France Télévisions* operates channels France 2,
France 3, France 4, France 5 and Ô - the latter being a special
service for the overseas territories, which pay a reduced
redevance. The *redevance* is never questioned nor is its relevance
in a digital epoch ever mentioned. *France Télévisions* is an
enormous bureaucracy with 10,000 employees, primarily
concerned with its own survival, deferentially covering the
presidency, broadcasting some lively chat shows but also
much appalling drivel. The customers do not get to decide if
this is value for money or not, because unless they sign a
declaration to the tax authorities that they do not own a
television set, they must pay, whether they like it or not.

TERRORISME
FRENCH SPECIALITY

It is hard to pin the invention of terrorism exclusively on the
French but the French have been innovative terrorists since at
least the 13th century, when Pope Innocent III launched a 20-
year military campaign to eliminate the Cathar heresy from the
Languedoc, leaving the province soaked in blood. The papal
armies employed dramatic techniques to exterminate the gnostic
Cathars, laying siege to their castles, catapulting the dead bodies
of captives over their walls, burning prisoners alive and finally
herding the entire population of Béziers into the cathedral and
setting it on fire in 1209. I have looked carefully around the
gloomy, fortress-like cathedral at Béziers rebuilt at the site of
this massacre, but have found no memorial or recognition of
this draconic history. The *Catholic Encyclopaedia* does concede the
campaign may have been excessive.

Subsequent French wars of religion built on the idea of
terrorism as not merely violence but violence as a form of
popular entertainment. Notable is the celebrated massacre of

St Bartholomew's Day in 1572 resulting in between 5,000 and 30,000 deaths and provoking the exile of the protestant Huguenots to England and Holland. It was only natural that the French revolution would build on the established foundation of terrorism, although substituting revolutionary for religious ideology and the technology of the QUILLOTINE for the cruder methods of the past. The reign of terror from 1793-94 was the first modernist terrorism in which the spectacle of terror was itself central to the project, the heads of aristocrats and priests being paraded on stakes and vast crowds gathering to watch the executions. The Islamic State still has some catching up to do.

TGV
PERK FOR THE RICH

Although the TGV is hailed by the French as an emblematic achievement, it's really transport for quite wealthy people, paid for by the taxes of people who do not use it. The high-speed lines bypass many cities (if they stopped along the way they would no longer be high-speed) and the economic benefits are hard to discern. It is certainly far less costly to transport people over medium distances by air than by trains (as long as this is done by Easyjet, not Air France). The union grip on railways in France makes costs high and efficiencies low. TGV drivers who work in air-conditioned cabs still get a retirement *prime* (bonus) for exposure to coal. Exports of TGV technology have been slow. Certainly, many other nations have now mastered it, including the Chinese.

TOILETTES
WHO STEALS FRENCH TOILET SEATS?

Nobody who has travelled the Hexagon can fail to have noticed the absence of toilet seats in many bars, restaurants and public conveniences (that is, when there is an actual toilet, since the un-ornamented hole in the ground of the so-called Turkish toilet is by no means extinct). To be fair, there are more clean loos in France than there used to be. But to say standards are mixed is to be generous. The English get the word loo from the French word, *l'eau* (water). Perhaps to avoid the foul, malodorous *chiottes* (slang, equivalent to the English 'bog'), French men are uninhibited in peeing by the side of the road, and I have seen women doing this, too.

TOUR DE FRANCE
CORRUPTION ON WHEELS

The first tour was run in 1903 and by 1904 riders were being dis-qualified for taking the train. In 1937, rider Roger Lapébie was caught being towed uphill by a car. There have been bombings by Basque separatists, the hurling of stink bombs by demon-strating firemen, blockades by farmers, numerous deaths of riders, spectators, officials and journalists and physical assaults by riders against one another. Since 1998 the race has been completely corrupted by doping, with disqualifications and expulsions in 1998, 2006, 2007, 2008, 2010, 2011, and 2012, when Lance Armstrong was stripped of all seven of his titles. In 2015, British cyclist Chris Froome was spat at and had urine thrown on him as French spectators accused him of being a doper, without a shred of evidence. The Tour often passes near my village and every summer we all go to watch it, scooping up the *tchotchkes* (Yiddish: trinkets) hurled from the publicity caravan then heartily cheering the magnificent men on their carbon-fibre racing machines as they whizz past. If they are doped to the gills, *tant pis* (so what). A magnificent spectacle - what could be more French? The tour has not been won by a French rider in 30 years.

TOURISTES
PARIS PRO TOTO

In 2015 the government launched a campaign to persuade the French to be polite to visitors. The government is to train the border police to say thank-you when tourists hand them their passports and offer sweets to well-behaved children. This quickly ran aground when the police union objected. 'We are not confectioners,' they said. Other measures include a plan to introduce announcements in English on inter-city trains and to set up a phone line to help Chinese people. To be fair, in most of France, people are already polite. The problem is Paris. Even many French people dislike Parisians. Parisians have been urged before to be polite to tourists, without apparent effect. Einstein said doing the same thing over and over and expecting different results is the definition of insanity.

TRAVAIL DOMINICAL
HOLY SUNDAY

The French are not necessarily work-shy although many are out of the habit. But even when they want to work, they are not allowed to. A recent reform pushed by industry minister Emmanuel Macron may allow French superstores to open on Sundays up to 12 times per year. The unions are strongly opposed although many of the members are happy to work on Sunday and be compensated at premium rates.

TRENTE-CINQ HEURES
FRANCE'S WAR AGAINST JOBS

The idea of the *35 heures* (35-hour week), implemented in 2000 by prime minister Lionel Jospin during the presidency of JACQUES CHIRAC, was that with everyone working less, there would be more work to be shared around, hence unemployment would fall. The author of the legislation was MARTINE AUBRY, then minister of social affairs. The idea was originally proposed by President FRANÇOIS MITTERRAND as part of his *110 propositions pour la France* (110 proposals for France) which also included retail price controls on books. It may be his greatest toxic legacy. The law was passed during a French period of *cohabitation* in which a supposedly conservative president (Chirac) had to govern with a socialist parliament. Chirac was too economically ignorant or (probably) lazy to see the danger. The Anglo-Saxon ultraliberals who gasped at this folly were ignored. The 35-hour week is straight out of the Marxist economic playbook, specifically the lump of labour fallacy, which holds that there is a finite amount of work, and this can be distributed among the available workers. This insane fantasy has been one of the principal destroyers of prosperity for the French. I debated with a French advocate of the *trente-cinq heures* on the BBC World Service while the law was going through in 2000, who accused me of French-bashing.

What followed was an approximate 11 per cent fall in economic activity concentrated in the public and unionised sectors of the economy and a reorganisation in France's tiny private sector to automate or delocalise production. There was very little replacement hiring, with the exception of the public sector. In short, it meant taxpayers paying more to hire more people to do the same amount of work. The services sector was more or less burned to the ground as whatever surplus value an employer might have found by hiring someone had been summarily confiscated. It was the beginning of the exodus of talented French people.

The project has been comprehensively demolished by Thierry Desjardins, the former deputy editor of *Le Figaro*, in his book *Laissez-nous travailler!* (*Let Us Work*, 2004) which is replete with case historie, economic analysis and facts proving every element of the scheme to have been nonsense. His book concludes with an interview with the president of an enterprise with 620 employees who concludes, *'Ce pays est foutu'* (this country is fucked). The most influential union, the CGT, knows a steal when it sees one and is demanding a 32-hour week. What is not to like?

TRENTE GLORIEUSES
LUCKY YEARS

It all seems long ago but once upon a time, the French economy sizzled. The 30 glorious years of the French economic miracle are said to have started soon after the Second World War and continued until 1974 when the *choc pétrolier* (oil crisis) hit the country, after OPEC raised prices and the era of cheap energy came to an end. To be born in France from the late 1940s to mid-1950s was to come of age at a time of full employment and deep and broad prosperity and optimism. The years of deficit, slow growth, unemployment and sclerosis that ensued were supposed to have ended with the introduction of the euro in 1999 but the sunlit uplands of European prosperity have yet to be gained and so it has really been 35 years of going nowhere for the French economy.

TRIERWEILER, VALÉRIE
FRANCE'S INTEREST IN PRIVATE LIVES

Briefly first lady of France. Claims she was sedated to stop her from making a fuss after she discovered that PRESIDENT FRANÇOIS HOLLANDE was being conducted on the back on a motor scooter to an affair with an actress. Revenge is a dish best eaten cold and she retaliated with *Merci pour ce moment* (2014), a highly readable book albeit not literature, that became a bestseller in France despite attacks on it from all quarters. It claimed that the president was a habitual liar and hypocrite and had behaved contemptuously towards her humble family. The commentariat considered *Merci pour ce moment* to be a betrayal of private life. In

Britain, she was condemned in the *Guardian,* on France Inter and in *Le Monde,* and some high-minded Paris bookshops refused to sell her book. The issue of *Paris Match* with extracts from her book was a bestseller.

TUNNEL SOUS LA MANCHE
THE CHANNEL TUNNEL

The noblest prospect that an enterprising Frenchman ever sees is the submarine tunnel to England. A French dream since the 18th century, it was resisted by the English who feared continental invasion. This has turned out to be true in the end as it has become the conduit for thousands of migrants who break into the lorries that use it daily. The tunnel is supposed to be one of the most secure sites in France but is like anything else proclaimed by officials nothing of the kind. The security is repeatedly breached by a handful of port workers from Calais, causing chaos on both sides of the channel and by migrants, seeking passage to the promised land of England. If a French union can invade the perimeter, one wonders what the feeble French police might do in the event it was attacked by terrorists. The first serious Channel tunnelling effort in 1874 quickly ground to a halt as did several subsequent attempts. The modern 50km/33 mile triple-bore tunnel was finally started in 1988 and completed in 1994, late and over-budget. Opened by the Queen and President FRANÇOIS MITTERRAND in May 1994, *Le Figaro* pronounced the tunnel to be the end of British insularity, but perhaps the opposite was also true. At the opening ceremony, the Queen noted that although it was a Frenchman who first flew over the channel, it was an Englishman who had first swum it. The French and the English cannot even agree what to call the strait separating us. For the French it is *La Manche* (the sleeve). See CALAIS.

TUTOYER, VOUVOYER
AN ENDLESS PROBLEM FOR ANGLOPHONES

To *tutoyer* someone is to address them with the familiar form of the pronoun for you: *tu*. To *vouvoyer* them is to use the more formal pronoun *vous*. This can be a minefield. Inadvertently addressing someone as *tu* can be considered to be taking a liberty or even an insult. Sometimes, however, even those very familiar with one another, including old married couples, will use *vous*, as a mark of respect or even affection. One of General de Gaulle's closest colleagues is said to have asked him, after many years, whether it might be time to *tutoyer*. '*Si vous voulez*,' (if you wish) replied the general. The safe rule for an anglophone is to stick with *vous*, except when addressing children, who are always *tu*. It is wise to wait before your French acquaintance or friend employs the familiar *tu* before using it yourself. There is evidence that the rigorous application of these protocols is falling out of favour with millennials.

U

ULTRA-LIBÉRALISME
FRENCH TABOO

Margaret Thatcher remains the ur-example of an ultra-liberal, even if she has been dead since 2013. Ultra-liberals are blamed for exploitation, banksterism, debt, untrammelled free trade, destruction of public services, competition, deregulation and much else. 'If a French person describes you as an ultra-liberal, they are not paying you a compliment,' says *E!Sharp*, the Brussels blog, in its dictionary of EU jargon. 'If you are ever branded an Anglo-Saxon ultra-liberal you really have upset someone.' See *langue de bois*.

URSSAF
GIANT FEEDING TROUGH

Unions de eecouvrement des cotisations de sécurité sociale et d'allocations Familiales (organisations for the payment of social security and family benefit contributions). The group of 100 organisations collects social security *cotisations* and two other taxes. Each organisation is responsible for a particular sector such as artists, farmers, taxi drivers, café owners, freelance writers, etc. The administrative overhead of these organisations, ostensibly private but in every respect acting as an agent of the state, is estimated to be 40 per cent of all the contributions received. Private suppliers of pensions are not permitted to compete. Cotisations almost double the cost of employing anyone in France.

V

VACHEMENT
EMPHASIS

A word implying cow-like but meaning decidedly, absolutely or without doubt. Often used to describe something particularly good to eat, e.g. *vachement bon*. Some claim this originates with an iconic TV commercial for Laughing Cow cheese (*La vache qui rit*), described as *vachement bon*. But this may be a false memory because YouTube has an old French TV commercial for milk, also using the phrase *vachement bon*. *Vachement* can also be employed if you think something is amazing (*vachement surprenant*) or in any other context in which one might wish to lay a special emphasis.

VALLS, MANUEL
SOCIALIST POLITICIAN, MISTRUSTED BY SOCIALISTS

President FRANÇOIS HOLLANDE's second prime minister, not at all the product of the golden circle, is the son of Catalan immigrants, has a Jewish wife, was formerly the interior minister. He is regarded by the French as hard-nosed and by the left as dangerously reformist. But I don't think anyone need fear for their job. He is not so reformist as to eschew the trappings of political power, having commandeered an air force Falcon jet to take him to the Champions League final in Berlin in June 2015, to watch his favourite team, Barcelona, win the European Champions League against Juventus. He took his two sons along for the ride, which was estimated to have cost French taxpayers 25,000 euros. Rachida Dati, a spokesman for the opposition, posted the obvious tweet: '*La reality, c'est que le vol familial Paris-Berlin a bien décollé. Mais l'emploi, toujours pas*' (the reality is that the family flight Paris-Berlin has taken off. But employment, not yet). One must suppose he will be discarded quickly if Hollande sees an advantage to himself. Valls has spoken plainly in ways that were previously inconceivable for a French prime minister (see GHETTOS, APARTHEID) and must certainly be a politician to watch but he lacks much of a constituency amongst Socialist party activists. Hollande plainly regards him as someone who can ultimately be forced to carry the can for the manifold failures of his presidency.

VÉLIB'
SYMBOL OF SOCIAL DIVISION

Paris has pioneered bike-sharing and the idea has been widely copied in France and beyond. But the scheme is troubled by widespread vandalism and theft. In 2013, 8,000 of the bikes were vandalised, 40 per cent of the fleet. In one night, 367 had their tyres slashed. The vandalism is concentrated in the deprived northeast of the city where the bikes are regarded as a manifestation of *bobo* culture. Vandalism of shared bikes in London is reported to be negligible. Paris is also pioneering electric scooter and electric car sharing schemes.

VERLAN
SLANG

The *Verlan* argot is no longer much used but has bequeathed some words that have come into common use. *Verlan* words are formed by somewhat approximately reversing the syllable-order words, with liberal licence, hence a *meuf* is *une femme* (woman) and a *keuf* is *un flic* (cop). Verlan itself is a good example: *l'envers* (reverse) becoming *vers-l'an*. *Verlan* is now more likely to be used by middle-aged people trying to be hip than by urban youth on the linguistic cutting edge. They prefer to sprinkle their discourse with anglicisms.

VGE (VALÉRY GISCARD d'ESTAING)
PRINCESS DIANA FAN

Initials alone suffice to identify Valéry Giscard d'Estaing. Born in Germany in 1926, during the French occupation of the Rhineland. De Gaulle's finance minister, president of the Republic from May 1974 to May 1981, impossibly grand and ancient figure, not just a *polytechnicien* (see X) but also a graduate of the ENA. From 2003 a member of the *ACADÉMIE FRANÇAISE*. A member of the resistance, he participated in the liberation of Paris in 1944. He may be clever, but his literary achievements are debatable. His proposed European Constitution, rejected by French voters in 2005 (but imposed anyway, relabelled as a treaty), was widely regarded as incomprehensible. Perhaps this obscurity was deliberate. VGE's concept of democratic legitimacy was expressed when he said that European 'public opinion will be led to adopt, without knowing it, the proposals we dare not present to them directly.' Post-Elysée, a writer. Author, inter alia, of *La princesse et le président* (*The Princess and the President*, 2009) positing a sentimental relation between Princess Diana and a thinly-disguised himself that provoked some derision.

VIADUC DE MILLAU
THE MOST BEAUTIFUL CONTEMPORARY BRIDGE IN THE WORLD

Magnificent structure spanning the Tarn gorge, one hour from my house, cutting an hour off my journey time to Paris. Thanks for that. The second of its seven pillars is the tallest structure in France, even higher than the Eiffel Tower. Designed by the French structural engineer Michel Virlogeux and the British architect Sir Norman Foster. Was briefly closed shortly after opening by a blockade of angry builders.

VIGIPIRATE
ANSWER TO TERRORIST THREATS

Internal counter-terrorism program launched in 2003 involving deployment of soldiers at airports, train stations, and outside synagogues. France is typically under an alert status called *vigilance* (vigilance) which signifies a generalised threat, with frequent escalations to the level *alerte attentat* (attack alert), indicating a reinforced alert against a specific threat. *Vigipirate* is not entirely convincing as there is no evidence that any *Vigipirate* unit has ever been deployed to counter an actual terrorist action. A typical *Vigipirate* formation at Montpellier airport is composed of three baby-faced soldiers carrying Famas assault rifles and sidearms. This seems more theatrical than a serious counter to the terrorist threat. There is also an air force *Vigipirate* squadron on 24-hour alert tasked with shooting down any hijacked aircraft that threaten to crash into sensitive infrastructure or populated areas. If the French cannot keep open the Channel tunnel against a handful of thuggish trade unionists from the port of Calais, it is hard to imagine them doing much better against an organised group of terrorists and indeed as the *Charlie Hebdo* incident demonstrated, they have not.

VIN
WHAT TO SAY?

'A subject of conversation among men,' said Flaubert. 'The best is Bordeaux because doctors prescribe it. The worse it is, the more natural.' This is no longer true given the renaissance in natural, organic wine although much of the Bordeaux remains good. I am biased because I live in a less distinguished, though enormous winemaking region, so I see the industry close-up, and it is not always a pretty story. France makes some of the best wine in the world, some of the worst, and a lot that falls between. The great houses do very well. But many of the smaller producers are frankly hopeless, and even when the wine is good they are clueless how to sell it. Tourists show up at the cellar doors of producers in the Languedoc, eager to take home a case of two of the delicious wine on offer, only to find that the winemaker is unable to accept credit cards and has never heard of PayPal.

For every grand vintage there are dozens of smaller producers whose products are often very good, but the mentality of the winemakers can be pretty detached from the harsh demands of a global market. Many of my neighbours think their competition is the vineyard on the other side of the valley and cannot imagine a supermarket in England or China where consumers have a choice of bottles from all over the world. I was at an organic wine fair in London, organised by an enterprising (and exiled-in-London) Frenchwoman, with one of my winemaking friends from the village. He's a *fou de vin* (a fanatic, for whom wine is an art more than a business). I dragged him into a Tesco to show him what he is up against. His jaw dropped at the sight of bottles from Argentina, Australia, Chile, Italy, New Zealand, South Africa, the United States and even England. These choices simply do not exist at supermarkets in France. At the best wine merchant in Pézenas, it is impossible to find a single bottle of imported wine. Some are even more extreme in their refusal to accept that they must compete in a global market. A Lidl supermarket here was actually bombed by militant local winemakers, for having dared to offer Spanish wine.

My own region of Languedoc-Roussillon boasts of being *le plus grand vignoble du monde* (largest vineyard in the world). Here, the peasant producer of grapes, selling them to the co-operative, is a declining model. The co-ops are being attacked on all fronts: by small-scale independents and larger commercial groups with more sophisticated production and marketing skills. But all winemakers complain that the harsh tax regime, unsympathetic regulations and brutal commercial tactics of the major distributors and supermarkets make it hard to compete. Many of the best of the smaller producers are incapable of communicating in English. Yes, French wines still have incredible prestige. At a top wine merchant that I visited in Hong Kong, it was the grand French labels that occupied pride of place - the great vintages of Bordeaux like Château Cheval Blanc and Pétrus, at breath-taking prices. But there was very little from the less-known French regions. Hope lies with an emerging generation of French producers who are learning to master the dark arts of marketing, like my friend Jean-Claude Mas in Pézenas, who is spinning off hot new global wine brands all the time, selling 25 million bottles a year all over the world, including millions exported to Australia, which is itself a major producer. But the trends are ominous. France was the largest producer of wine in Europe as recently as 2012 but has now fallen behind both Italy and Spain.

VIVENDI
SEMI-GOVERNMENTAL ORGAN

France's not very impressive digital media champion, indeed its only native global digital media giant with activities in film, music and television. Vivendi's origins are in the *Compagnie générale des eaux* (General Water Company) created by an imperial decree of Napoléon III with monopoly concessions in Lyons and Paris. After a century focused mainly on municipal water provision, the company diversified into waste disposal, energy and transport and by 1983 was a founder of Canal+, eventually dumping the boring old water and sewage businesses to become a media company. Canal+ has used its monopoly profits in France to expand internationally but seems to be lagging globally against new platforms such as Netflix. Vivendi had a near-death experience after a failed adventure in Hollywood and abandoned mobile telephony in France after failing against Orange, its state-sponsored competitor. Yet it continues to enjoy considerable protection in France because of its role as a financier of French films. The chairman is VINCENT BOLLORÉ, a friend of NICOLAS SARKOZY. *Monday Note*, an intelligent French media newsletter, attributes Vivendi's success solely to it having made it almost impossible for consumers to cancel Canal+. I can testify this is true.

VOITURES
CARS

The French are divided into three tribes: the *Citroënistes*, the *Renaultistes* and the *Peugeotistes*. The tribe of Citroën is considered somewhat dashing, that of Renault somewhat middle-of-the-road while the Peugeot driver is more likely to be an accountant or civil servant. Native French people do not choose to join one sect or another, but are born into them. As a foreigner, I am a *Citroëniste* by adoption, having bought a 1951 Traction Avant on eBay from a retired general in the Belgian army (who knew that Belgium had an army?). She is called Modestine, after the donkey in Robert Louis Stevenson's *Travels with a Donkey in the Cévennes*. Even though the car is French, it took five months to register her at the local *préfecture,* requiring the production of a fat dossier including *attestations, certificats, déclarations de conformité* and proof that all taxes had been paid. I finally succeeded in persuading a bureaucrat to affix his *tampon* (rubber stamp) to my application by showing him a picture of the vehicle. '*Voilà,*' he said, '*c'était la voiture de mon grand-père*' (my grandfather had one of those - a phrase I have subsequently heard a thousand times). This proves that while French bureaucrats are hopelessly rigid, they can be susceptible to romantic sentiment. Driving my glorious restored car through France, I make friends everywhere.

Although imports are taking an increasing share of the French market, the big three French manufacturers still account for more than half of all sales. Particularly favoured are the utility vehicles (Citroën Berlingo, Renault Kangoo) that look like garden sheds with wheels. French cars are eccentric, often fabulous, not always terribly reliable but still endowed with a certain eccentric *je ne sais quoi*. Despite its glorious heritage the industry's future is not so clear. Though Bugatti is located in France and Mercedes makes its SMART cars here, Renault is aggressively outsourcing production to its Romanian subsidiary, Dacia. Iconic cars of the past like the Citroën 2CV, Traction Avant and DS-21, and the dashing Renault Alpine and Caravelle, have not been replaced with similarly admired successors. In a global car market French companies must make huge investments in new vehicle technologies but do not seem to have achieved leadership in electric vehicles, driverless cars or hybrid powertrains. An exception is Michelin, the tyre-maker, which remains a worldwide powerhouse and impressive technological innovator. All the French motor industry giants share the problem that input costs are high, capacity too great and domestic consumer demand suppressed by the country's economic stagnation. And then there is the government. Flexibility demands closing inefficient plants but is hampered by continual government interference. Renault is in practice a PARAÉTATIQUE (semi-governmental) arm of the French state, which holds double voting rights for its shareholding, while Nissan, another major shareholder, is excluded from voting altogether.

VOLTAIRE
SURPRISINGLY MODERN WRITER

French writer (1694-1778) dead more than 200 years yet still relevant, perhaps more so than ever. Surprisingly, lived to a ripe and prosperous old age (83) despite having the authorities on his heels for much of his life. Always wilier than his pursuers. Of his 2,000 books and pamphlets and 20,000 letters, only a handful are consulted now but these include the eternally classic anticlerical manifesto *Candide, ou l'optimisme*. This reads freshly even today. Dr Pangloss, the eternally optimistic character in the novel, gave his name to the adjective Panglossian, a state of naïve optimism, which characterises much French political discourse even today. He also wrote some wonderful letters from England. Voltaire was a brilliant mathematician who made a fortune exploiting the national lottery. He was a figure in the court of Frederic the Great in Prussia. He finally invested in Swiss watchmaking, which was a bit like the Silicon Valley of his day.

'Famous for his repellent cold smile. Science superficial,' said Flaubert, summarising the opinion of his day. *Traité sur la tolérance* - Voltaire's attack on religious fanaticism (1763) - became a surprise bestseller in France following the Charlie Hebdo shootings. His *Letters Concerning the English Nation* (1733), written in English during his exile in London, remain an enduring parody of English society and also a solid appreciation of the value put by the English on commerce. 'I cannot say which is most useful to a nation; a Lord, powder'd in the tip of the Mode…or a Merchant, who enriches his Country, dispatches Orders from his Compting-House to *Surat* and *Grand Cairo*, and contributes to the Felicity of the World.' Supposedly asked on his deathbed if he would renounce the devil, he is supposed to have replied: 'This is no time to be making new enemies.' His ghost is reported to haunt his chateau at Ferney on the outskirts of Geneva and has a reputation for making itself known to selected visitors, especially pretty young women.

W

THERE ARE NO NATIVE FRENCH WORDS BEGINNING WITH THE LETTER W

All French words beginning with W are cognates, most from English. Some examples:

wagon-lit - railway sleeping car.

WC - toilet.

waterproof - waterproof garment.

wattman - electric-tram driver. Obsolete, but Frenchmen of a certain age still recall the signs on trams: *il est interdit de parler au wattman* (Speaking to the driver is forbidden).

web - *idem*.

webcam - *idem*.

week-end - weekend, made French by the insertion of a hyphen.

westerns - adored American movies.

whisky - admired tipple.

wok - used to make Chinese food.

And most sensitive of all:

Waterloo - in 2015 the French government boycotted the 200th anniversary commemorations of the battle and forced Belgium to abandon the idea of issuing a special two-euro coin to mark the defeat of Napoléon Bonaparte. (They issued a 2.5 euro coin anyway, although it is not legal tender in France.) *The New York Times* found several French people who claimed that Napoléon had actually won and Martin Kettle, associate editor of the *Guardian* is among those distressed that he had not.

X

'X'

ENGINEERING SCHOOL WHOSE STUDENTS ARE SOLDIERS

The grandest engineering school in France is more formally called *L'École Polytechnique*. The *grande école* at Palaiseau south of Paris graduates those who go on to become France's technocratic elite. Students are members of the military and wear uniforms. The school boasts a heritage of magnificent achievements by its graduates since it was founded in 1794. But there are doubts whether it is fully versed in the technologies of the information economy. No global analysis on the role of the school has been undertaken by the state for more than 40 years, according to a French parliamentary report in 2014. The French ability to master difficult material technologies (aircraft, jet engines, nuclear power stations, shipbuilding, the list is pretty long) is credited to graduates of this prestigious school but in the Internet age X has not spun out a French Silicon Valley. This may be because students are not permitted to harbour any subversive ideas that after graduation they might get involved in a start-up, or go work wherever they want. They are required to spend 10 years as civil servants, working for the state, by which time they will have been completely absorbed into the French way of thinking, or else pay a *pantoufle* (exit fee) of 40,000 euros to reimburse the cost of their education.

Y

YAOURT
STRATEGIC PRODUCT
Strategic bacterial fermentation. The French government responded to rumours that Pepsi or Nestlé might seek to acquire yogurt-maker Danone by passing a law, known as the Danone Law, to protect such 'strategic' industries from perfidious foreign ownership.

YACHT
CAPITALIST SYMBOL
Hated symbol of inequality. Former president Nicolas Sarkozy was mercilessly attacked for vacationing on a yacht owned by the plutocrat Vincent Bolloré.

YVETOT
NUL POINTS
A once beautiful city at the centre of the *pay de Caux*, region of Normandy that was the setting of Gustave Flaubert's *Madame Bovary*. '*Voir Yvetot et mourir*' (see Yvetot and die), advised Flaubert in his *Dictionnaire des idées reçus*, evoking Naples, but mainly, I suspect, looking for something beginning with the letter 'y'. The town of 12,000 in the Seine-Maritime was largely destroyed during the Second World War and not all the rebuilding has been sympathetic. So feel free to skip it.

Z

ZADISTES
ECO WARRIORS

A ZAD is technically a *zone d'aménagement différé,* that's to say a protected space where the government can seize land so that it cannot be developed. *Zadistes* are a militant and confrontational ecological movement that is involved in numerous protests across France in opposition to large infrastructure projects. These include the extension of the TGV to Bordeaux, the proposed giant airport at Notre-Dame-des-Landes near Nantes, and the Sivens dam in the Tarn Department, a project physically attacked by *Zadistes* determined that the habitat take priority over the farmers' demands for water. Police are not so tender with the *Zadistes* as they are with trade unionists. A young man was killed by a police flash-bang grenade in a protest at the Sivens site, provoking further violent demonstrations. The political wing of this movement is the green party, *Europe Écologie Les Verts* (EELV), an ultra-leftist movement hostile to capitalism, Anglo-Saxon *ultra-libéralisme,* genetically modified crops, cars (except their own), fracking for gas, nuclear power, and in favour of 70 per cent taxes on high incomes. EELV signed a coalition agreement with the socialists before the last elections but left the government in a reshuffle.

ZEMMOUR, ERIC
FRENCH GAD FLY

A columnist for *Le Figaro* magazine whose protracted attack on the state of the Republic, *Suicide Français (French Suicide),* was a bestseller in France in 2014 as the country crawled through its slough of despond. The son of an Algerian Jewish family that settled in France after the ceasefire, he is accused of Bonapartist, Jacobin, Gaullist, Pétainist and nationalist tendencies by his critics, who are numerous. His angry denunciations of the conceits of the French intellectual, political, corporate and political establishments have won him few friends. But he has little to contribute on the practical questions of how to deliver jobs, prosperity and happiness to the French people who actually exist, rather than those he imagines. The eagerness with which his critics wish to shut him up, keeping him off the TV and even trying to ban him from speaking, suggests, to his credit, that he is at least annoying them.

ZEP
ALPHABET SOUP

Zones d'éducation prioritaire were launched in 1981 as the education establishment recognised that it was failing to educate certain students. They were relaunched in 1990 when the measures of 1981 were found to be not working, and then relaunched again in 1998 when the failure of the 1990 reforms was finally acknowledged. The ZEPs still exist in the popular mind and ZEP continues to be used as a synonym for a zone of educational deprivation. In fact the ZEP has been supplanted by an alphabet soup of other acronyms (APV, RAR, CLAIR, ECLAIR, etc.) representing supposed reforms for which the results have also been invisible to modest. After the *Charlie Hebdo* massacre, hundreds of classes of mainly Muslim students in the ZEPs refused to join their teachers in a Republican moment of silence, provoking yet another anguished debate about the failure of French education. Teachers get paid more for working in ZEPs. But they usually strike each time a new reform is attempted.

ZIDANE, ZINÉDINE YAZID ('ZIZOU')

GREATEST EVER FRENCH FOOTBALLER

Born in Marseille in 1972, Zizou is believed by many to have been the best European footballer in history, although he blotted his career by being sent off in the 110th minute of his second world cup final in 2006 for a *coup de boule* (head-butting) against Italy's Marco Materazzi. France lost the game. In retirement he has occupied himself in numerous sporting and charitable activities. He could be a greater role model for young French people if he chose to live in France rather than Spain.

ZOLA, ÉMILE
IMMORTAL FRENCH WRITER

Oscar Wilde said of Zola, 'if he has not got genius, he can at least be dull'. Totally unfair since his work is magnificent. Zola was a crusader against social injustice, a friend of FLAUBERT and may well have been killed for his role in the Dreyfus AFFAIRE. He memorialised his friend Cézanne in *L'œuvre* (*The Work*), as wrenching a piece of writing as anything ever written about art. His first major novel, *Thérèse Raquin* (1867), was the beginning of the cycle called *Les Rougon Macquart*, the chronicle of a family during the Second Empire. Like Dickens, Zola (1840-1902) was often paid by the word, hence with little incentive to brevity. Zola exposed the worst excesses of France's industrial revolution, the horror of the Franco-Prussian war (*La débâcle*, 1892) and the anti-semitic persecution of Alfred Dreyfus, (*J'accuse*, 1898) for which he was convicted of criminal libel and stripped of the Legion of Honour. He fled to London where he was unhappy, and returned to Paris, where he was pardoned although not fully exonerated until after his death. Zola's exposé of the excesses of 19th-century capitalism inoculated French people with an enduring suspicion of money and business. I suspect Zola today would be goring the underachieving French state with the same enthusiasm that he applied to the robber barons of his age. Zola was possibly murdered by enemies he made during the Dreyfus affair, but there's no conclusive evidence. He died of carbon monoxide poisoning after his chimney was blocked. It was not satisfactorily explained whether this was an accident or by design, although I suspect the latter, since there were plenty of people who wished him ill.

Afterword

HOW TO SAVE A PEOPLE WHO DON'T WANT TO BE SAVED?

Is France capable of finding a formula for getting richer, not poorer? Is there any prospect of a viable project to re-launch France? Is any leader or circumstance likely to lead to such an outcome? As one reform after another tumbles, or is watered down, or put into the too-hard-to-do basket, it is easy to imagine that France is hopeless, the contradictions too deep, the tentacles of *clientélisme* too deeply embedded, infecting France like a *tique* (tick) with an incurable malaise. It is tempting to call for a restoration of the monarchy if not the empire, and admit that the revolution was a terrible mistake, although I doubt this would fly.

The fundamental problem is the belief in exceptionalism that has produced the psychosis that France is safer isolated within its interior and European bubbles, rather than punching harder in the wider world. France clings to a *code du travail* (employment code) that destroys jobs and a monstrous, infantalising, unreformed *état providence* (welfare state), without ever saying how they intend to keep on paying for it. Wage overheads are four times higher than in Britain, and they can't understand why the people have no jobs (let them toss burgers at McDonald's?) The ruling Socialists offer a prospectus that is literally incredible - pretend reforms achieving nothing. The National Front offers less, a prospectus even more *dirigiste* (centrally managed) than the Socialists, with toxic added nationalism. The *républicains* (formerly the UMP), party of the right, has never felt strong enough to challenge the statist shibboleths and as it tacks to the leftish centrist consensus, seems unlikely ever to do this. Even though the French know they must change, they can only talk about it. These self-proclaimed revolutionaries are really just the most conservative people in Europe. They seem incapable of serious reform.

The first article of the French constitution speaks of a Republic 'indivisible, secular and social.' This is holy scripture in the French mentality but there's room for interpretation and the current interpretation is self-destructive. It's hard to argue with a state claiming the right to be indivisible. Secularism (treated in the text: see *laïcité*) is a difficult idea, in practice. But the social element has been hijacked. There are elements to French society that are profoundly and delightfully social, but 'social' also implies socialism, where it gets more problematic, in a society where socialism too often is interpreted to mean conformity, dependency, hierarchy and *dirigisme*. France can be admired as a country that values a social dimension, but not so much for its unquestioning acceptance of an ultra-socialism in which resources are redistributed from both the rich and the poor to the bottomless pit of a state that knows few limits and in which self-reliance, enterprise and the private sector have been widely demonised and punished.

Nevertheless, having delivered my pathology of France, I shall try to offer a prescription to save it, even though I am at but the humblest level of elected office in France, and unlikely to rise higher.

1. STOP TAXING JOBS

This is going to require going much, much further than the feeble reforms currently proposed. It means taking a chainsaw to the thicket of rules, anti-competitive practices, special privileges for the elite and restraints of trade and labour that crush enterprise. Payroll taxes are completely out of kilter with France's competitors, even as they benefit the institutions that collect them at the expense of those who are nominally supposed to benefit.

None of the reliefs so far proposed cut to the depth of the problem. Nobody seems to like capitalism in France but that's because they mistake for capitalism what in France is too often corporatism and clientelism.

The state in France will never be shrunk to the size of a pea but its 54 per cent share of the economy is wildly out of line compared to its main competitors. The French state with its crushing burdens on business, punishment of the enterprising and disincentives to investment and employment is, bluntly, toxic for investors. France must stop treating its citizens like children by promising that the state can do everything. It must allow businesses to grow and hire (and also fire) and in this way might inspire the best and brightest of its younger generation to stay in France, rather than fleeing on the Eurostar to London, like latter-day Huguenots.

2. STOP PLAYING SECOND FIDDLE TO THE GERMANS

The visceral French objections to any idea of reforming the EU serve nobody but the French elite. Ordinary people are far less convinced that the EU project is delivering them benefits. For a time, when the EU's priority was opening markets to competition, the European project did force some reforms onto the French economy, such as slightly more competitive energy and telecommunications markets. But the government has retained its command of the economy and the EU has morphed into a corporatist monster. The *débâcle* of the euro, cooked up by François Mitterrand and the corrupt German chancellor Helmut Kohl, has been a catastrophe for French competitiveness. It is too late to exit the euro, but not too late for the French to re-evaluate their relationship with the Germans.

There is an obvious alternative and that is to embrace the idea of EU reform, to use a reformed EU to help France to reform itself, and to accept the United Kingdom as a partner, not an adversary. A more welcoming investment climate for clever, agile

British companies in France could help, but not until the labour market is reformed. The same is true for other potential foreign investors terrified, like Titan Tyres, of the crazy employment conditions in France. The French must see that a British exit from the EU would be a disaster - not necessarily for Britain, but certainly for the French. It would leave the French even more exposed to a Germany that is already too dominant. There has never been a better time to renew the *entente cordiale*.

3. DEFINE A NEW REPUBLIC

Early in his mandate, President François Hollande asked his ministers to present their ideas for the future, resulting in hundreds of feeble propositions, almost all of which have apparently now been forgotten. The inability of France to define and get behind some kind of grand national project of renewal is partly the consequence of cynicism, partly of doubt that it is necessary but largely because no convincing project is being offered. Former president Nicolas Sarkozy promised a break with the past and didn't deliver. Hollande promised immediate change but the economy has become worse, even as he has become distracted by his idea of himself as a war president in the crusade for *laïcité*. On the stage of the EU, he mouths platitudes about solidarity with the Greeks and their need to reform while turning his back on the economic disaster of France itself. Tinkering reforms are not enough, France needs to be inspired and that is going to take big ideas and a leader with actual guts.

There is much talk of a 6th Republic, but no coherent idea of what this could be. So in the absence of any ideas from French politicians, here is my own version. France must reconsider what it means by *liberté, égalité, fraternité*, which has become an alibi for a toxic social project that valorises sloth, envy, dependence and crushed ambition. Talent must be liberated, and equality must become equality of opportunity not of outcome. The state must retire from the micromanagement of every aspect of life and give space to the genius of the French people to create a future for themselves. A new republic must be future-pointing, outward-looking and dynamic, not reactionary, isolationist and protection-ist. It must explicitly speak to young people who are so systemat-ically excluded from participation in the economy. This doesn't mean ultra-liberalism or abandoning the poor to starve. But it does mean that the French state must stop pandering to its clients, the unions and its civil servants.

Is any of this possible? Perhaps not. France seems to me to be trapped in an economic death spiral in which those responsible do nothing effective because like the aristocrats, until they were deposed by the revolution, they do not suffer at all. French people have put up with this too long. They need to take responsibility. There must either be a *révolution tranquille* (quiet revolution) in the French mentality or the country risks being plunged into a much less benign upheaval.

Vive la France!

Acknowledgements

This book was inspired by Ambrose Bierce's caustic and funny *Devil's Dictionary*, exquisitely crafted between 1881 and 1906; by Gustave Flaubert's *Dictionnaire des idées reçues* (Dictionary of Conventional Wisdom), a sardonic masterpiece, never finished but reconstructed from his notes, and published posthumously in 1913, and finally by Walter Benjamin's *Arcades Project*, a magisterial study of Paris, also never completed, also posthumously published.

Bierce, a great, slashing journalist, who died in Mexico in murky circumstances in 1914, was a scholar of the French and much else. He dedicated his book to those 'enlightened souls who prefer dry wines to sweet, sense to sentiment, wit to humour and clean English to slang.' He left numerous pertinent reflections on France, referenced here and there in this book, and left a splendid poem on France, identifying its hopeless contradictions:

Unhappy State! with horrors still to strive:
Thy Hugo dead, thy Boulanger alive;
A Prince who'd govern where he dares not dwell,
And who for power would his birthright sell
Who, anxious o'er his enemies to reign,
Grabs at the sceptre and conceals the chain;
While pugnant factions mutually strive
By cutting throats to keep the land alive.
Perverse in passion, as in pride perverse
To all a mistress, to thyself a curse;
Sweetheart of Europe! every sun's embrace
Matures the charm and poison of thy grace.
Yet time to thee nor peace nor wisdom brings:

In blood of citizens and blood of kings
The stones of thy stability are set,
And the fair fabric trembles at a threat.

Bierce's and Flaubert's works were presented ostensibly as dictionaries, or *abécédaires,* although neither are really dictionaries, but a series of reflections and meditations, revelations and insights, organised alphabetically. Benjamin also toyed with alphabetisation, but his work was encyclopaedic more than definitional and in volume almost overwhelming. I dedicate this book to the memories of all three of them.

Many people helped with inspiration, criticism, suggestions, corrections and encouragement, not least the scores if not hundreds of French people who have shared their stories with me in my 15 years in France. I must thank in particular the warm and generous people of Caux, Hérault, my adopted home. Nestled between the Mediterranean and the Cévennes mountains, Caux has been inhabited for more than 1,000 years - probably much longer, as some of the most ancient traces of human civilisation in Europe have been discovered just a few kilometres from here. Its people have welcomed, fed and befriended me and even elected me to their municipal council.

For practical help, Jean Martinez, a brilliant professor of biochemistry and Mayor of Caux, kindly reviewed various drafts. He has been tolerant of my efforts to inject an Anglo-Saxon gust of ideas into the functioning of our community, though he has no responsibility for my conclusions here. Marie-Jo Morelle, a French expatriate, translator and inspiring teacher of French and French culture at the University of Surrey, was a fountain of suggestions and welcome contestations. Jacques Kuhnlé, a retired professor in Lorraine, and Karen Robinson, who failed to teach me how to spell at *The Sunday Times*, wore out red pencils patiently correcting my errors and drawing my attention to alternative points of view.

Other kind counsellors included Susan Douglas, my former colleague at *The Sunday Times*, Peter and Dominique Glynn-Smith, an Anglo-French couple with a unique insight into *entente cordiale*, Norman Berke, a wise American, his Irish wife Stephanie and her daughter Wumps, all of whom have seen a great deal of life in France, and Frank Russell, who keeps an eye on the French for me from a vantage point in the 21st *arrondissement* of Paris (Kensington). I thank my neighbours Benoît and Andrea Yveline, Jocelyne and Jean-Pierre Vanel, and Bertrand and Cristel Laugeri for feeding me and revealing many insights to French life. Yvette Angelats, Rupert and Helena Wright, Edward Muller, Jane Reed, Christopher Ludow, Françoise Ellery, Alan Pearce, and Barry Strum contributed many valuable ideas. Special thanks to Marie-Trinité Lopez, whose village *salon de thé* has become a second home.

Above all I must thank Daniel, my son, who told me to write this book; my wife, Terry, who tolerated my disappearance while I wrote it and my daughter Alysen, for tolerating me in general. Also Ringo, foundling Labrador, who helped me explore the glorious countryside surrounding Caux. Walking the flanks of the ancient volcanos among the endless vines, the orchids, the wild fennel and the abundant fig trees, has been inspirational and therapeutic. I am indebted to many others for corrections and advice. And then there are some who had better not be mentioned. All the errors and misunderstandings are my own.

Jonathan Miller
Caux, Hérault

'Risks reigniting the Hundred Years' War.'
The Mayor of Jonathan Millers' village